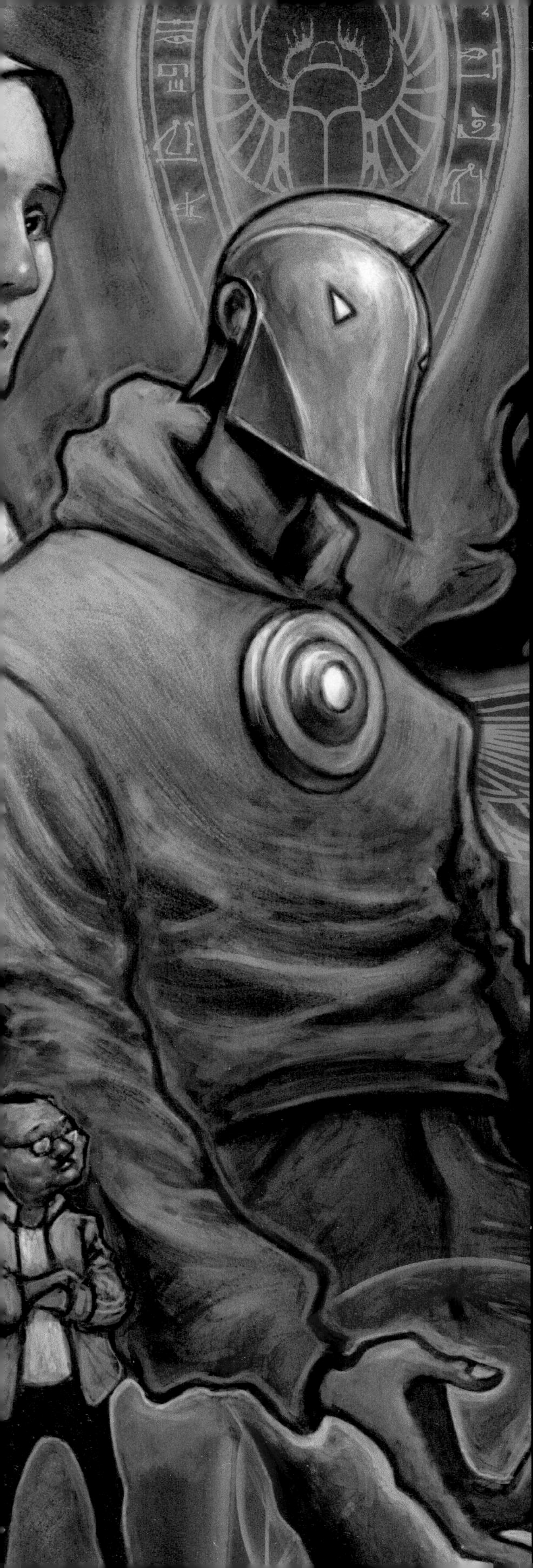

PRISONERS OF THE PAST

OCTOR FATE

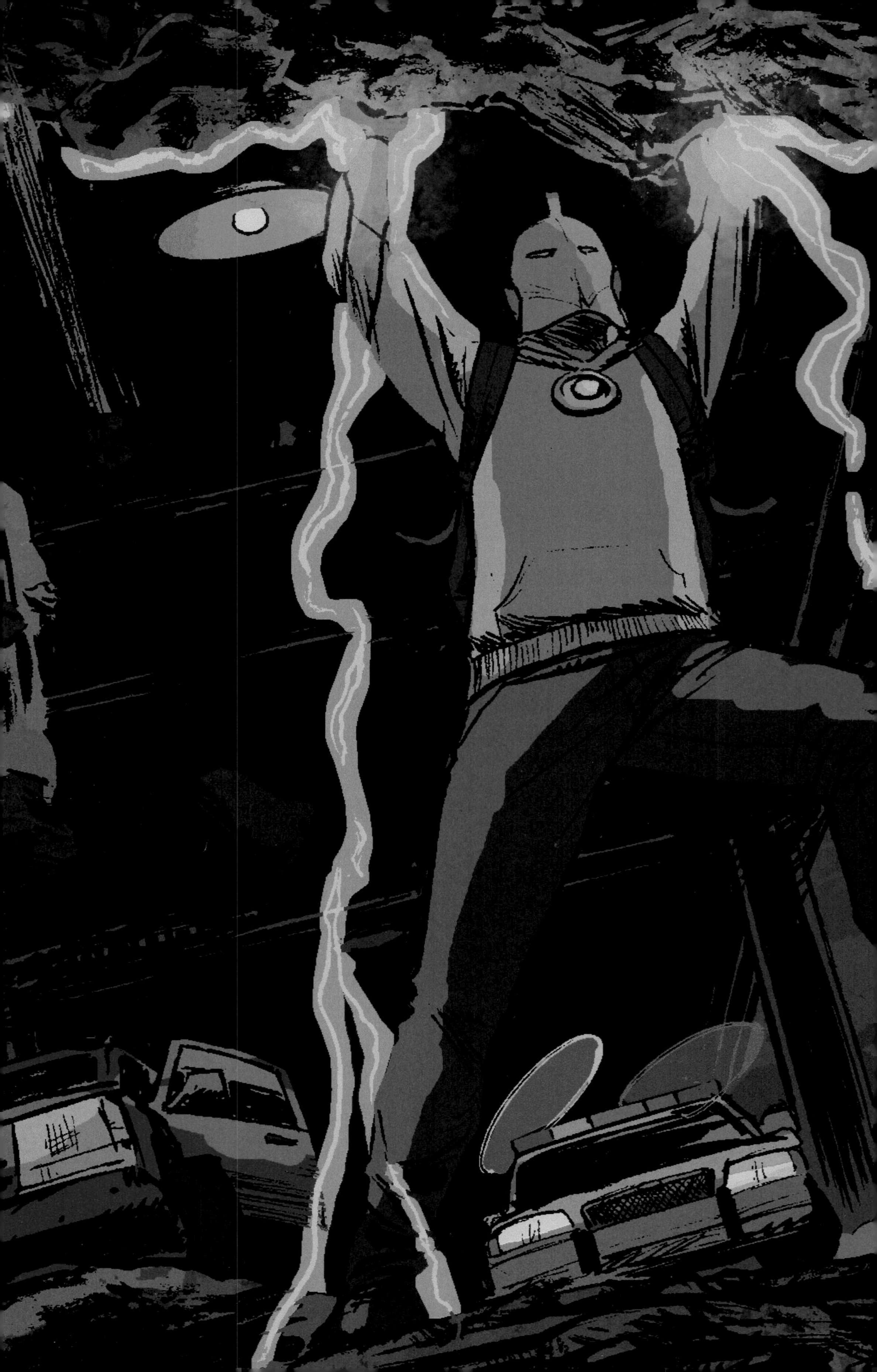

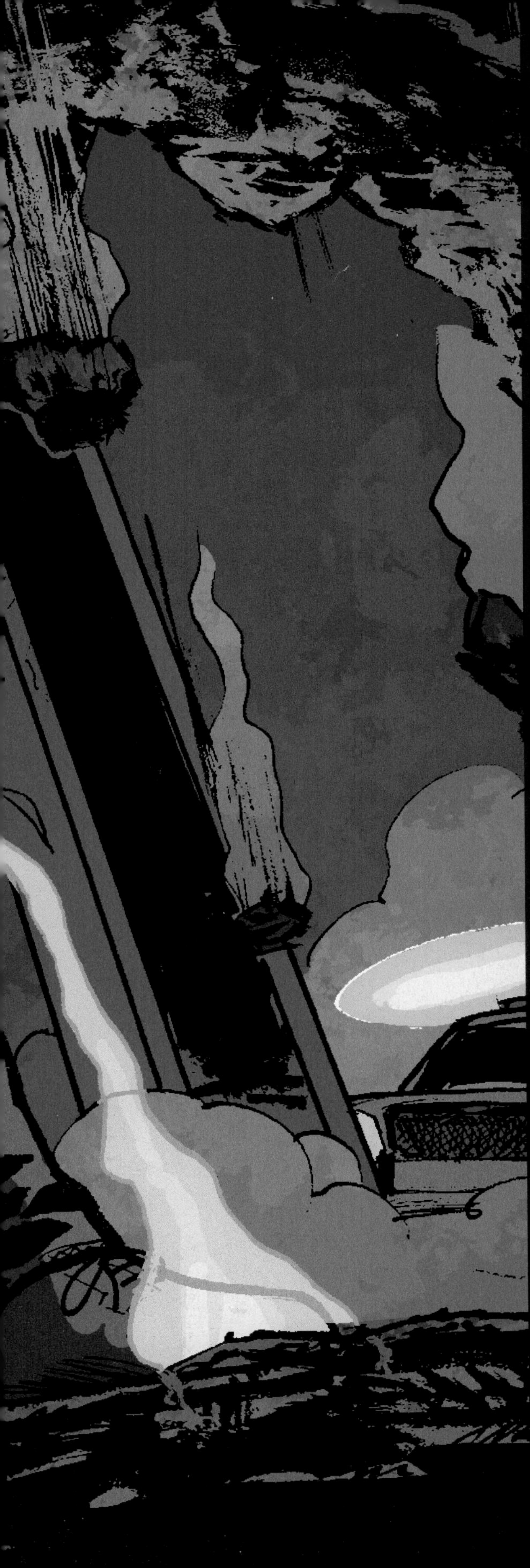

DOCTOR FATE

VOLUME 2
PRISONERS OF THE PAST

WRITTEN BY
PAUL LEVITZ

ART BY
SONNY LIEW
IBRAHIM MOUSTAFA

COLOR BY
LEE LOUGHRIDGE

LETTERS BY
SAIDA TEMOFONTE

COLLECTION COVER ART BY
SONNY LIEW

ANDY KHOURI DAVID WOHL Editors – Original Series
JEB WOODARD Group Editor – Collected Editions
LIZ ERICKSON Editor – Collected Edition
STEVE COOK Design Director – Books
DAMIAN RYLAND Publication Design

BOB HARRAS Senior VP – Editor-in-Chief, DC Comics

DIANE NELSON President
DAN DiDIO and JIM LEE Co-Publishers
GEOFF JOHNS Chief Creative Officer
AMIT DESAI Senior VP – Marketing & Global Franchise Management
NAIRI GARDINER Senior VP – Finance
SAM ADES VP – Digital Marketing
BOBBIE CHASE VP – Talent Development
MARK CHIARELLO Senior VP – Art, Design & Collected Editions
JOHN CUNNINGHAM VP – Content Strategy
ANNE DEPiES VP – Strategy Planning & Reporting
DON FALLETTI VP – Manufacturing Operations
LAWRENCE GANEM VP – Editorial Administration & Talent Relations
ALISON GILL Senior VP – Manufacturing & Operations
HANK KANALZ Senior VP – Editorial Strategy & Administration
JAY KOGAN VP – Legal Affairs
DEREK MADDALENA Senior VP – Sales & Business Development
JACK MAHAN VP – Business Affairs
DAN MIRON VP – Sales Planning & Trade Development
NICK NAPOLITANO VP – Manufacturing Administration
CAROL ROEDER VP – Marketing
EDDIE SCANNELL VP – Mass Account & Digital Sales
COURTNEY SIMMONS Senior VP – Publicity & Communications
JIM (SKI) SOKOLOWSKI VP – Comic Book Specialty & Newsstand Sales
SANDY YI Senior VP – Global Franchise Management

DOCTOR FATE VOLUME 2: PRISONERS OF THE PAST

Published by DC Comics. Compilation and all new material Copyright © 2016 DC Comics. All Rights Reserved.

Originally published in single magazine form in DOCTOR FATE 8-12 Copyright © 2016 DC Comics. All Rights Reserved. All characters, their distinctive likenesses and related elements featured in this publication are trademarks of DC Comics. The stories, characters and incidents featured in this publication are entirely fictional. DC Comics does not read or accept unsolicited ideas, stories or artwork.

DC Comics, 2900 West Alameda Ave., Burbank, CA 91505
Printed by RR Donnelley, Salem, VA, USA. 9/16/16. First Printing.
ISBN: 978-1-4012-6492-5

Library of Congress Cataloging-in-Publication Data is available

PEFC Certified

Printed on paper from
sustainably managed
forests and controlled
sources

PEFC

PEFC/29-31-75   www.pefc.org

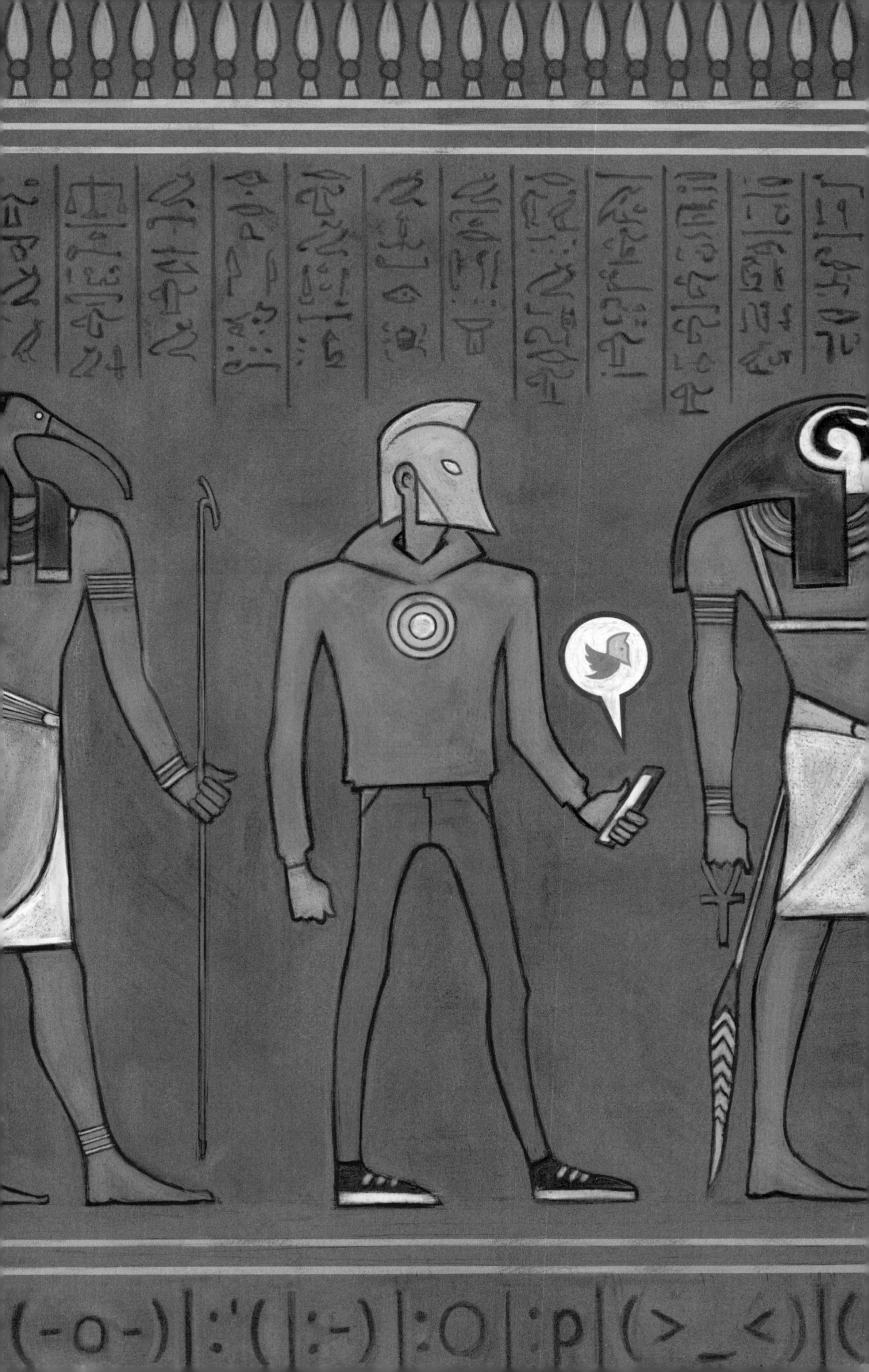
(-o-) | :'(| :-) | :O | :p | (>_<) | (

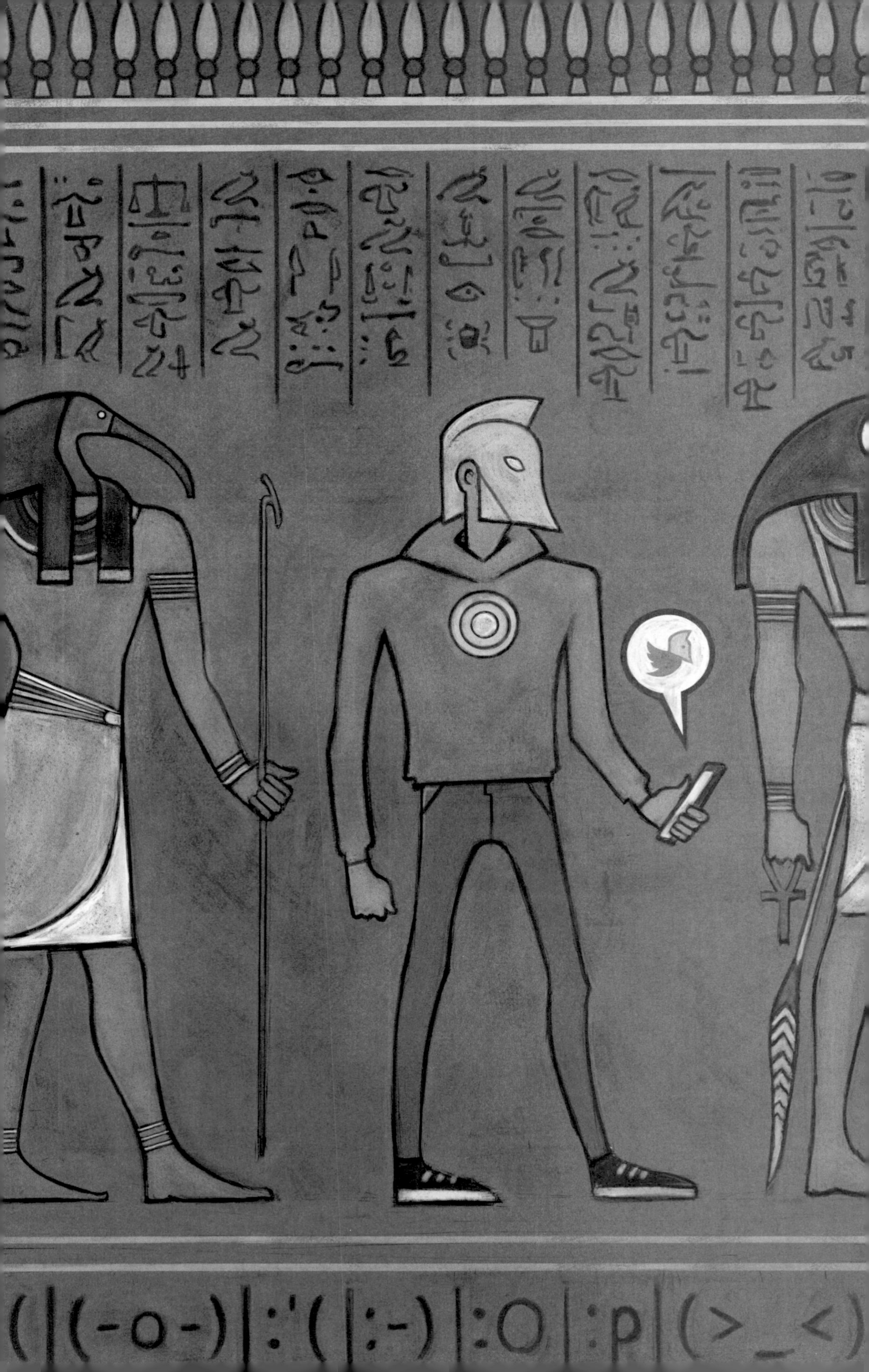
(| (-o-) | :'(| :-) | :O | :p | (>_<)

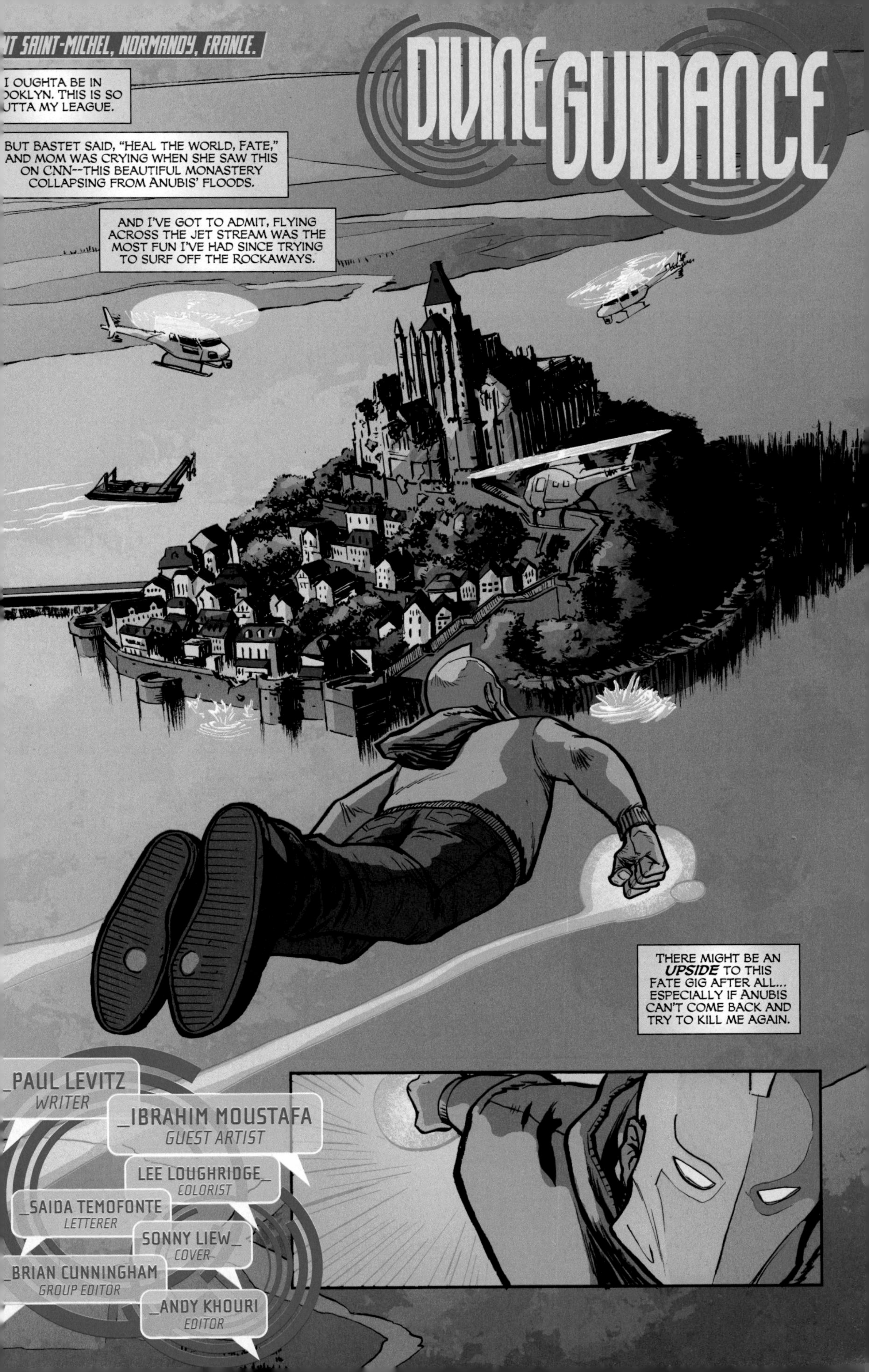

NT SAINT-MICHEL, NORMANDY, FRANCE.
DIVINE GUIDANCE
I OUGHTA BE IN
OOKLYN. THIS IS SO
UTTA MY LEAGUE.
BUT BASTET SAID, "HEAL THE WORLD, FATE," AND MOM WAS CRYING WHEN SHE SAW THIS ON CNN--THIS BEAUTIFUL MONASTERY COLLAPSING FROM ANUBIS' FLOODS.
AND I'VE GOT TO ADMIT, FLYING ACROSS THE JET STREAM WAS THE MOST FUN I'VE HAD SINCE TRYING TO SURF OFF THE ROCKAWAYS.
THERE MIGHT BE AN UPSIDE TO THIS FATE GIG AFTER ALL... ESPECIALLY IF ANUBIS CAN'T COME BACK AND TRY TO KILL ME AGAIN.
_PAUL LEVITZ WRITER
_IBRAHIM MOUSTAFA GUEST ARTIST
LEE LOUGHRIDGE_ COLORIST
_SAIDA TEMOFONTE LETTERER
SONNY LIEW_ COVER
_BRIAN CUNNINGHAM GROUP EDITOR
_ANDY KHOURI EDITOR

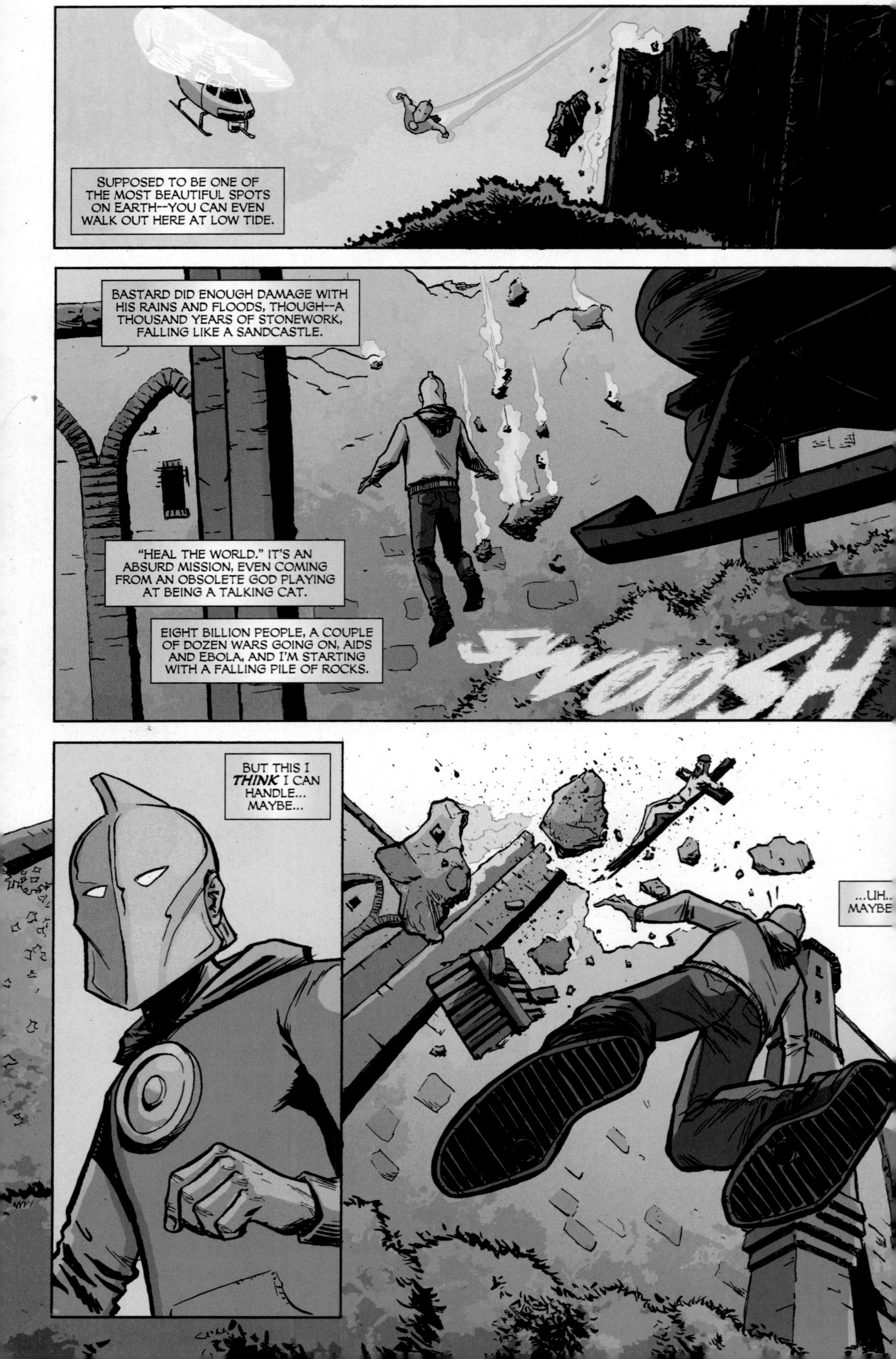

SUPPOSED TO BE ONE OF THE MOST BEAUTIFUL SPOTS ON EARTH--YOU CAN EVEN WALK OUT HERE AT LOW TIDE.
BASTARD DID ENOUGH DAMAGE WITH HIS RAINS AND FLOODS, THOUGH--A THOUSAND YEARS OF STONEWORK, FALLING LIKE A SANDCASTLE.
"HEAL THE WORLD." IT'S AN ABSURD MISSION, EVEN COMING FROM AN OBSOLETE GOD PLAYING AT BEING A TALKING CAT.
EIGHT BILLION PEOPLE, A COUPLE OF DOZEN WARS GOING ON, AIDS AND EBOLA, AND I'M STARTING WITH A FALLING PILE OF ROCKS.
SWOOSH
BUT THIS I *THINK* I CAN HANDLE... MAYBE...
!!
...UH.. MAYBE

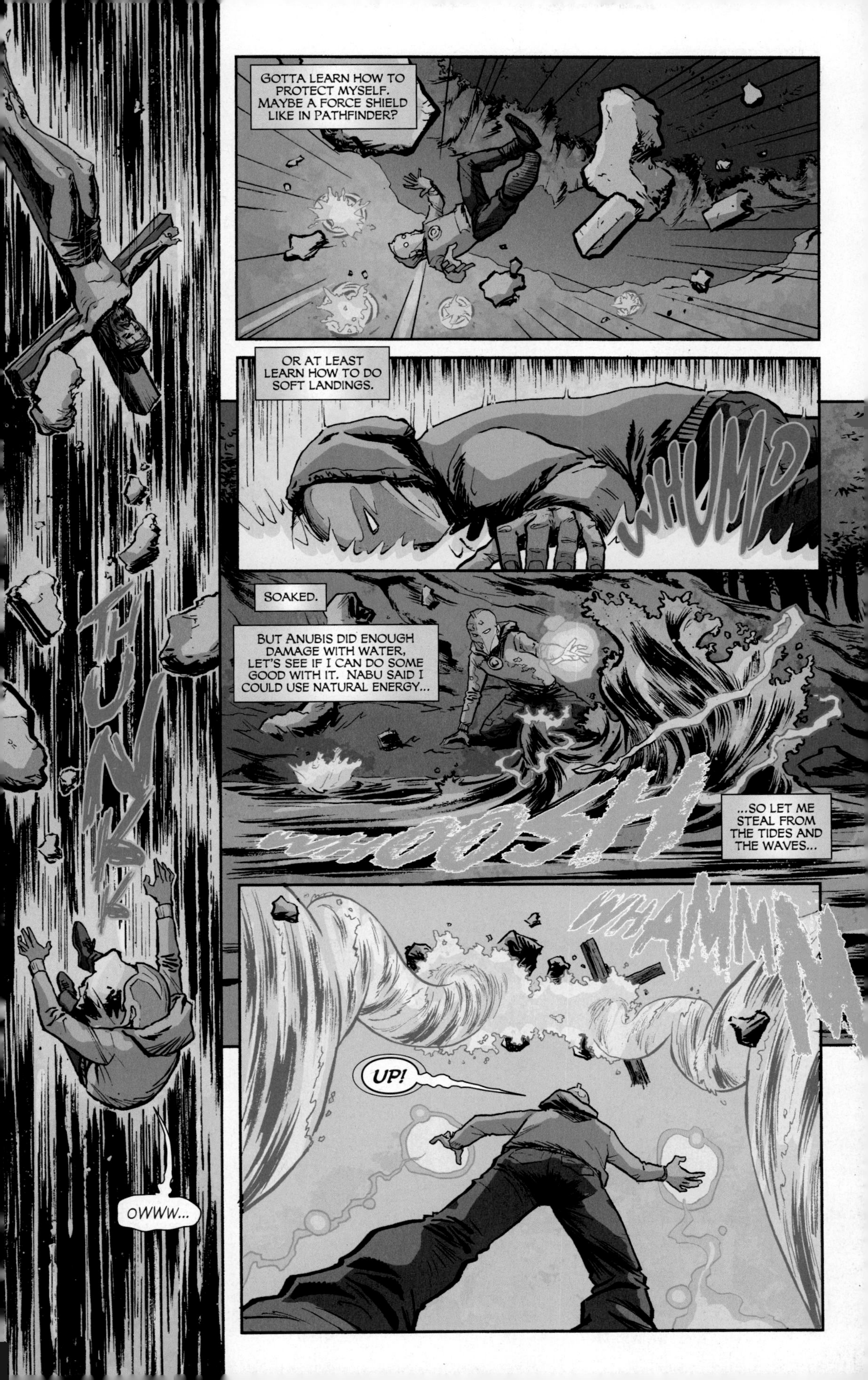
THUNK
OWWW...
GOTTA LEARN HOW TO PROTECT MYSELF. MAYBE A FORCE SHIELD LIKE IN PATHFINDER?
OR AT LEAST LEARN HOW TO DO SOFT LANDINGS.
WHUMP
SOAKED.
BUT ANUBIS DID ENOUGH DAMAGE WITH WATER, LET'S SEE IF I CAN DO SOME GOOD WITH IT. NABU SAID I COULD USE NATURAL ENERGY...
WHOOOSH
...SO LET ME STEAL FROM THE TIDES AND THE WAVES...
WHAMMM
UP!

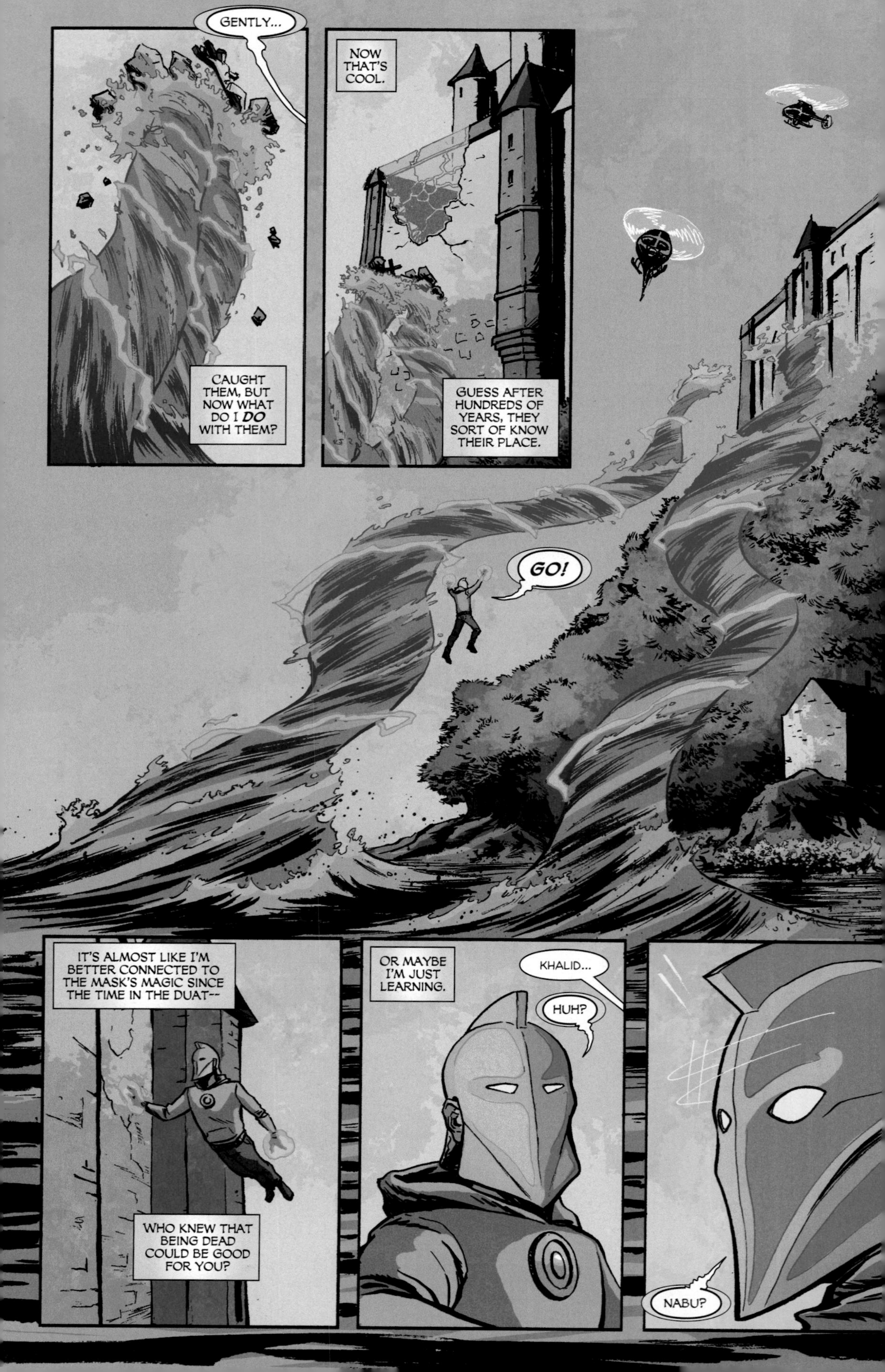
GENTLY...
CAUGHT THEM, BUT NOW WHAT DO I DO WITH THEM?
NOW THAT'S COOL.
GUESS AFTER HUNDREDS OF YEARS, THEY SORT OF KNOW THEIR PLACE.
GO!
IT'S ALMOST LIKE I'M BETTER CONNECTED TO THE MASK'S MAGIC SINCE THE TIME IN THE DUAT--
WHO KNEW THAT BEING DEAD COULD BE GOOD FOR YOU?
OR MAYBE I'M JUST LEARNING.
KHALID...
HUH?
NABU?

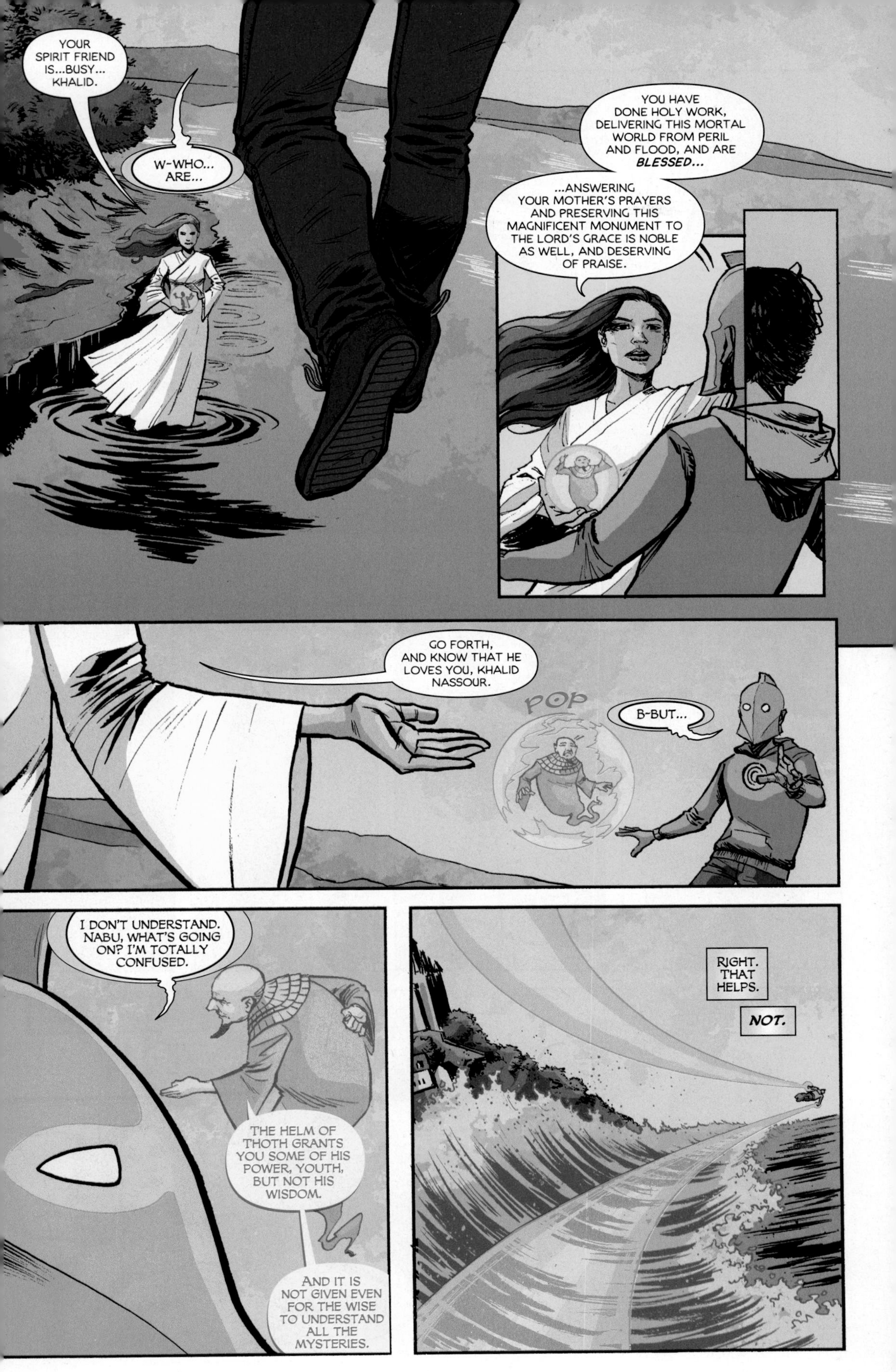
YOUR SPIRIT FRIEND IS...BUSY... KHALID.
W-WHO... ARE...
YOU HAVE DONE HOLY WORK, DELIVERING THIS MORTAL WORLD FROM PERIL AND FLOOD, AND ARE *BLESSED...*
...ANSWERING YOUR MOTHER'S PRAYERS AND PRESERVING THIS MAGNIFICENT MONUMENT TO THE LORD'S GRACE IS NOBLE AS WELL, AND DESERVING OF PRAISE.
GO FORTH, AND KNOW THAT HE LOVES YOU, KHALID NASSOUR.
POP
B-BUT...
I DON'T UNDERSTAND. NABU, WHAT'S GOING ON? I'M TOTALLY CONFUSED.
THE HELM OF THOTH GRANTS YOU SOME OF HIS POWER, YOUTH, BUT NOT HIS WISDOM.
AND IT IS NOT GIVEN EVEN FOR THE WISE TO UNDERSTAND ALL THE MYSTERIES.
RIGHT. THAT HELPS.
NOT.

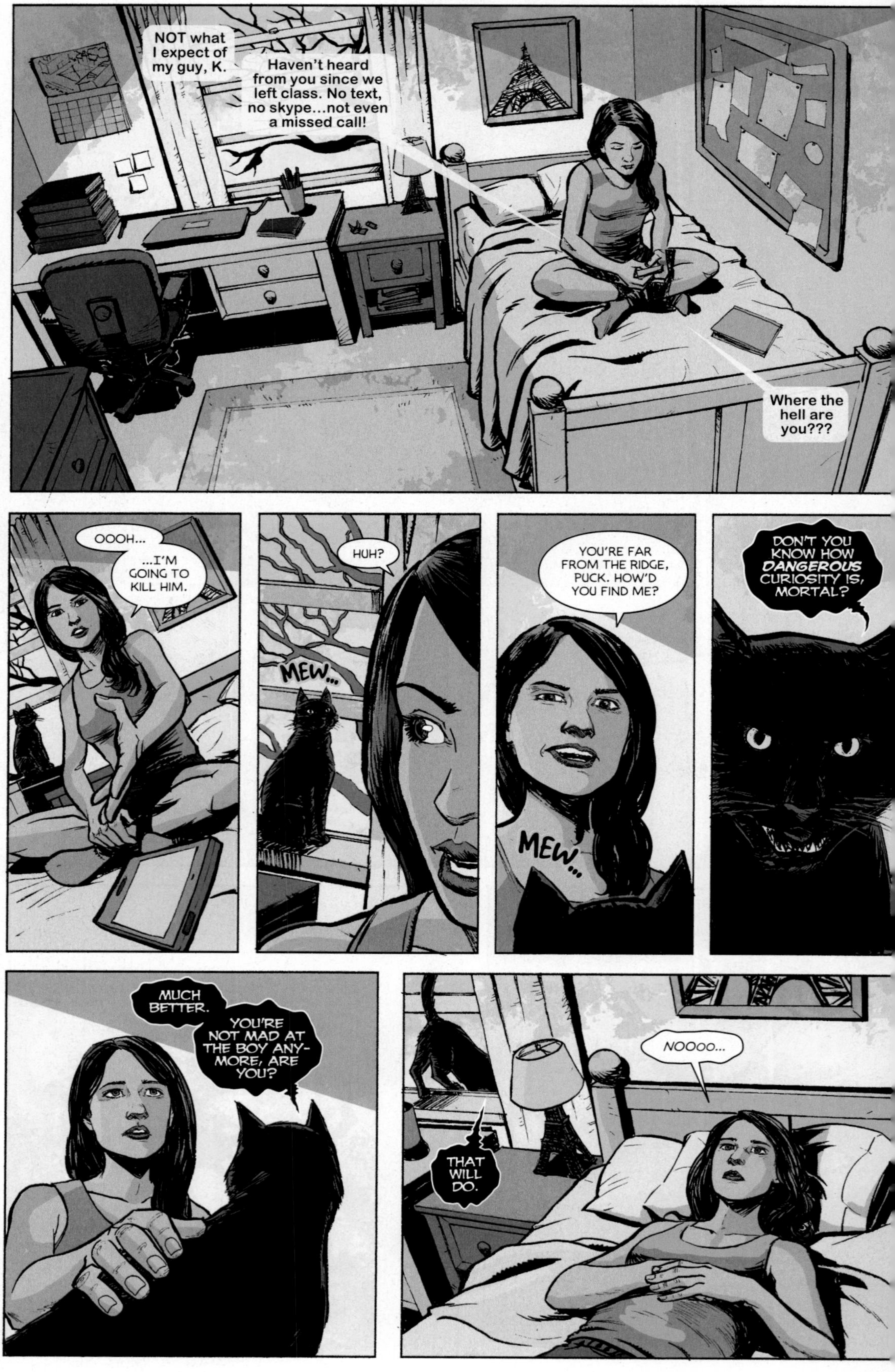
NOT what I expect of my guy, K.
Haven't heard from you since we left class. No text, no skype...not even a missed call!
Where the hell are you???
OOOH...
...I'M GOING TO KILL HIM.
HUH?
MEW...
YOU'RE FAR FROM THE RIDGE, PUCK. HOW'D YOU FIND ME?
MEW...
DON'T YOU KNOW HOW DANGEROUS CURIOSITY IS, MORTAL?
MUCH BETTER.
YOU'RE NOT MAD AT THE BOY ANYMORE, ARE YOU?
NOOOO...
THAT WILL DO.

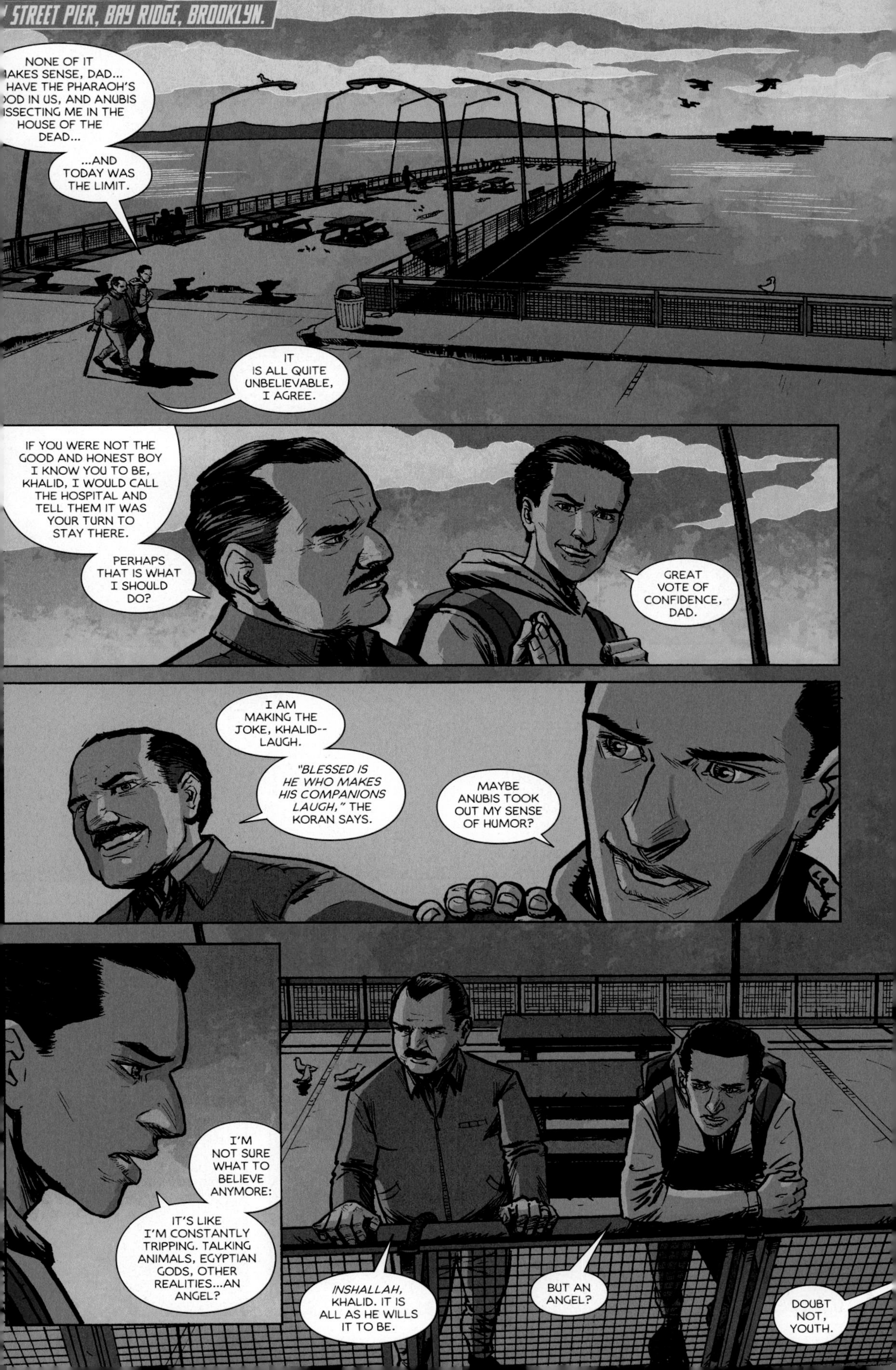
STREET PIER, BAY RIDGE, BROOKLYN.
NONE OF IT AKES SENSE, DAD... HAVE THE PHARAOH'S OOD IN US, AND ANUBIS ISSECTING ME IN THE HOUSE OF THE DEAD...
...AND TODAY WAS THE LIMIT.
IT IS ALL QUITE UNBELIEVABLE, I AGREE.
IF YOU WERE NOT THE GOOD AND HONEST BOY I KNOW YOU TO BE, KHALID, I WOULD CALL THE HOSPITAL AND TELL THEM IT WAS YOUR TURN TO STAY THERE.
PERHAPS THAT IS WHAT I SHOULD DO?
GREAT VOTE OF CONFIDENCE, DAD.
I AM MAKING THE JOKE, KHALID--LAUGH.
"BLESSED IS HE WHO MAKES HIS COMPANIONS LAUGH," THE KORAN SAYS.
MAYBE ANUBIS TOOK OUT MY SENSE OF HUMOR?
I'M NOT SURE WHAT TO BELIEVE ANYMORE:
IT'S LIKE I'M CONSTANTLY TRIPPING. TALKING ANIMALS, EGYPTIAN GODS, OTHER REALITIES...AN ANGEL?
INSHALLAH, KHALID. IT IS ALL AS HE WILLS IT TO BE.
BUT AN ANGEL?
DOUBT NOT, YOUTH.

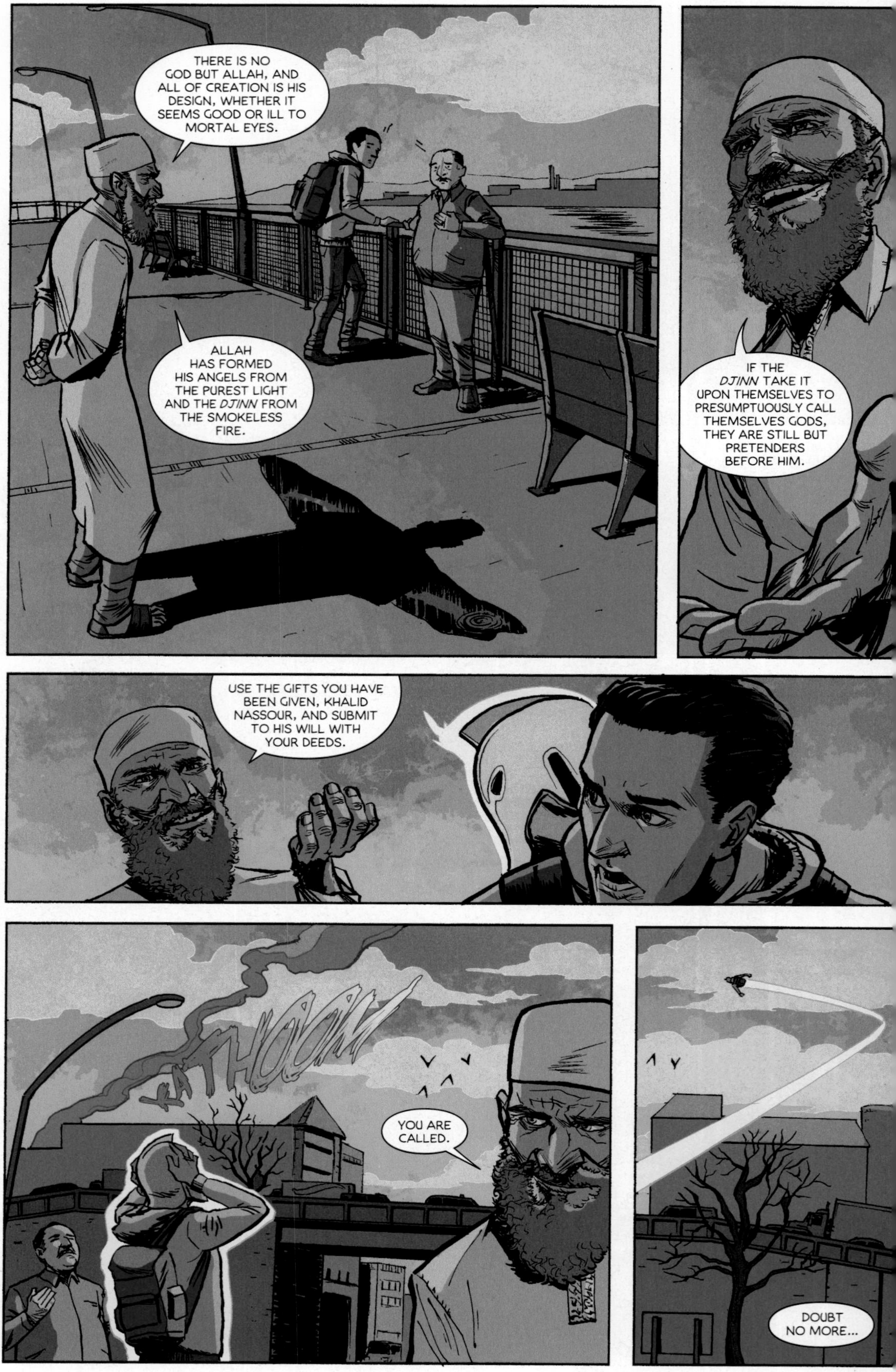
THERE IS NO GOD BUT ALLAH, AND ALL OF CREATION IS HIS DESIGN, WHETHER IT SEEMS GOOD OR ILL TO MORTAL EYES.
ALLAH HAS FORMED HIS ANGELS FROM THE PUREST LIGHT AND THE *DJINN* FROM THE SMOKELESS FIRE.
IF THE *DJINN* TAKE IT UPON THEMSELVES TO PRESUMPTUOUSLY CALL THEMSELVES GODS, THEY ARE STILL BUT PRETENDERS BEFORE HIM.
USE THE GIFTS YOU HAVE BEEN GIVEN, KHALID NASSOUR, AND SUBMIT TO HIS WILL WITH YOUR DEEDS.
KATHOOM
YOU ARE CALLED.
DOUBT NO MORE...

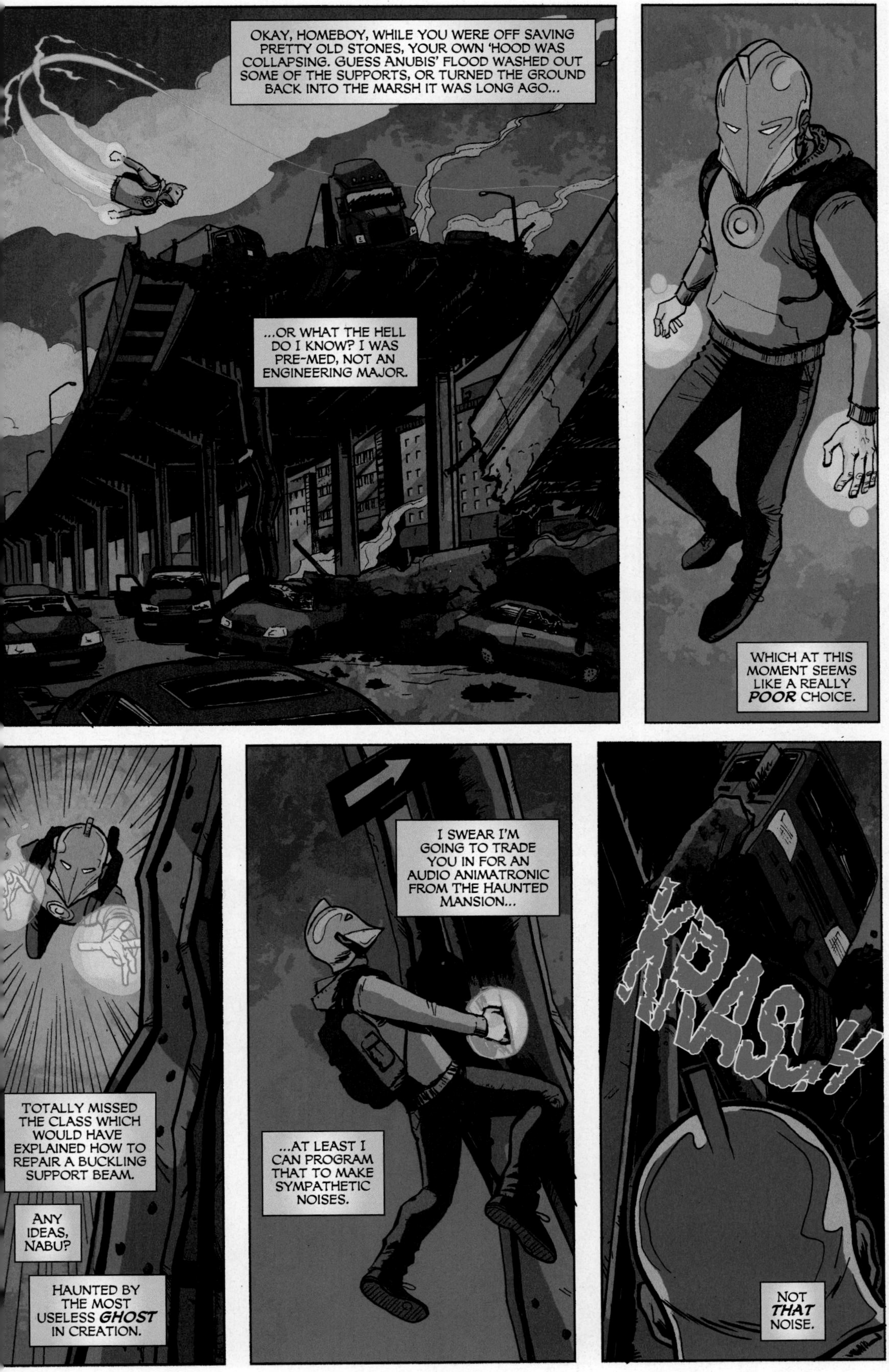
OKAY, HOMEBOY, WHILE YOU WERE OFF SAVING PRETTY OLD STONES, YOUR OWN 'HOOD WAS COLLAPSING. GUESS ANUBIS' FLOOD WASHED OUT SOME OF THE SUPPORTS, OR TURNED THE GROUND BACK INTO THE MARSH IT WAS LONG AGO...
...OR WHAT THE HELL DO I KNOW? I WAS PRE-MED, NOT AN ENGINEERING MAJOR.
WHICH AT THIS MOMENT SEEMS LIKE A REALLY *POOR* CHOICE.
TOTALLY MISSED THE CLASS WHICH WOULD HAVE EXPLAINED HOW TO REPAIR A BUCKLING SUPPORT BEAM.
ANY IDEAS, NABU?
HAUNTED BY THE MOST USELESS *GHOST* IN CREATION.
I SWEAR I'M GOING TO TRADE YOU IN FOR AN AUDIO ANIMATRONIC FROM THE HAUNTED MANSION...
...AT LEAST I CAN PROGRAM THAT TO MAKE SYMPATHETIC NOISES.
KRASSH
NOT *THAT* NOISE.

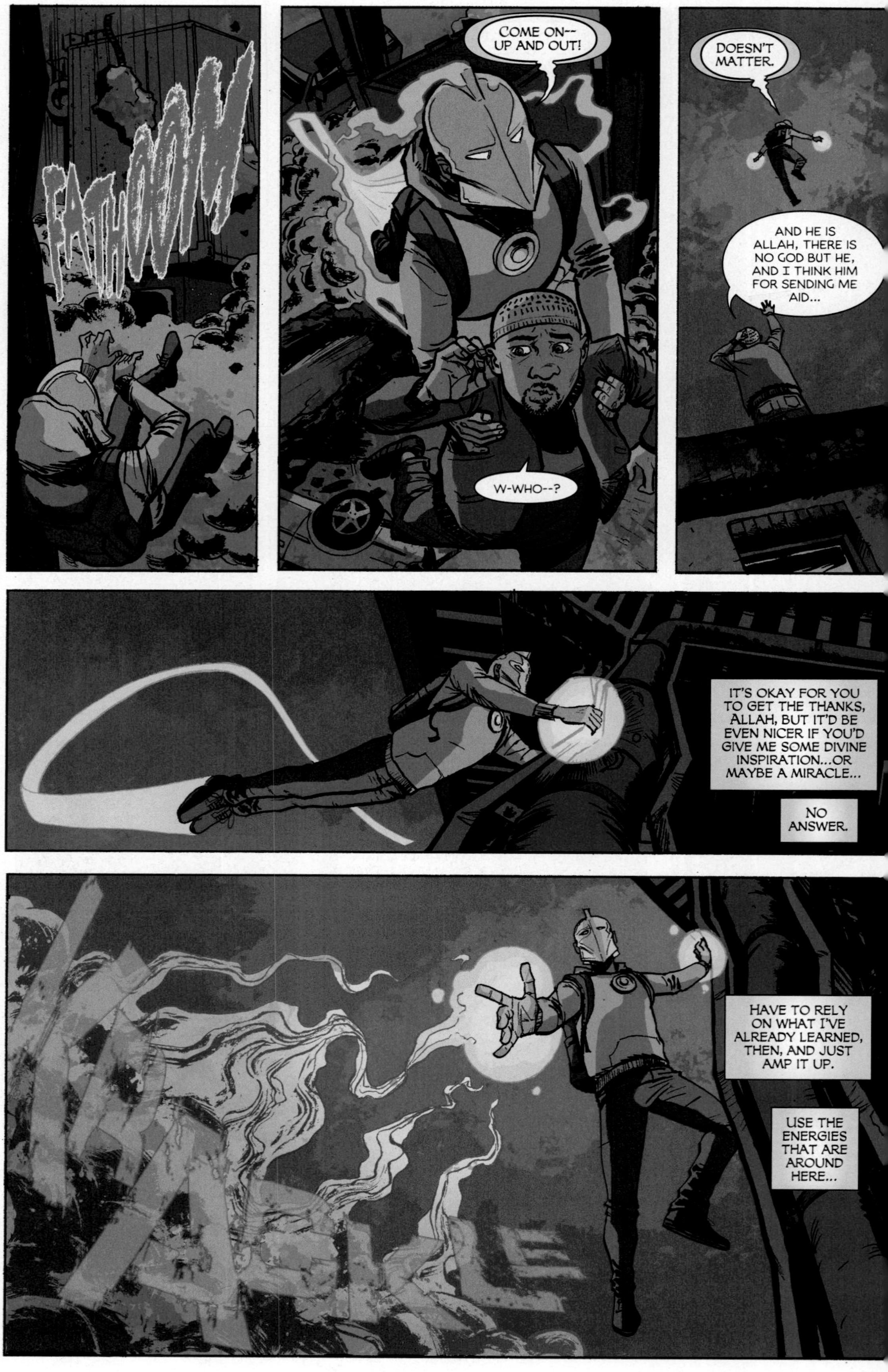
FATHOOM
COME ON-- UP AND OUT!
W-WHO--?
DOESN'T MATTER.
AND HE IS ALLAH, THERE IS NO GOD BUT HE, AND I THINK HIM FOR SENDING ME AID...
IT'S OKAY FOR YOU TO GET THE THANKS, ALLAH, BUT IT'D BE EVEN NICER IF YOU'D GIVE ME SOME DIVINE INSPIRATION...OR MAYBE A MIRACLE...
NO ANSWER.
HAVE TO RELY ON WHAT I'VE ALREADY LEARNED, THEN, AND JUST AMP IT UP.
USE THE ENERGIES THAT ARE AROUND HERE...

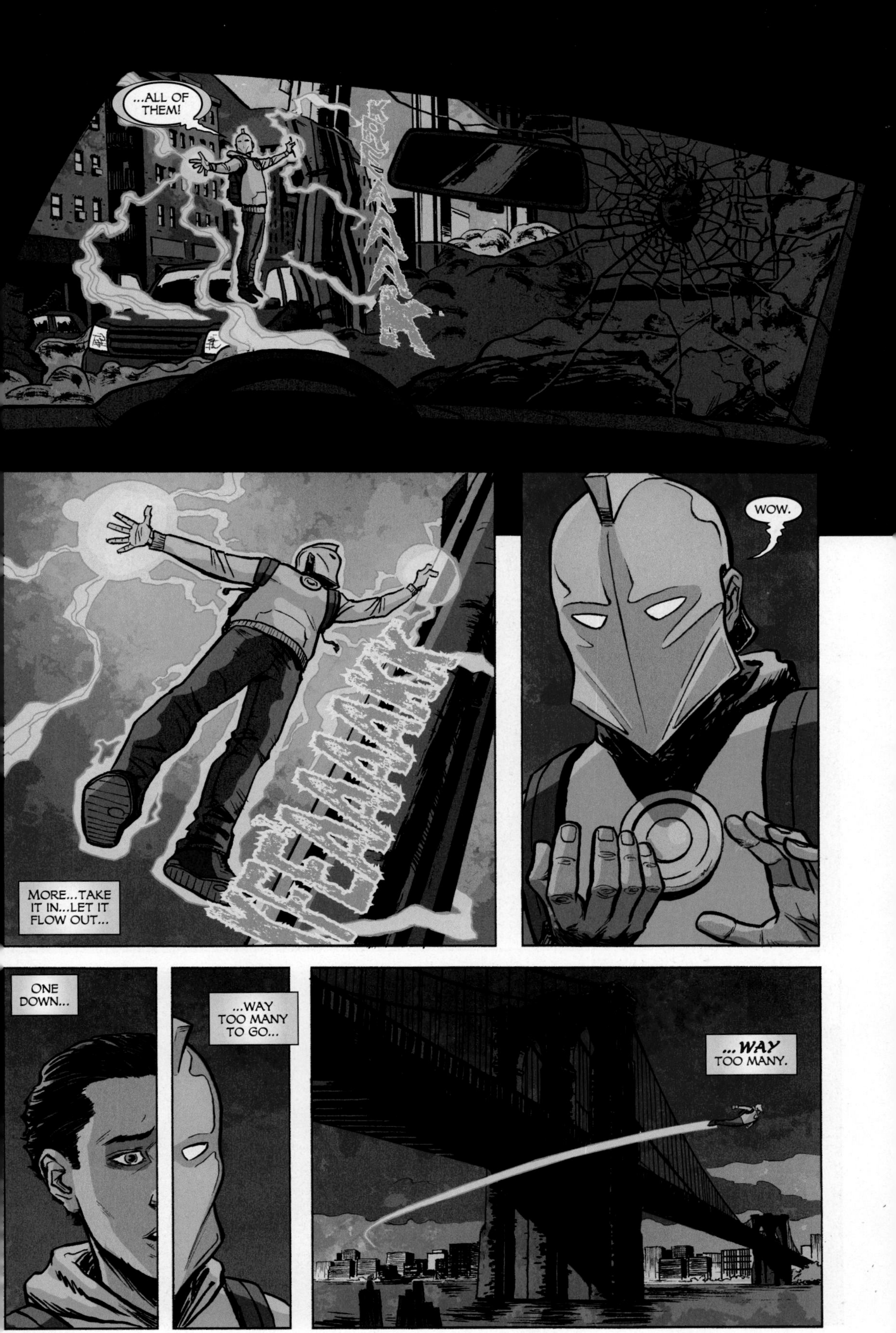
...ALL OF THEM!
MORE...TAKE IT IN...LET IT FLOW OUT...
WOW.
ONE DOWN...
...WAY TOO MANY TO GO...
...WAY TOO MANY.

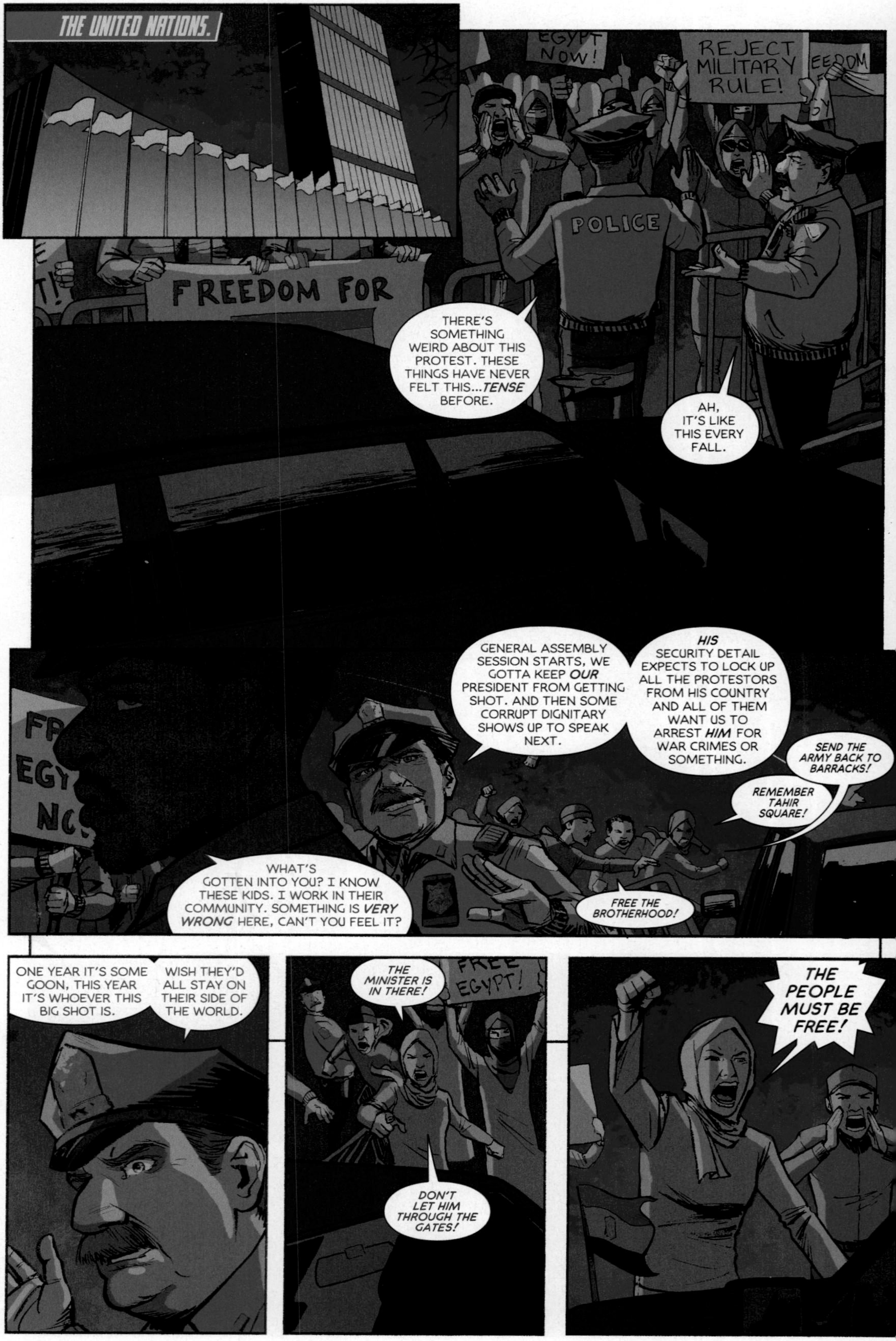
THE UNITED NATIONS.
EGYPT NOW!
REJECT MILITARY RULE!
POLICE
FREEDOM FOR
THERE'S SOMETHING WEIRD ABOUT THIS PROTEST. THESE THINGS HAVE NEVER FELT THIS...TENSE BEFORE.
AH, IT'S LIKE THIS EVERY FALL.
GENERAL ASSEMBLY SESSION STARTS, WE GOTTA KEEP OUR PRESIDENT FROM GETTING SHOT. AND THEN SOME CORRUPT DIGNITARY SHOWS UP TO SPEAK NEXT.
HIS SECURITY DETAIL EXPECTS TO LOCK UP ALL THE PROTESTORS FROM HIS COUNTRY AND ALL OF THEM WANT US TO ARREST HIM FOR WAR CRIMES OR SOMETHING.
SEND THE ARMY BACK TO BARRACKS!
REMEMBER TAHIR SQUARE!
WHAT'S GOTTEN INTO YOU? I KNOW THESE KIDS. I WORK IN THEIR COMMUNITY. SOMETHING IS VERY WRONG HERE, CAN'T YOU FEEL IT?
FREE THE BROTHERHOOD!
ONE YEAR IT'S SOME GOON, THIS YEAR IT'S WHOEVER THIS BIG SHOT IS.
WISH THEY'D ALL STAY ON THEIR SIDE OF THE WORLD.
THE MINISTER IS IN THERE!
FREE EGYPT!
DON'T LET HIM THROUGH THE GATES!
THE PEOPLE MUST BE FREE!

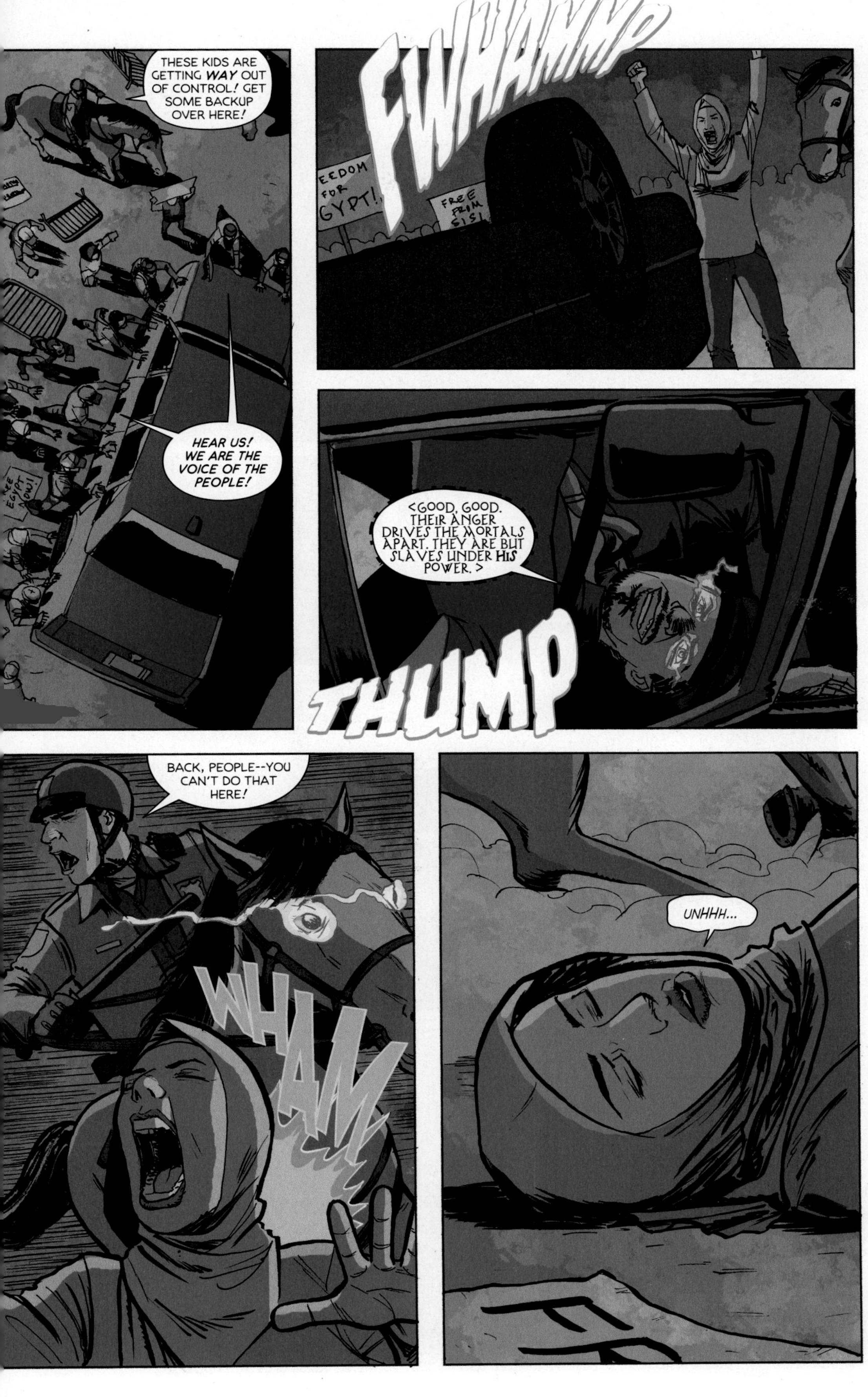
THESE KIDS ARE GETTING WAY OUT OF CONTROL! GET SOME BACKUP OVER HERE!
HEAR US! WE ARE THE VOICE OF THE PEOPLE!
EEDOM FOR GYPT!
FREE FROM SISI
FWHAMMMP
<GOOD, GOOD. THEIR ANGER DRIVES THE MORTALS APART. THEY ARE BUT SLAVES UNDER HIS POWER.>
THUMP
BACK, PEOPLE--YOU CAN'T DO THAT HERE!
WHAM
UNHHH...

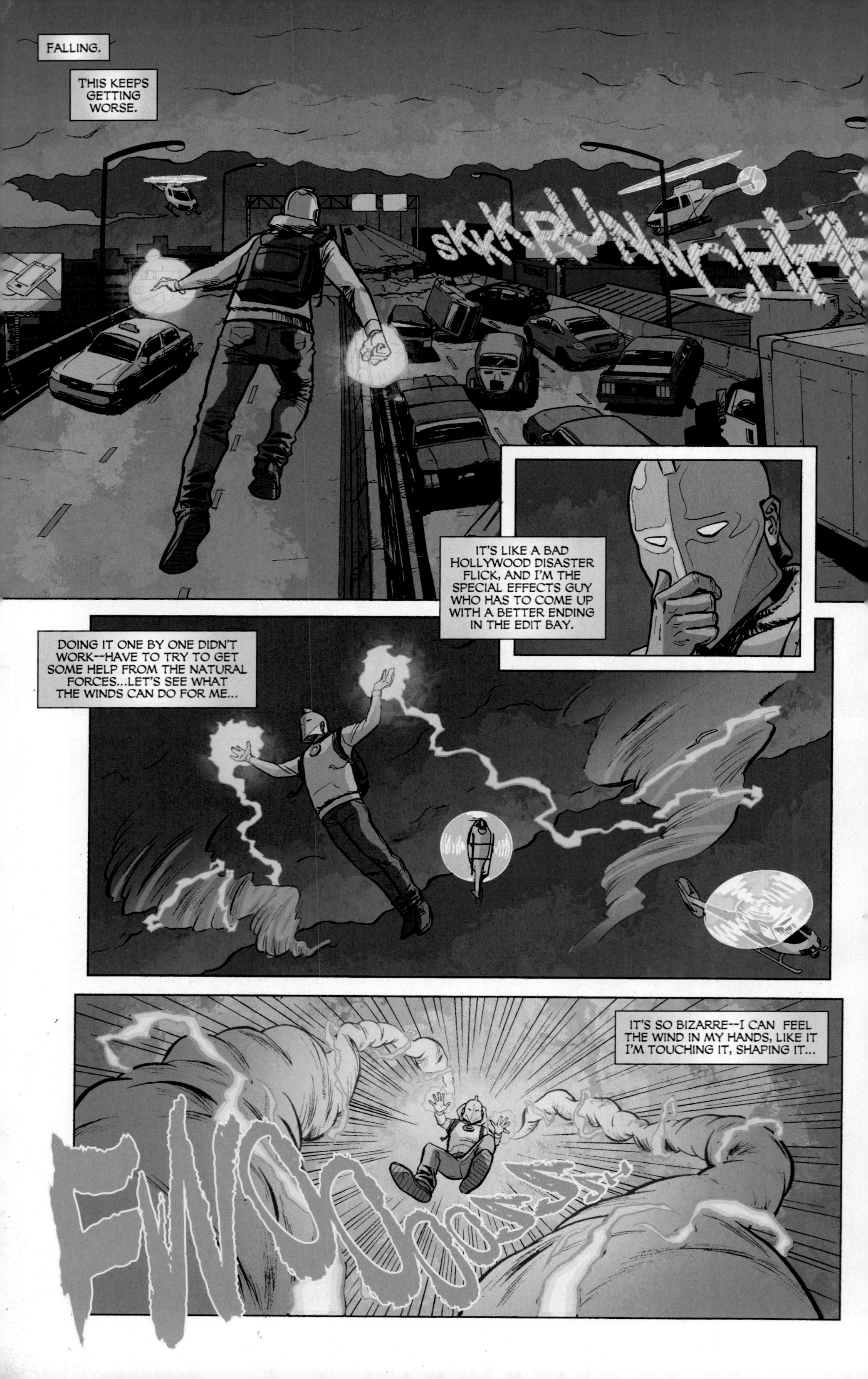

FALLING.
THIS KEEPS GETTING WORSE.
SKKKRUNNCHHH
IT'S LIKE A BAD HOLLYWOOD DISASTER FLICK, AND I'M THE SPECIAL EFFECTS GUY WHO HAS TO COME UP WITH A BETTER ENDING IN THE EDIT BAY.
DOING IT ONE BY ONE DIDN'T WORK--HAVE TO TRY TO GET SOME HELP FROM THE NATURAL FORCES...LET'S SEE WHAT THE WINDS CAN DO FOR ME...
IT'S SO BIZARRE--I CAN FEEL THE WIND IN MY HANDS, LIKE IT I'M TOUCHING IT, SHAPING IT...
FWOOOOSSSH

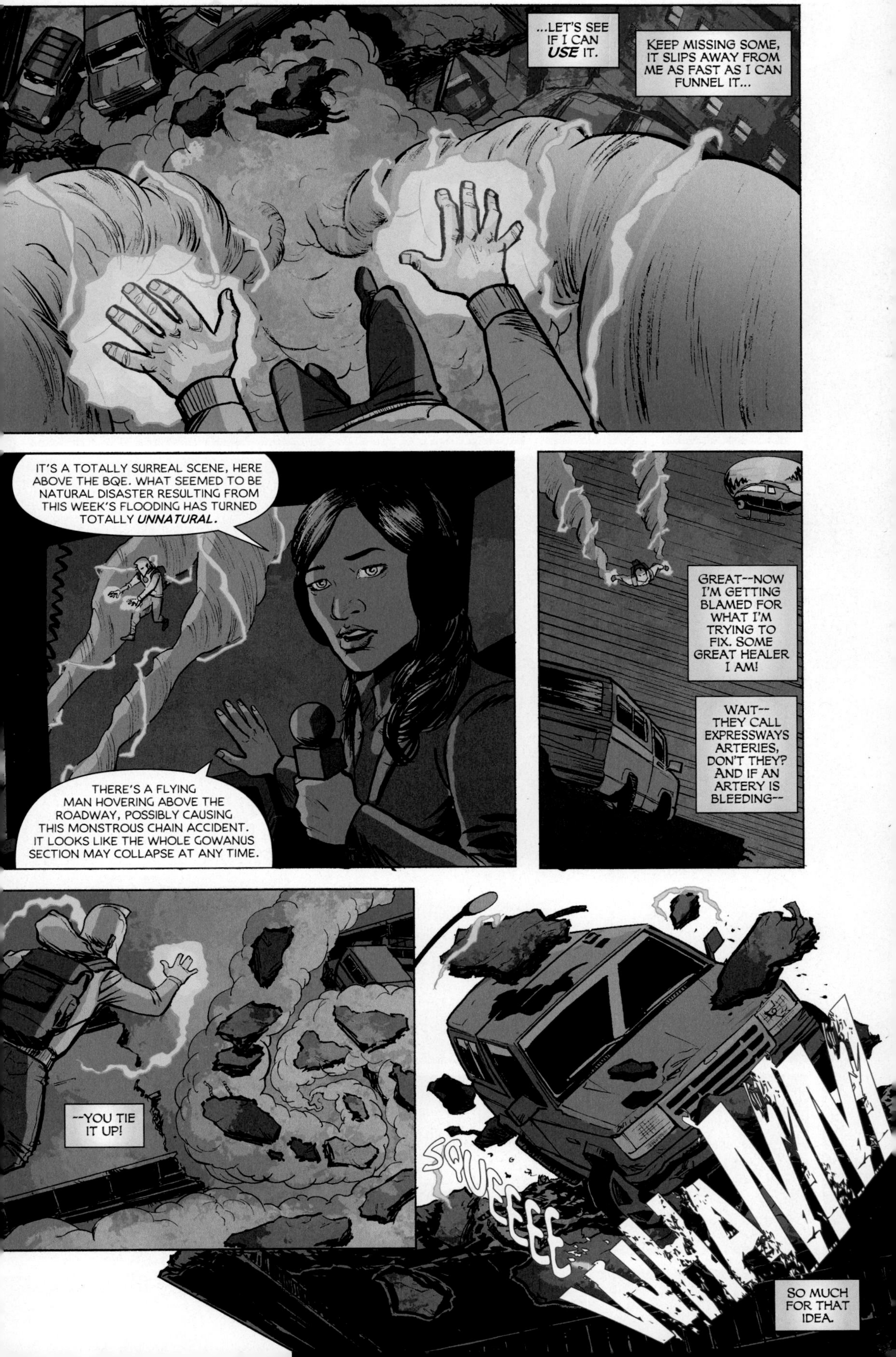
...LET'S SEE IF I CAN USE IT.
KEEP MISSING SOME, IT SLIPS AWAY FROM ME AS FAST AS I CAN FUNNEL IT...
IT'S A TOTALLY SURREAL SCENE, HERE ABOVE THE BQE. WHAT SEEMED TO BE NATURAL DISASTER RESULTING FROM THIS WEEK'S FLOODING HAS TURNED TOTALLY UNNATURAL.
THERE'S A FLYING MAN HOVERING ABOVE THE ROADWAY, POSSIBLY CAUSING THIS MONSTROUS CHAIN ACCIDENT. IT LOOKS LIKE THE WHOLE GOWANUS SECTION MAY COLLAPSE AT ANY TIME.
GREAT--NOW I'M GETTING BLAMED FOR WHAT I'M TRYING TO FIX. SOME GREAT HEALER I AM!
WAIT-- THEY CALL EXPRESSWAYS ARTERIES, DON'T THEY? AND IF AN ARTERY IS BLEEDING--
--YOU TIE IT UP!
SQUEEEEE
WHAMM
SO MUCH FOR THAT IDEA.

REW-UP
T THIS.
THE PYRAMIDS--
LOOK WITHIN!
IF THAT'S ALL YOU HAVE TO OFFER, NABU-- SHUT UP.
OR MAYBE...
HEY, YOU IN THE HALLOWEEN OUTFIT! GET YOUR HANDS UP!
THAT WILL NOT SOLVE ANYTHING, OFFICER.
THIS-- I HOPE-- SHALL!
THUNK
KRAKKOOOM

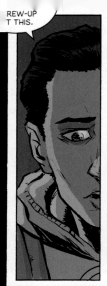

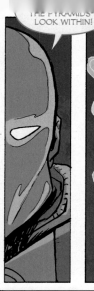

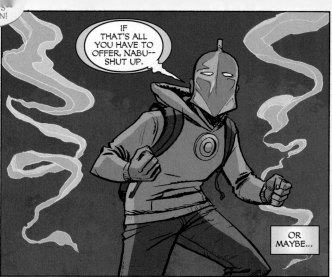

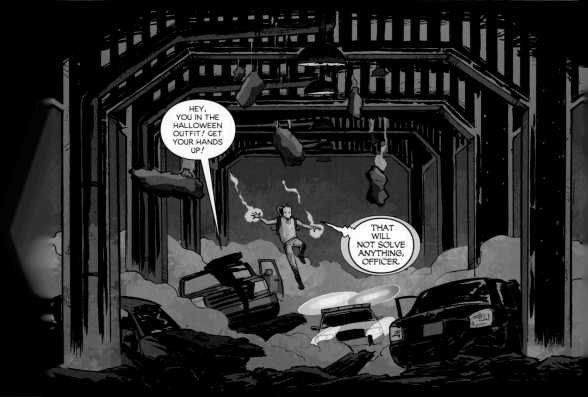

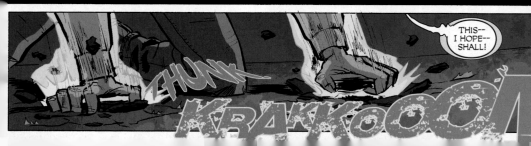

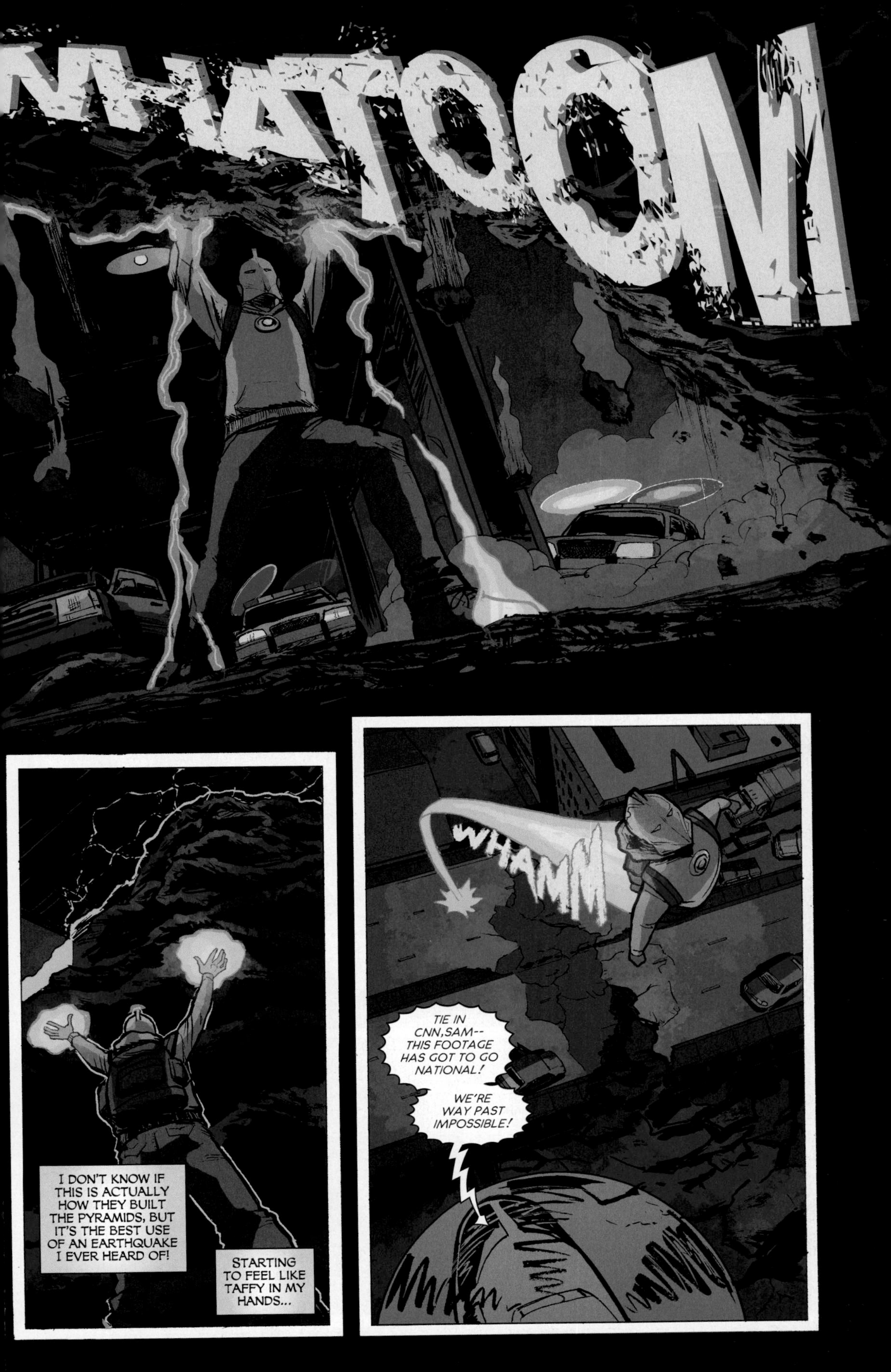
WHATOOM
I DON'T KNOW IF THIS IS ACTUALLY HOW THEY BUILT THE PYRAMIDS, BUT IT'S THE BEST USE OF AN EARTHQUAKE I EVER HEARD OF!
STARTING TO FEEL LIKE TAFFY IN MY HANDS...
WHAMM
TIE IN CNN, SAM-- THIS FOOTAGE HAS GOT TO GO NATIONAL!
WE'RE WAY PAST IMPOSSIBLE!

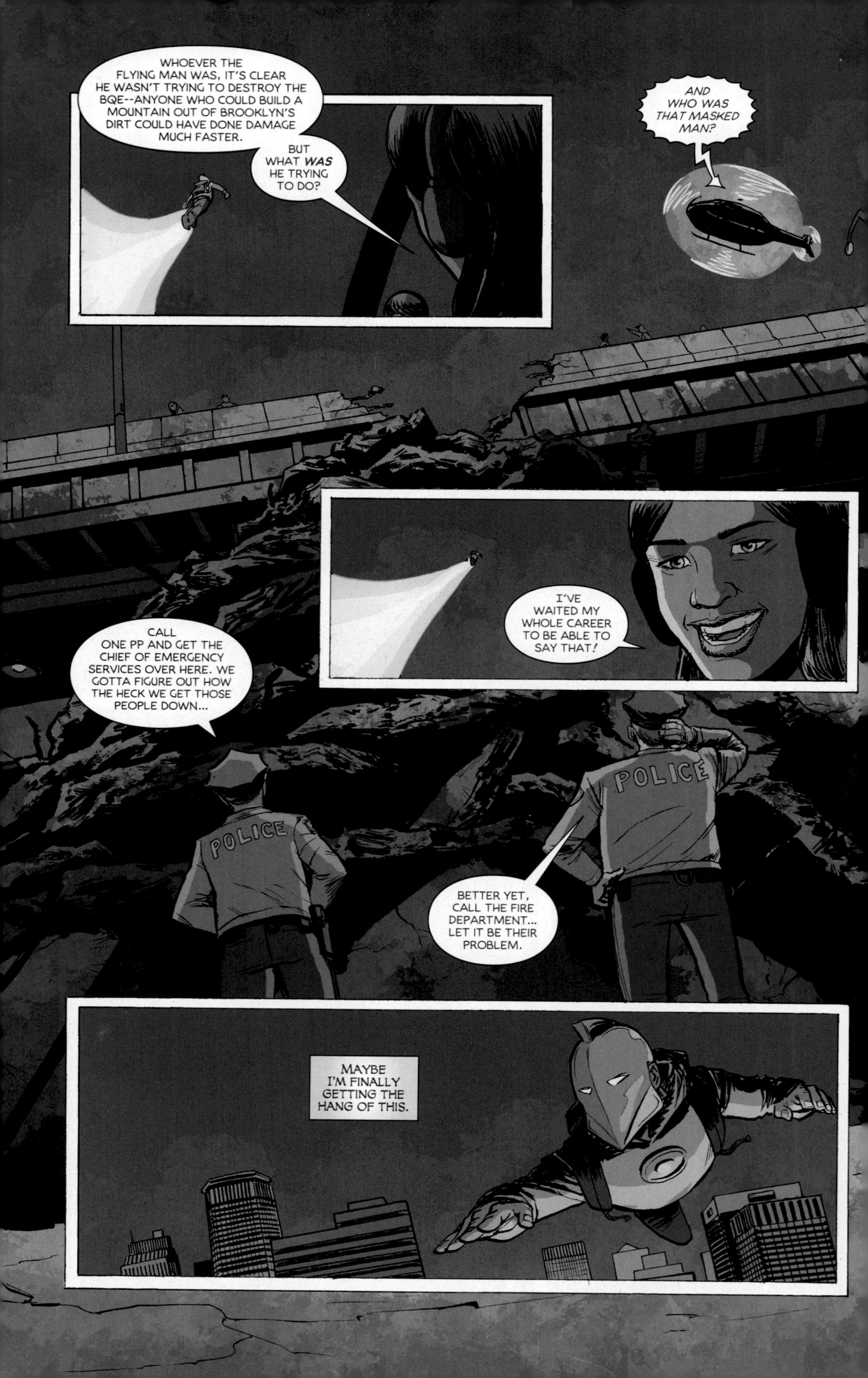
WHOEVER THE FLYING MAN WAS, IT'S CLEAR HE WASN'T TRYING TO DESTROY THE BQE--ANYONE WHO COULD BUILD A MOUNTAIN OUT OF BROOKLYN'S DIRT COULD HAVE DONE DAMAGE MUCH FASTER.
BUT WHAT *WAS* HE TRYING TO DO?
AND WHO WAS THAT MASKED MAN?
I'VE WAITED MY WHOLE CAREER TO BE ABLE TO SAY THAT!
CALL ONE PP AND GET THE CHIEF OF EMERGENCY SERVICES OVER HERE. WE GOTTA FIGURE OUT HOW THE HECK WE GET THOSE PEOPLE DOWN...
POLICE
POLICE
BETTER YET, CALL THE FIRE DEPARTMENT... LET IT BE THEIR PROBLEM.
MAYBE I'M FINALLY GETTING THE HANG OF THIS.

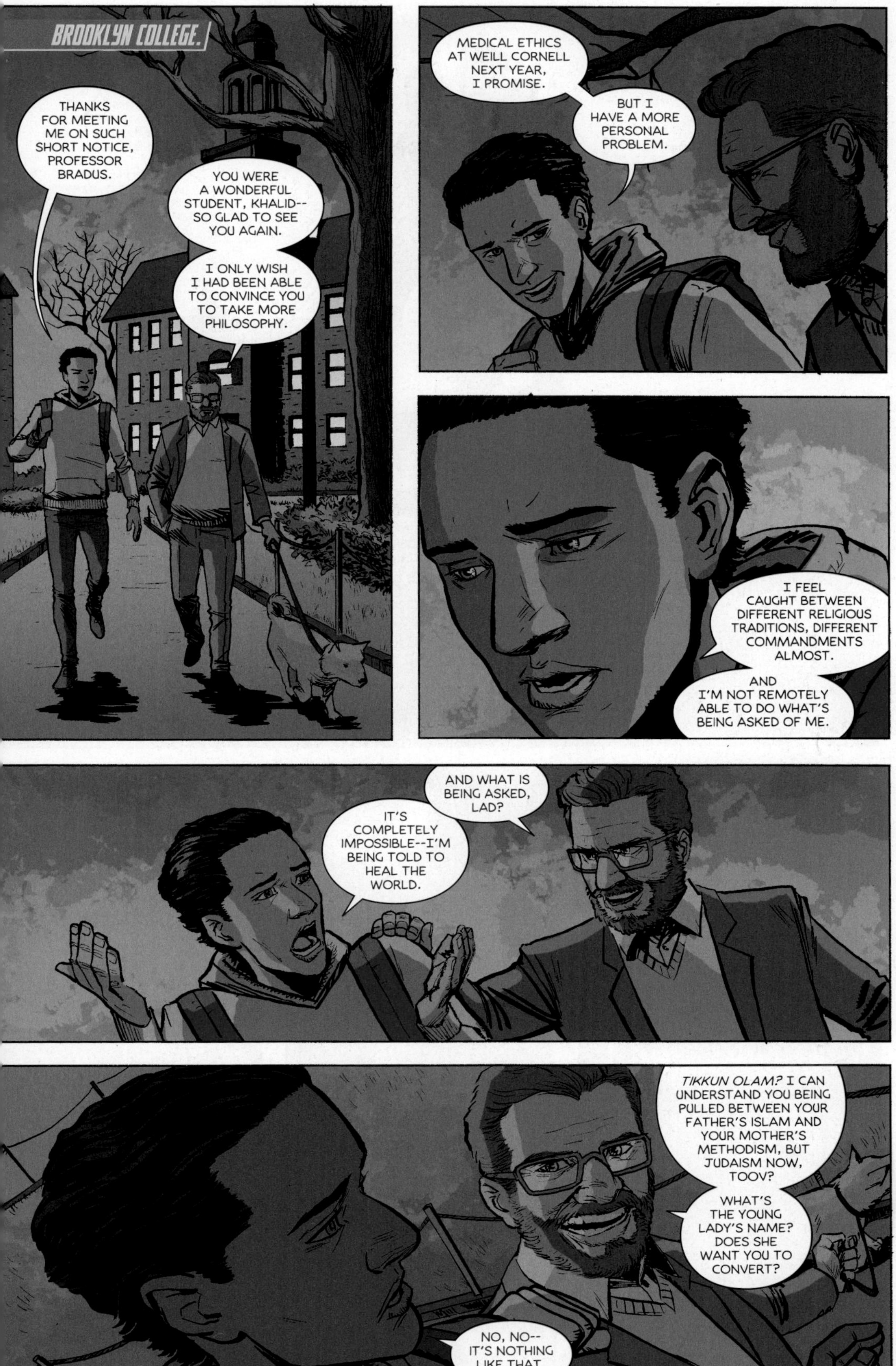
BROOKLYN COLLEGE.
THANKS FOR MEETING ME ON SUCH SHORT NOTICE, PROFESSOR BRADUS.
YOU WERE A WONDERFUL STUDENT, KHALID-- SO GLAD TO SEE YOU AGAIN.
I ONLY WISH I HAD BEEN ABLE TO CONVINCE YOU TO TAKE MORE PHILOSOPHY.
MEDICAL ETHICS AT WEILL CORNELL NEXT YEAR, I PROMISE.
BUT I HAVE A MORE PERSONAL PROBLEM.
I FEEL CAUGHT BETWEEN DIFFERENT RELIGIOUS TRADITIONS, DIFFERENT COMMANDMENTS ALMOST.
AND I'M NOT REMOTELY ABLE TO DO WHAT'S BEING ASKED OF ME.
AND WHAT IS BEING ASKED, LAD?
IT'S COMPLETELY IMPOSSIBLE--I'M BEING TOLD TO HEAL THE WORLD.
TIKKUN OLAM? I CAN UNDERSTAND YOU BEING PULLED BETWEEN YOUR FATHER'S ISLAM AND YOUR MOTHER'S METHODISM, BUT JUDAISM NOW, TOO?
WHAT'S THE YOUNG LADY'S NAME? DOES SHE WANT YOU TO CONVERT?
NO, NO-- IT'S NOTHING LIKE THAT.

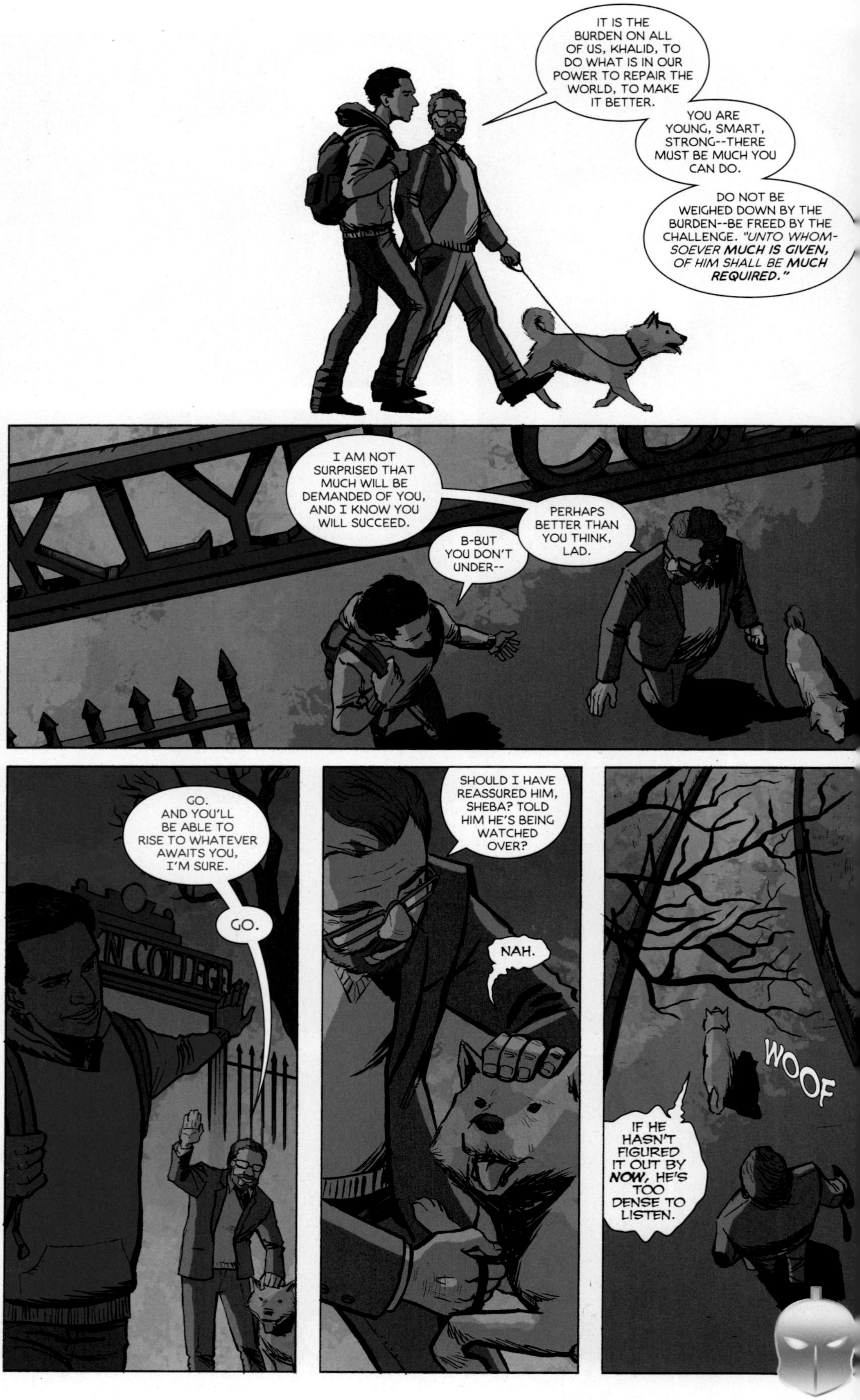
IT IS THE BURDEN ON ALL OF US, KHALID, TO DO WHAT IS IN OUR POWER TO REPAIR THE WORLD, TO MAKE IT BETTER.
YOU ARE YOUNG, SMART, STRONG--THERE MUST BE MUCH YOU CAN DO.
DO NOT BE WEIGHED DOWN BY THE BURDEN--BE FREED BY THE CHALLENGE. *"UNTO WHOMSOEVER* **MUCH IS GIVEN,** *OF HIM SHALL BE* **MUCH REQUIRED."**
I AM NOT SURPRISED THAT MUCH WILL BE DEMANDED OF YOU, AND I KNOW YOU WILL SUCCEED.
B-BUT YOU DON'T UNDER--
PERHAPS BETTER THAN YOU THINK, LAD.
GO. AND YOU'LL BE ABLE TO RISE TO WHATEVER AWAITS YOU, I'M SURE.
GO.
N COLLEGE
SHOULD I HAVE REASSURED HIM, SHEBA? TOLD HIM HE'S BEING WATCHED OVER?
NAH.
WOOF
IF HE HASN'T FIGURED IT OUT BY **NOW,** HE'S TOO DENSE TO LISTEN.

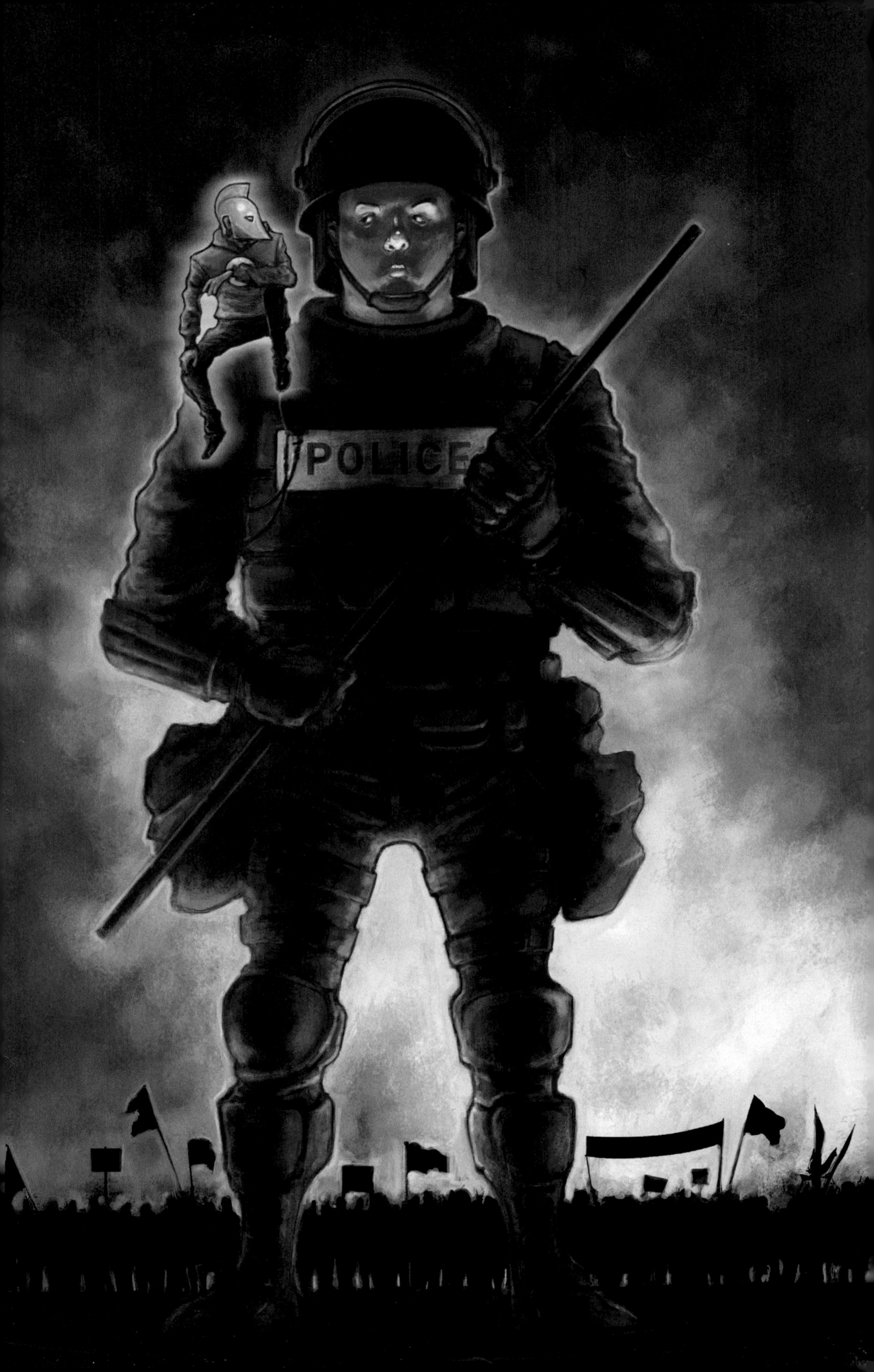
POLICE

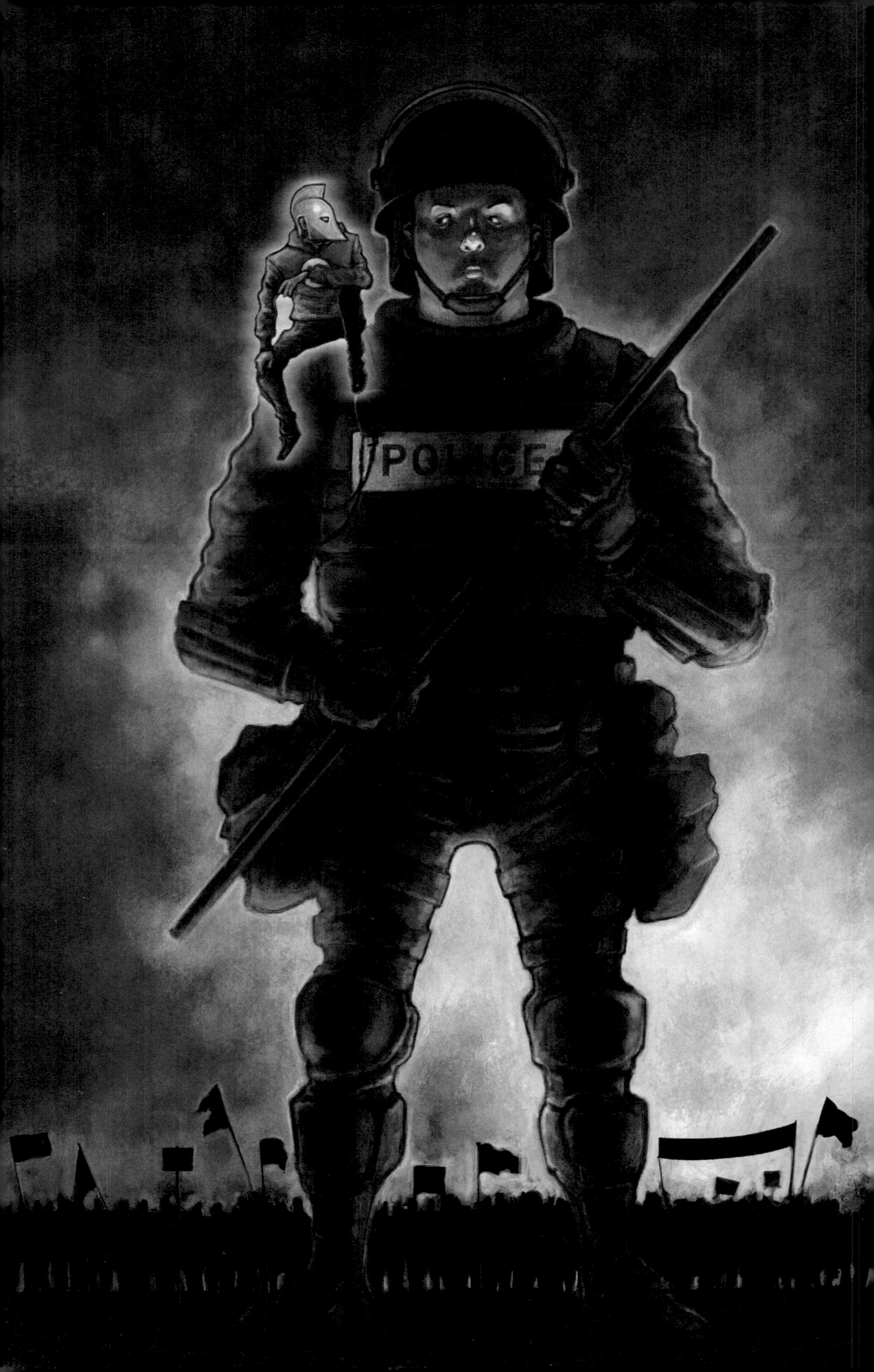
POLICE

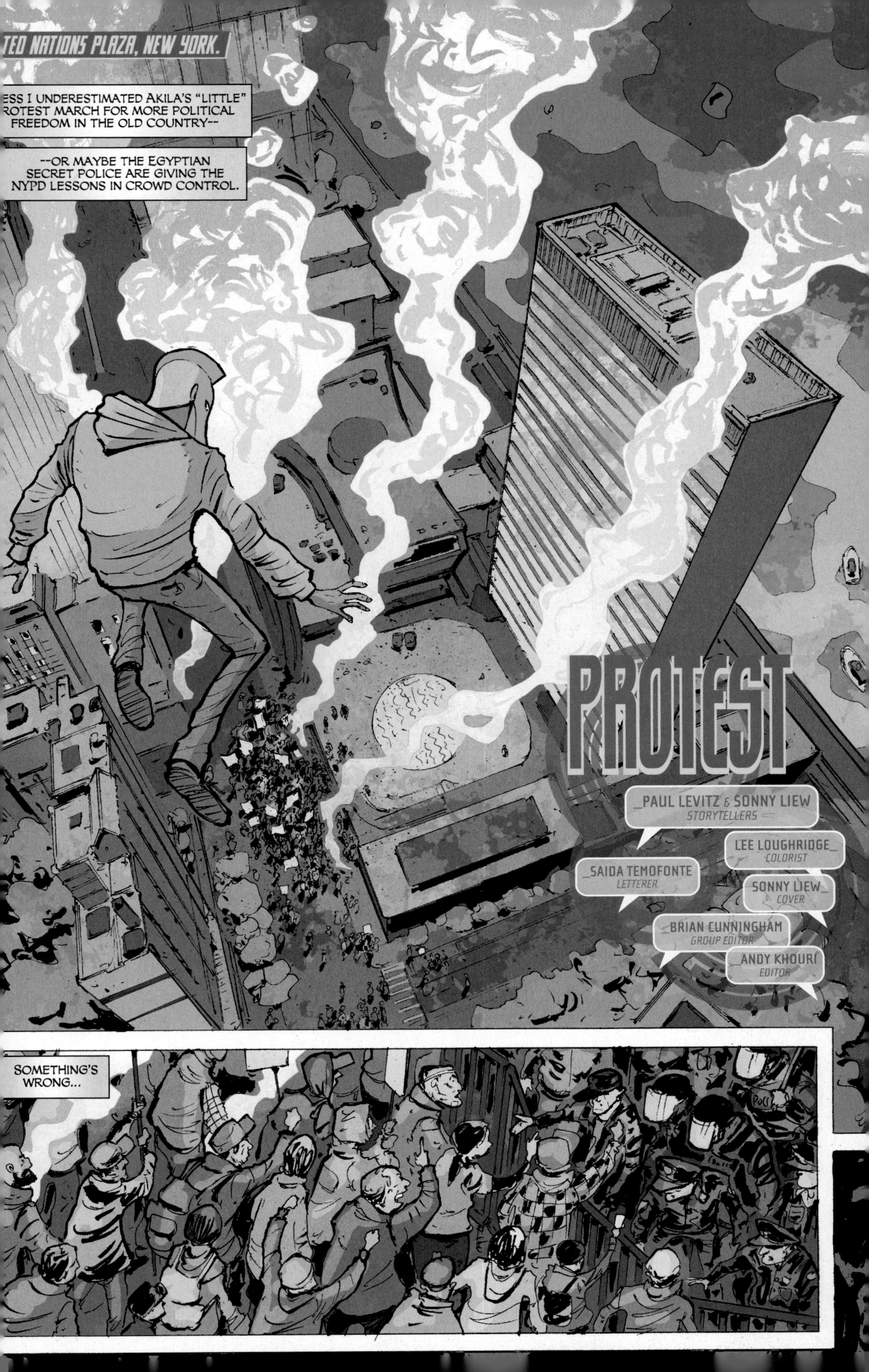

TED NATIONS PLAZA, NEW YORK.
ESS I UNDERESTIMATED AKILA'S "LITTLE" ROTEST MARCH FOR MORE POLITICAL FREEDOM IN THE OLD COUNTRY--
--OR MAYBE THE EGYPTIAN SECRET POLICE ARE GIVING THE NYPD LESSONS IN CROWD CONTROL.
PROTEST
_PAUL LEVITZ & SONNY LIEW
STORYTELLERS
LEE LOUGHRIDGE_
COLORIST
_SAIDA TEMOFONTE
LETTERER
SONNY LIEW_
COVER
_BRIAN CUNNINGHAM
GROUP EDITOR
_ANDY KHOURI
EDITOR
SOMETHING'S WRONG...

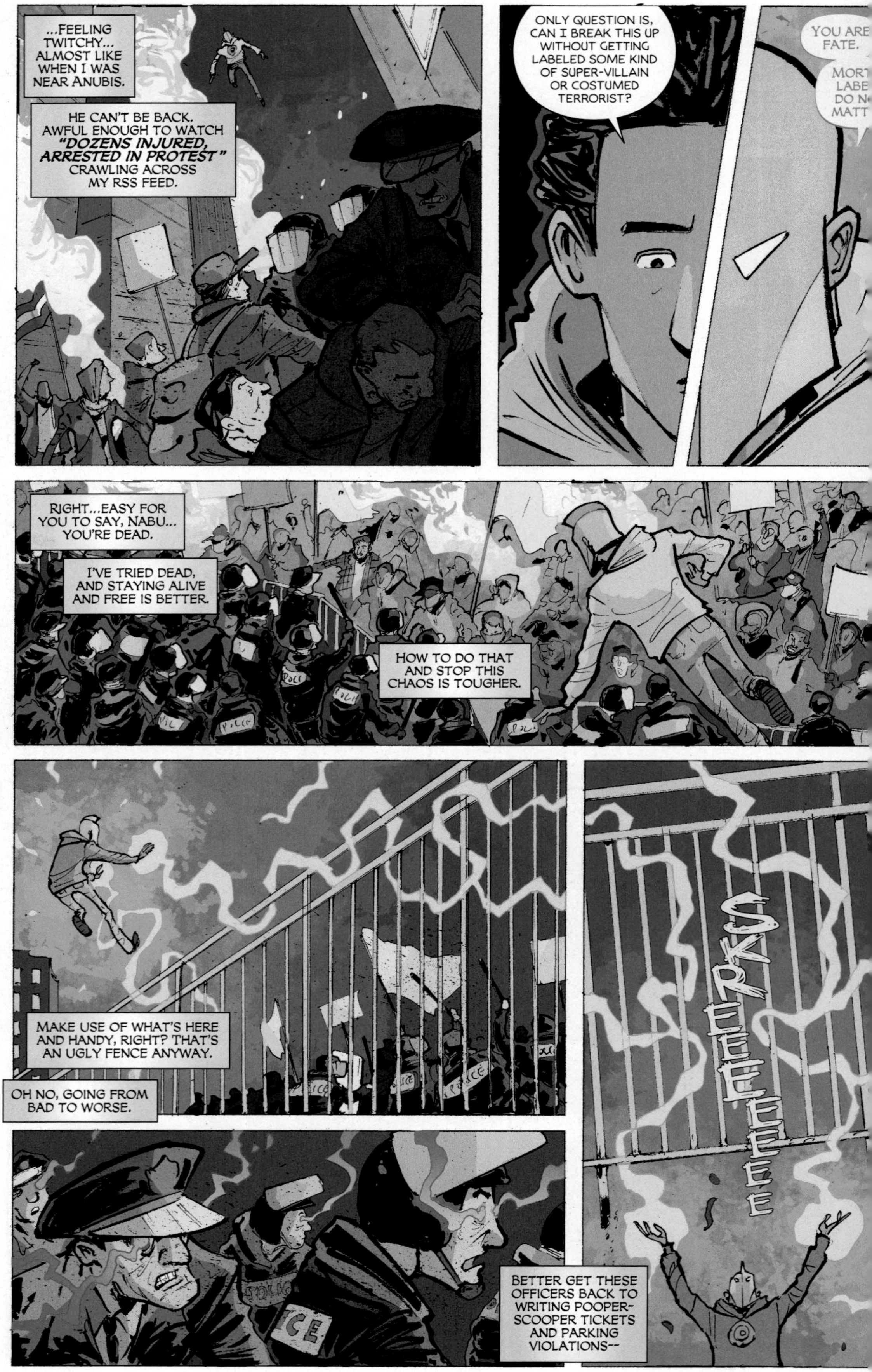

...FEELING TWITCHY... ALMOST LIKE WHEN I WAS NEAR ANUBIS.
HE CAN'T BE BACK. AWFUL ENOUGH TO WATCH *"DOZENS INJURED, ARRESTED IN PROTEST"* CRAWLING ACROSS MY RSS FEED.
ONLY QUESTION IS, CAN I BREAK THIS UP WITHOUT GETTING LABELED SOME KIND OF SUPER-VILLAIN OR COSTUMED TERRORIST?
YOU ARE FATE.
RIGHT...EASY FOR YOU TO SAY, NABU... YOU'RE DEAD.
I'VE TRIED DEAD, AND STAYING ALIVE AND FREE IS BETTER.
HOW TO DO THAT AND STOP THIS CHAOS IS TOUGHER.
MAKE USE OF WHAT'S HERE AND HANDY, RIGHT? THAT'S AN UGLY FENCE ANYWAY.
OH NO, GOING FROM BAD TO WORSE.
SKREEEEEEEE
BETTER GET THESE OFFICERS BACK TO WRITING POOPER-SCOOPER TICKETS AND PARKING VIOLATIONS--

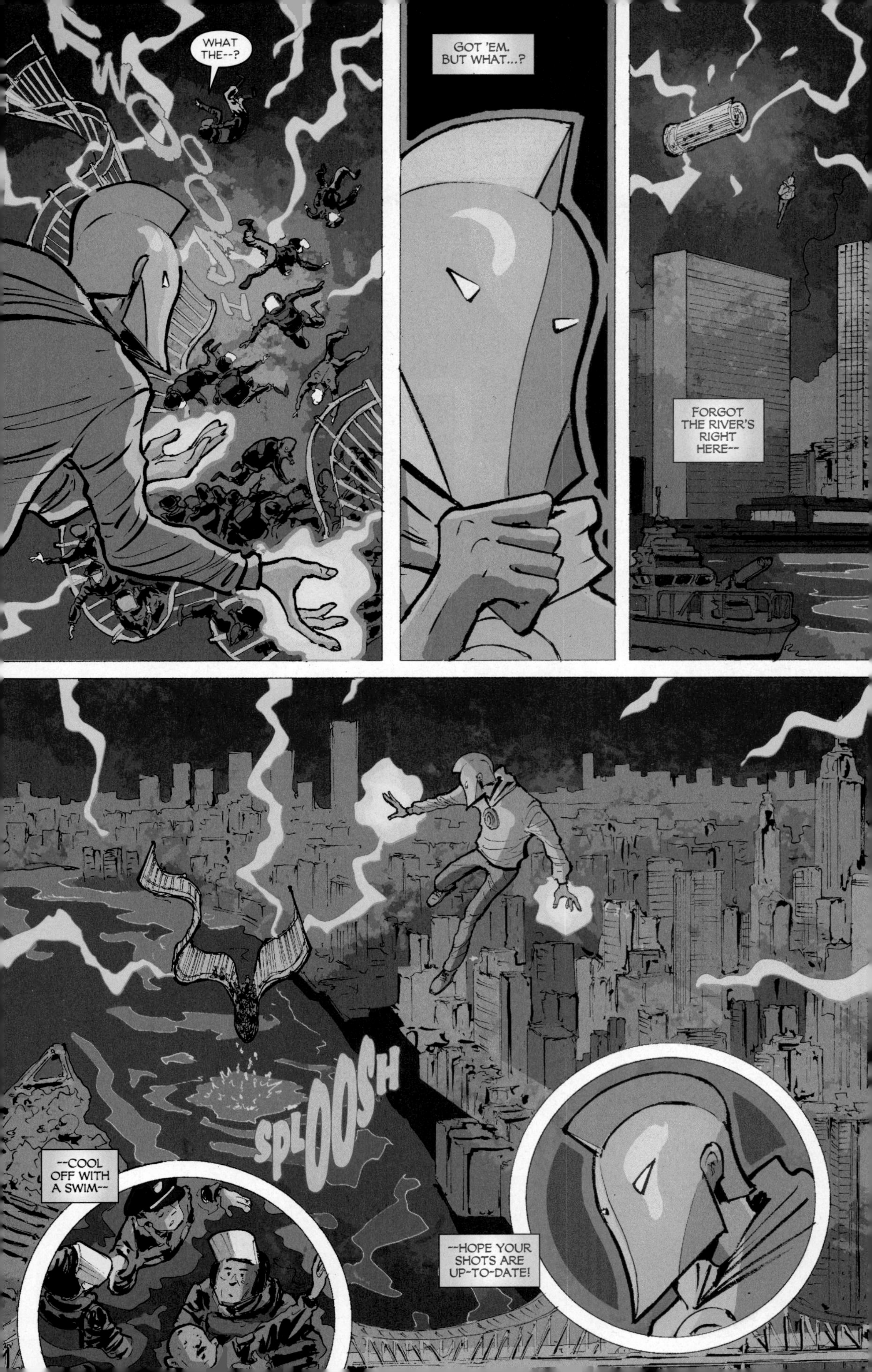
WHAT THE--?
WOOOOOOOSH
GOT 'EM. BUT WHAT...?
FORGOT THE RIVER'S RIGHT HERE--
SPLOOOSH
--COOL OFF WITH A SWIM--
--HOPE YOUR SHOTS ARE UP-TO-DATE!

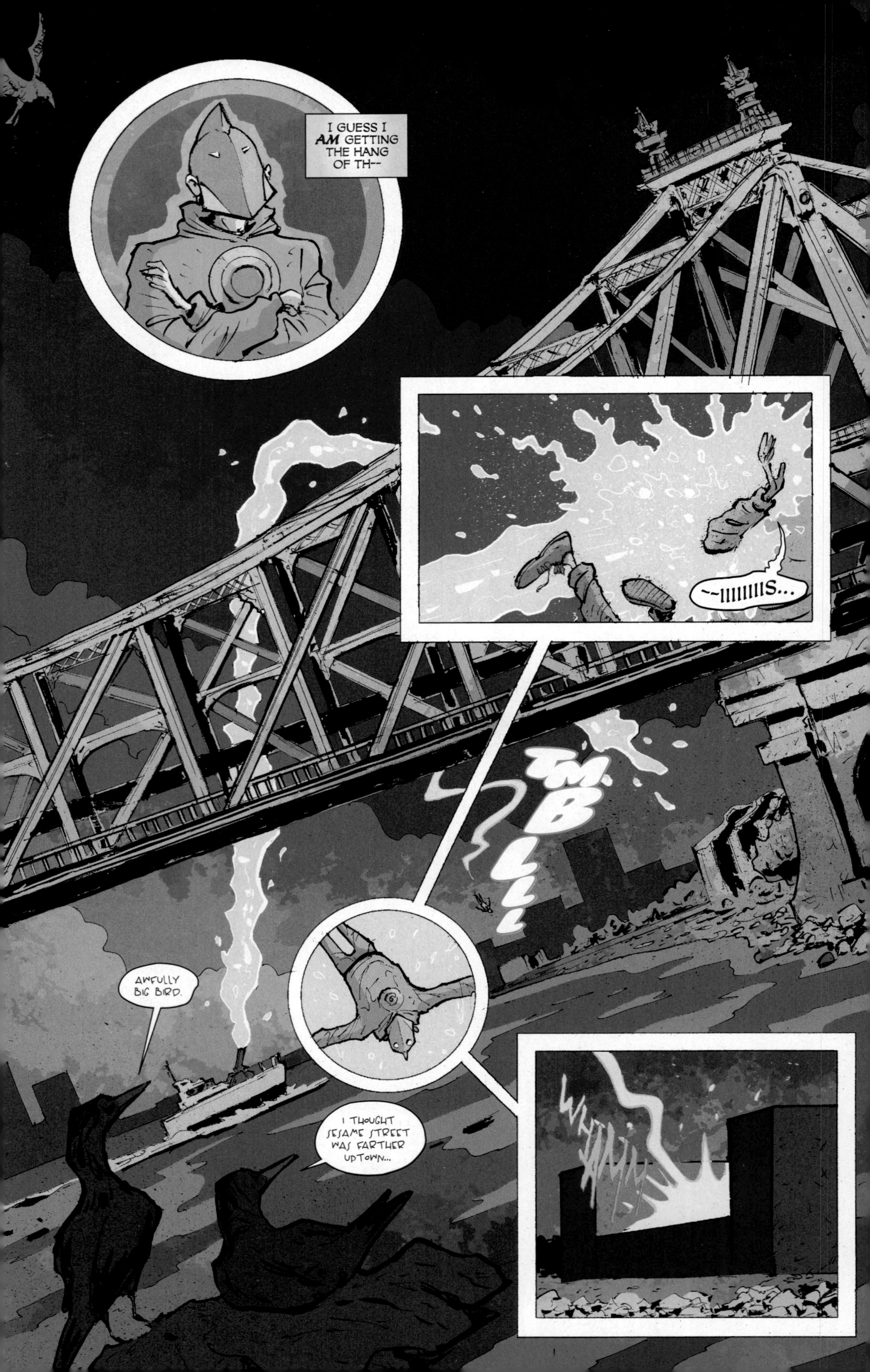
I GUESS I AM GETTING THE HANG OF TH--
--IIIIIIIS...
AWFULLY BIG BIRD.
I THOUGHT SESAME STREET WAS FARTHER UPTOWN...

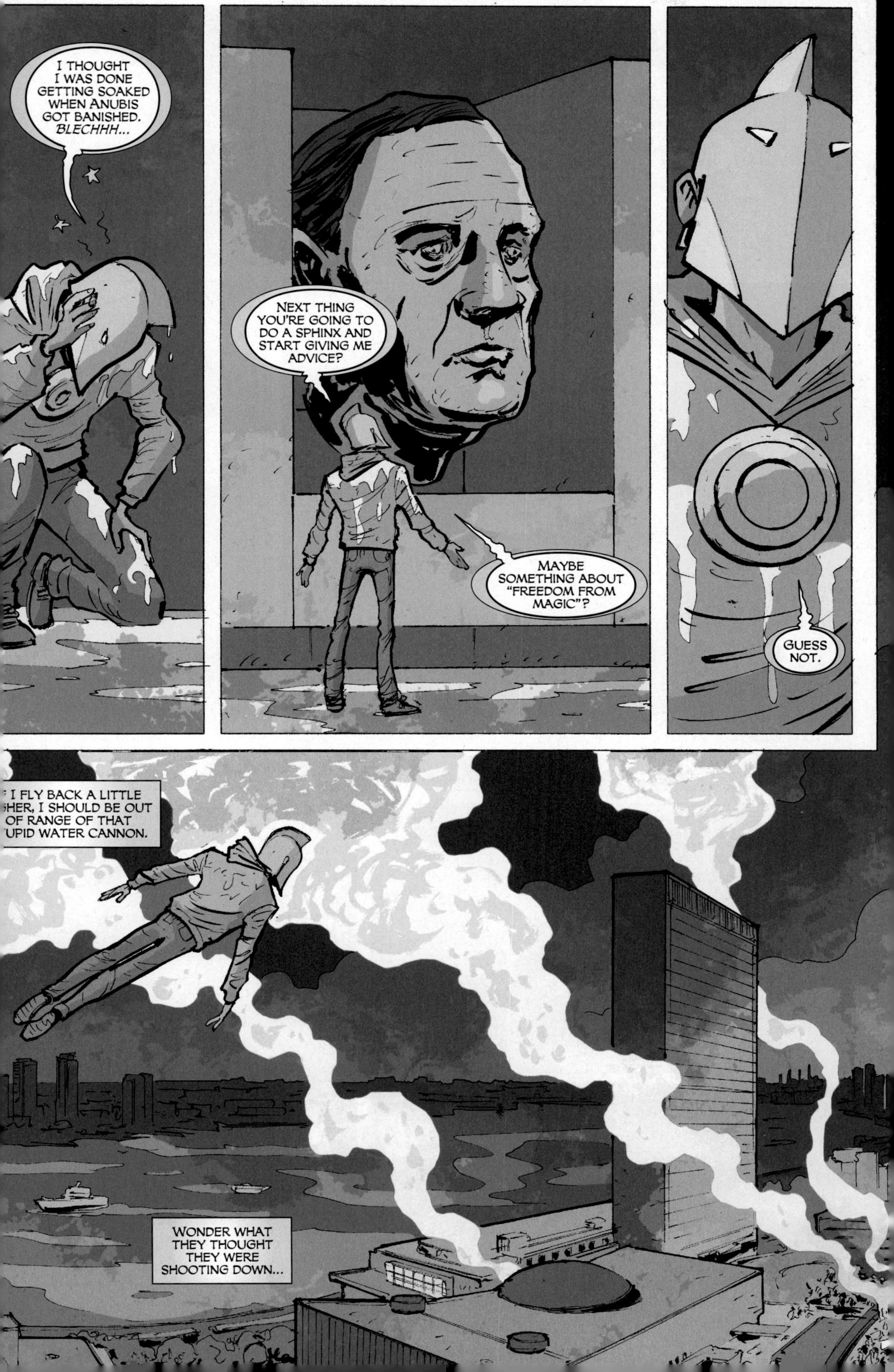
I THOUGHT I WAS DONE GETTING SOAKED WHEN ANUBIS GOT BANISHED. *BLECHHH...*
NEXT THING YOU'RE GOING TO DO A SPHINX AND START GIVING ME ADVICE?
MAYBE SOMETHING ABOUT "FREEDOM FROM MAGIC"?
GUESS NOT.
F I FLY BACK A LITTLE GHER, I SHOULD BE OUT OF RANGE OF THAT UPID WATER CANNON.
WONDER WHAT THEY THOUGHT THEY WERE SHOOTING DOWN...

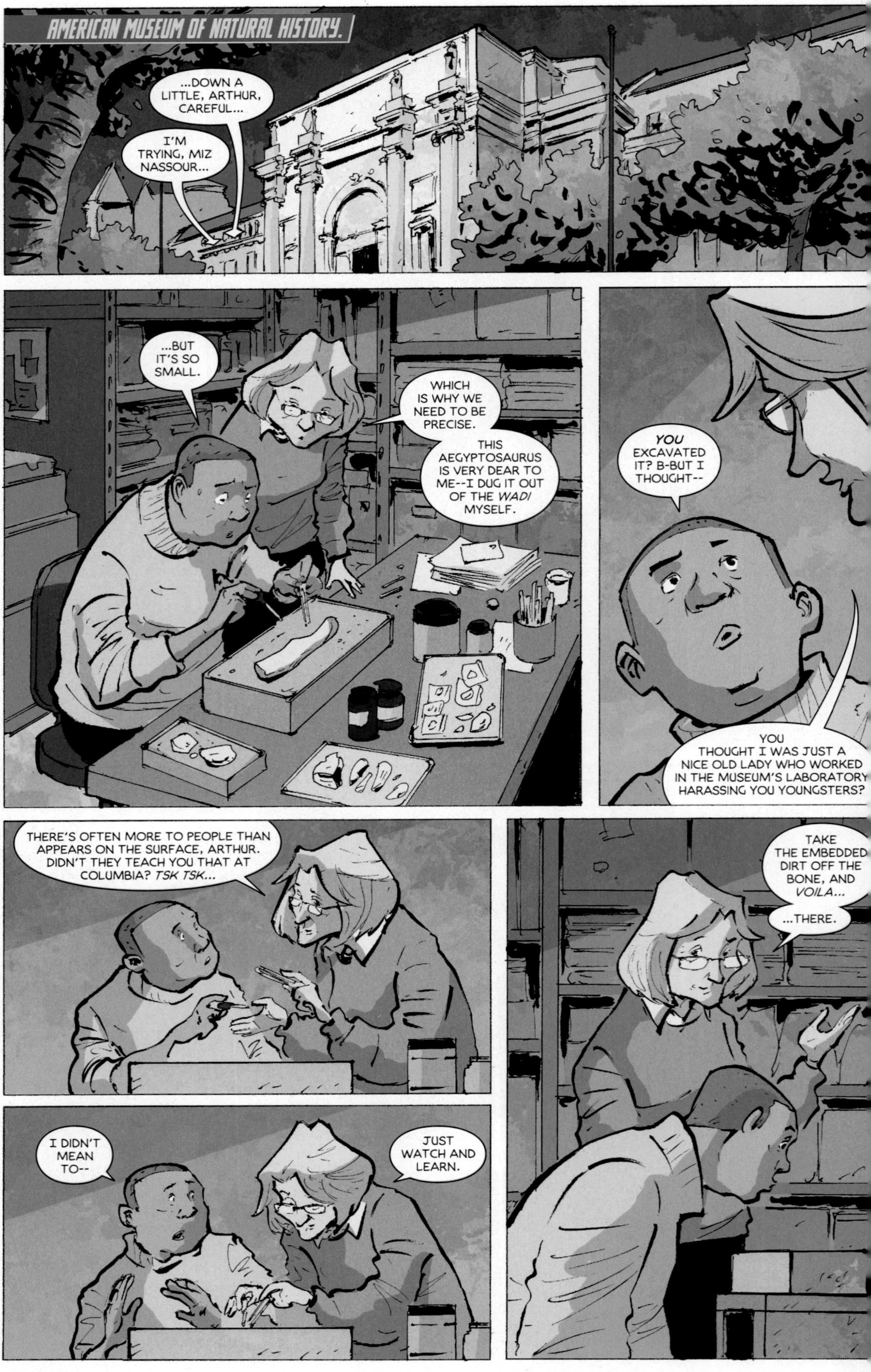
AMERICAN MUSEUM OF NATURAL HISTORY.
...DOWN A LITTLE, ARTHUR, CAREFUL...
I'M TRYING, MIZ NASSOUR...
...BUT IT'S SO SMALL.
WHICH IS WHY WE NEED TO BE PRECISE.
THIS AEGYPTOSAURUS IS VERY DEAR TO ME--I DUG IT OUT OF THE WADI MYSELF.
YOU EXCAVATED IT? B-BUT I THOUGHT--
YOU THOUGHT I WAS JUST A NICE OLD LADY WHO WORKED IN THE MUSEUM'S LABORATORY HARASSING YOU YOUNGSTERS?
THERE'S OFTEN MORE TO PEOPLE THAN APPEARS ON THE SURFACE, ARTHUR. DIDN'T THEY TEACH YOU THAT AT COLUMBIA? TSK TSK...
I DIDN'T MEAN TO--
JUST WATCH AND LEARN.
TAKE THE EMBEDDED DIRT OFF THE BONE, AND VOILA...
...THERE.

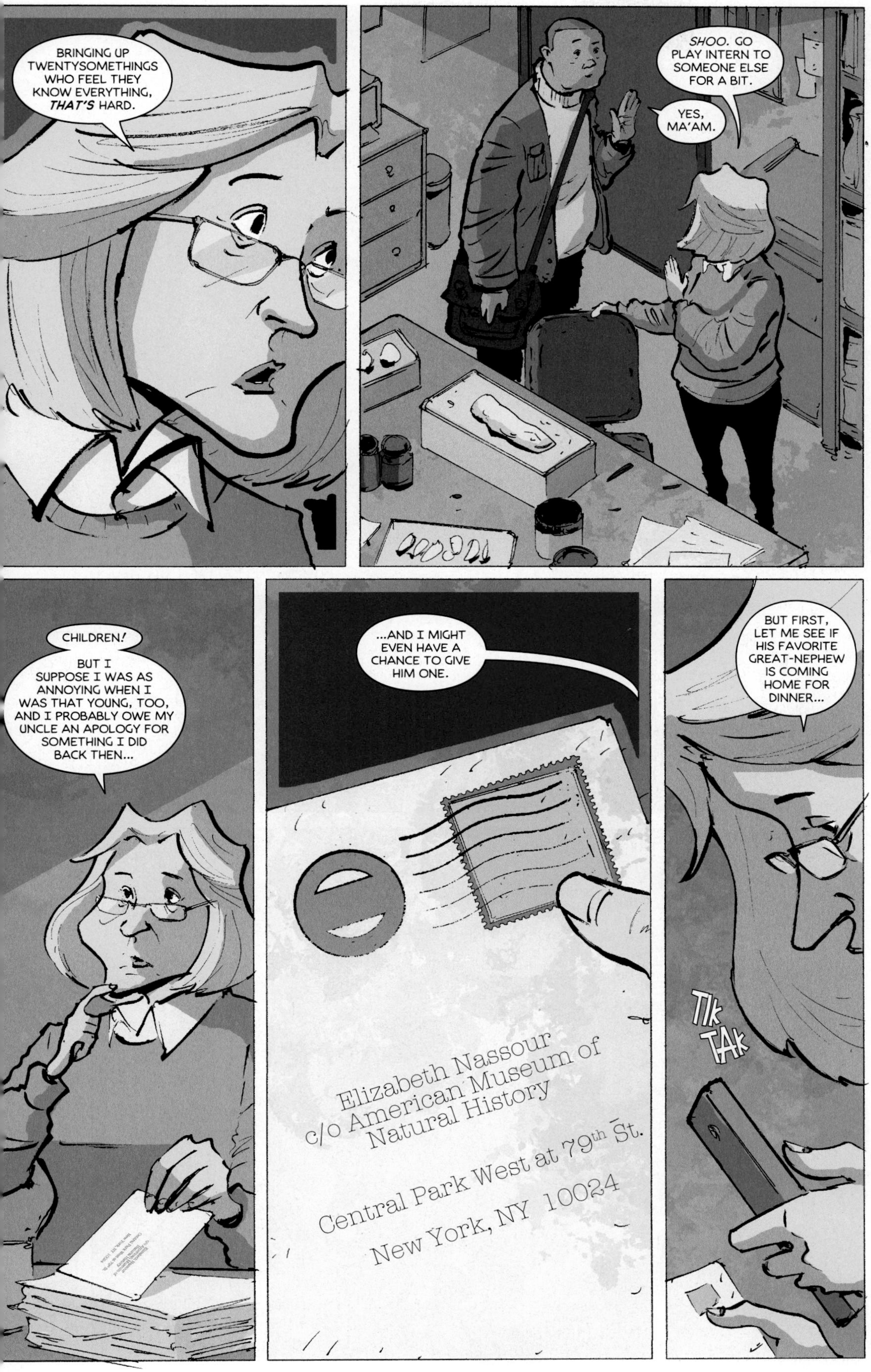
BRINGING UP TWENTYSOMETHINGS WHO FEEL THEY KNOW EVERYTHING, *THAT'S* HARD.
SHOO. GO PLAY INTERN TO SOMEONE ELSE FOR A BIT.
YES, MA'AM.
CHILDREN!
BUT I SUPPOSE I WAS AS ANNOYING WHEN I WAS THAT YOUNG, TOO, AND I PROBABLY OWE MY UNCLE AN APOLOGY FOR SOMETHING I DID BACK THEN...
...AND I MIGHT EVEN HAVE A CHANCE TO GIVE HIM ONE.
Elizabeth Nassour
c/o American Museum of
Natural History
Central Park West at 79th St.
New York, NY 10024
BUT FIRST, LET ME SEE IF HIS FAVORITE GREAT-NEPHEW IS COMING HOME FOR DINNER...
TIK
TAK

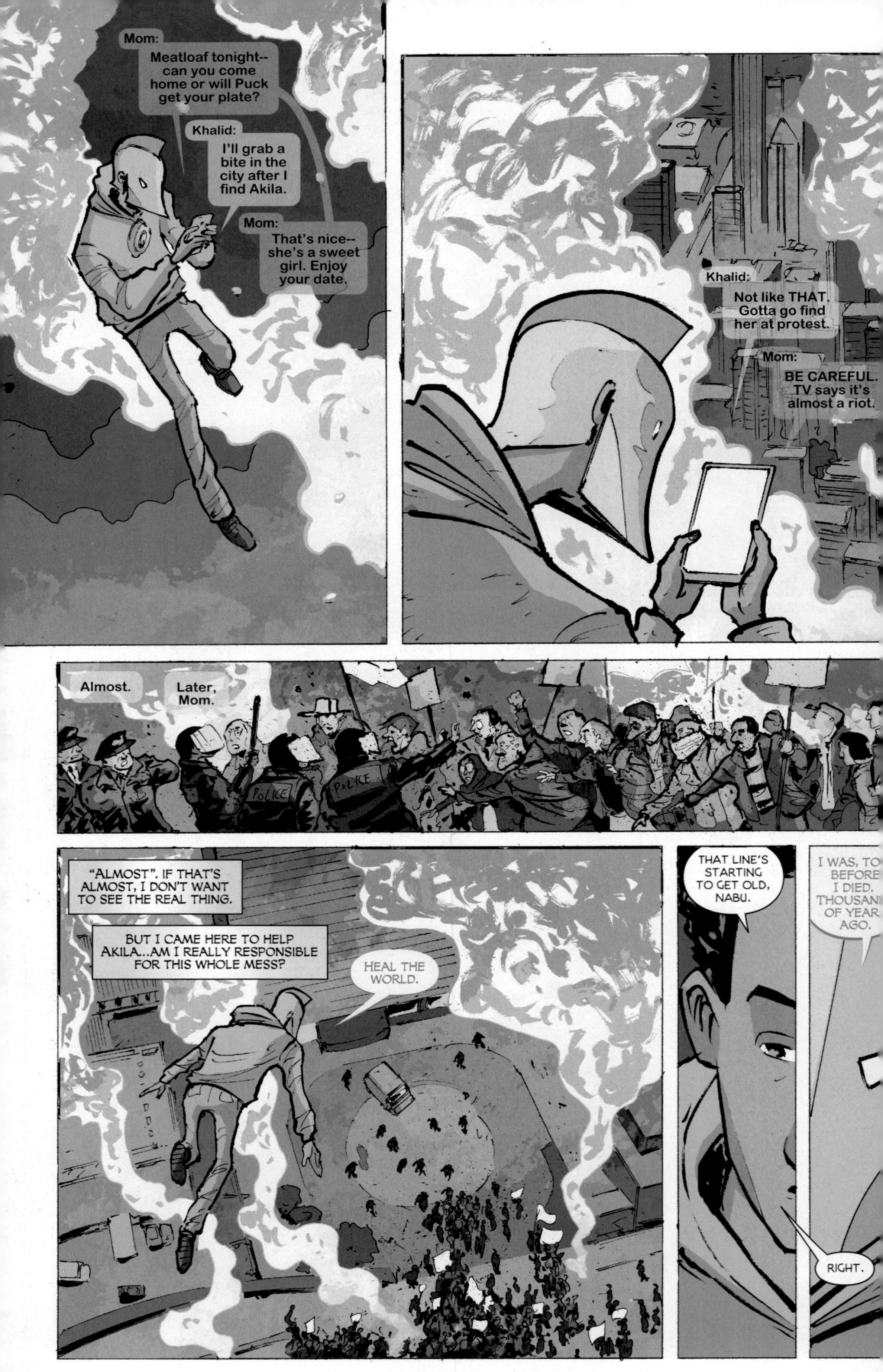
Mom:
Meatloaf tonight-- can you come home or will Puck get your plate?
Khalid:
I'll grab a bite in the city after I find Akila.
Mom:
That's nice-- she's a sweet girl. Enjoy your date.
Khalid:
Not like THAT. Gotta go find her at protest.
Mom:
BE CAREFUL. TV says it's almost a riot.
Almost.
Later, Mom.
POLICE
POLICE
"ALMOST". IF THAT'S ALMOST, I DON'T WANT TO SEE THE REAL THING.
BUT I CAME HERE TO HELP AKILA...AM I REALLY RESPONSIBLE FOR THIS WHOLE MESS?
HEAL THE WORLD.
THAT LINE'S STARTING TO GET OLD, NABU.
I WAS, TO BEFORE I DIED. THOUSAN OF YEAR AGO.
RIGHT.

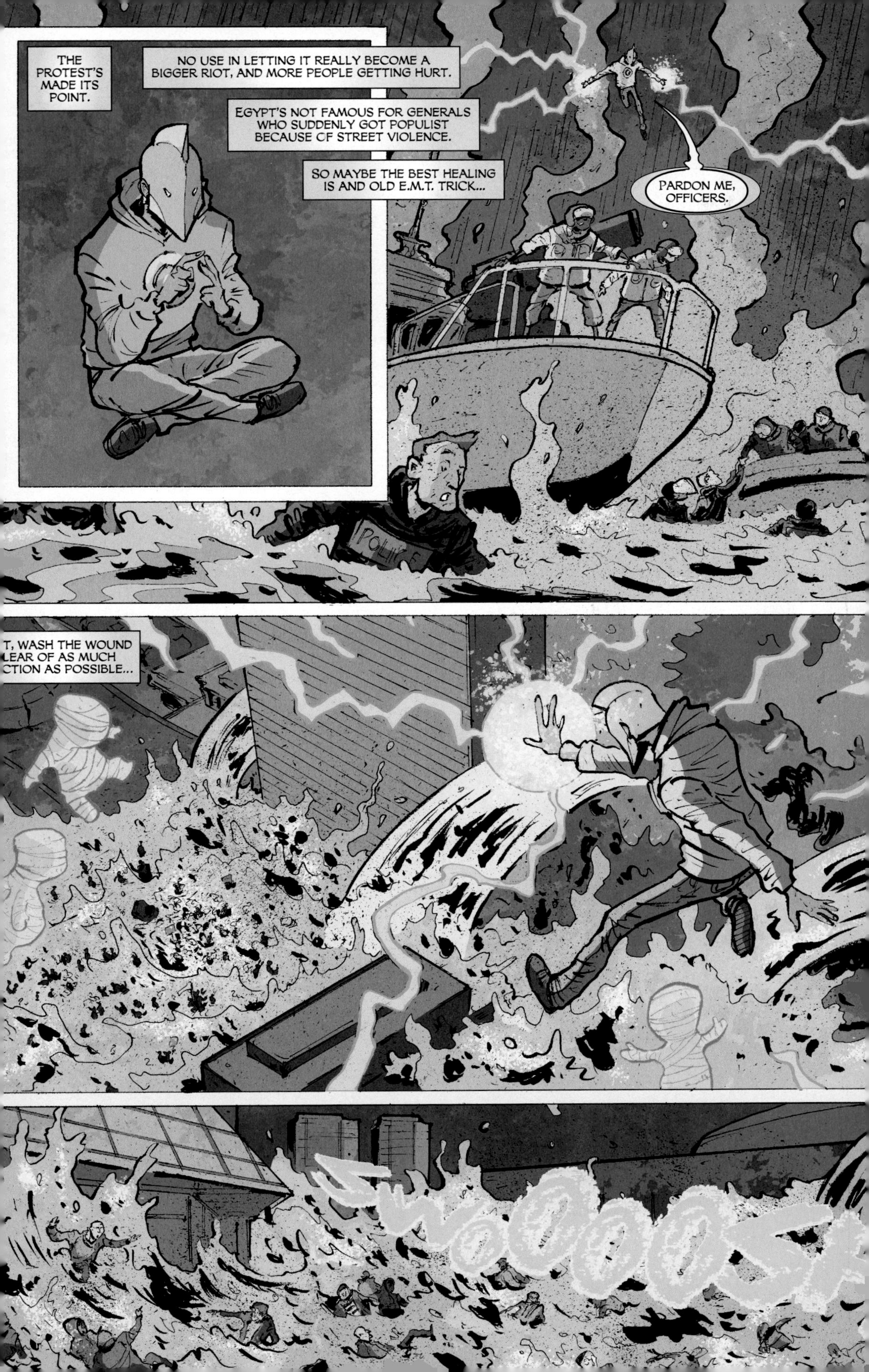
THE PROTEST'S MADE ITS POINT.
NO USE IN LETTING IT REALLY BECOME A BIGGER RIOT, AND MORE PEOPLE GETTING HURT.
EGYPT'S NOT FAMOUS FOR GENERALS WHO SUDDENLY GOT POPULIST BECAUSE OF STREET VIOLENCE.
SO MAYBE THE BEST HEALING IS AND OLD E.M.T. TRICK...
PARDON ME, OFFICERS.
POLICE
T, WASH THE WOUND
LEAR OF AS MUCH
CTION AS POSSIBLE...
SWOOOOSH

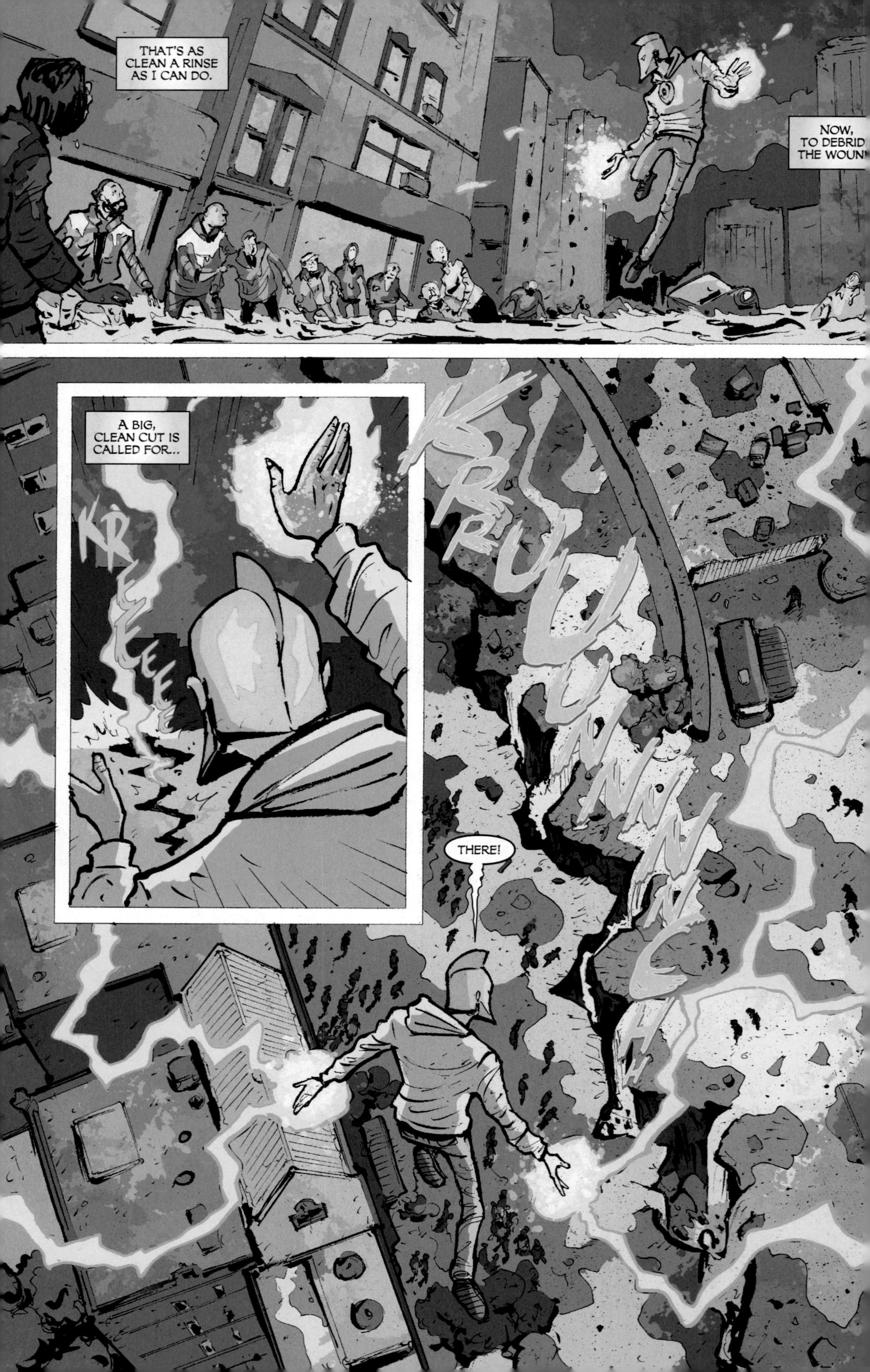
THAT'S AS CLEAN A RINSE AS I CAN DO.
NOW, TO DEBRID THE WOUN
A BIG, CLEAN CUT IS CALLED FOR...
THERE!

THAT'LL CALM TEMPERS LONG ENOUGH FOR THEM TO MARCH THE HALF MILE AROUND THE BREAK...AND MAYBE LONGER...

...BUT THERE'S STILL NO SIGN OF AKILA.

IS SHE HURT? IN A HOSPITAL? DRAGGED OFF SOMEWHERE?

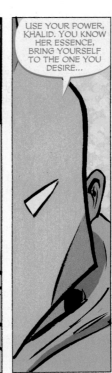

USE YOUR POWER, KHALID. YOU KNOW HER ESSENCE, BRING YOURSELF TO THE ONE YOU DESIRE...

IT'S NOT LIKE *THAT,* NABU--SHE'S A FRIEND.

I DON'T WANT HER HURT.

AKILA... WHERE *ARE* YOU?

OKAY. GUESS THIS IS THE WAY IT WORKS...

...BUT HOW'D YOU GET THAT FAR FROM THE PROTEST? WHERE ARE YOU?

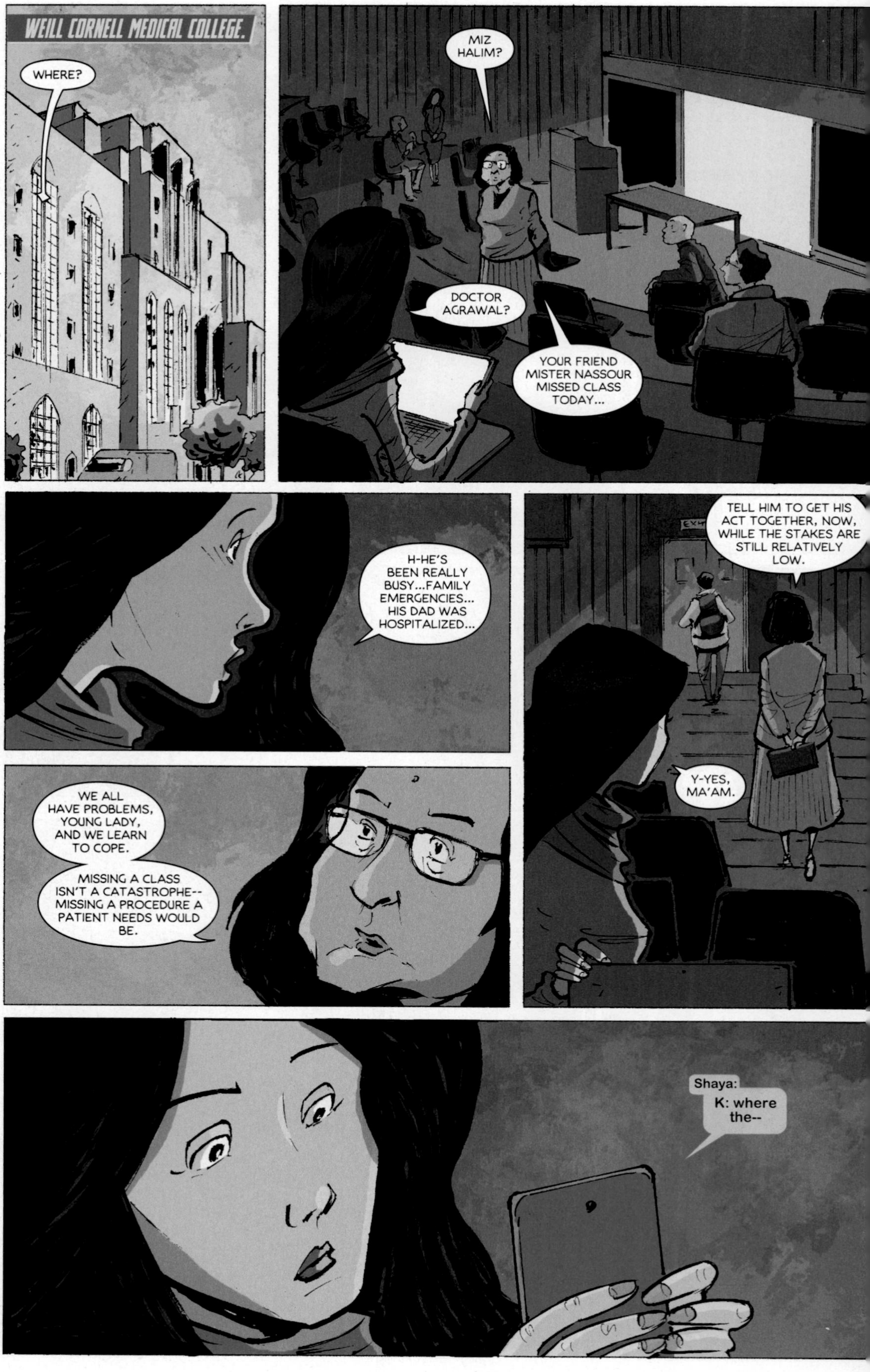
WEILL CORNELL MEDICAL COLLEGE.
WHERE?
MIZ HALIM?
DOCTOR AGRAWAL?
YOUR FRIEND MISTER NASSOUR MISSED CLASS TODAY...
H-HE'S BEEN REALLY BUSY...FAMILY EMERGENCIES... HIS DAD WAS HOSPITALIZED...
WE ALL HAVE PROBLEMS, YOUNG LADY, AND WE LEARN TO COPE.
MISSING A CLASS ISN'T A CATASTROPHE-- MISSING A PROCEDURE A PATIENT NEEDS WOULD BE.
TELL HIM TO GET HIS ACT TOGETHER, NOW, WHILE THE STAKES ARE STILL RELATIVELY LOW.
Y-YES, MA'AM.
Shaya:
K: where the--

WHERE'D SHE GO? AKILA'S THE LAST ONE I'D EXPECT TO CUT OUT FROM THE PROTEST AND GO FOR SOUP DUMPLINGS...

...BESIDES, SHE'S PRETTY STRICTLY *HALAL*, ANYWAY.

TELL ME SHE'S NOT IN THE TOMBS, PLEASE.

I CAN'T IMAGINE AKILA LOCKED UP WITH HALF THE HOOKERS AND CROOKS IN THE CITY...

SUBTLE. REAL SUBTLE.

PLOINK

STOP
DO NOT ENTER
UNTIL INSTRUCTED
→ BY OFFICER

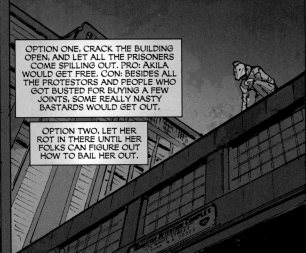

OPTION ONE, CRACK THE BUILDING OPEN, AND LET ALL THE PRISONERS COME SPILLING OUT. PRO: AKILA WOULD GET FREE. CON: BESIDES ALL THE PROTESTORS AND PEOPLE WHO GOT BUSTED FOR BUYING A FEW JOINTS, SOME REALLY NASTY BASTARDS WOULD GET OUT.

OPTION TWO, LET HER ROT IN THERE UNTIL HER FOLKS CAN FIGURE OUT HOW TO BAIL HER OUT.

NEITHER ONE SEEMS OKAY.

I'M SURE THERE'S *SOME* KIND OF MAGIC I COULD USE, BUT WHAT?

NABU, I THOUGHT YOU WERE SUPPOSED TO BE THE *HELPFUL* GUIDE TO THIS GIG...*NOT.*

LOOK.

HUH?

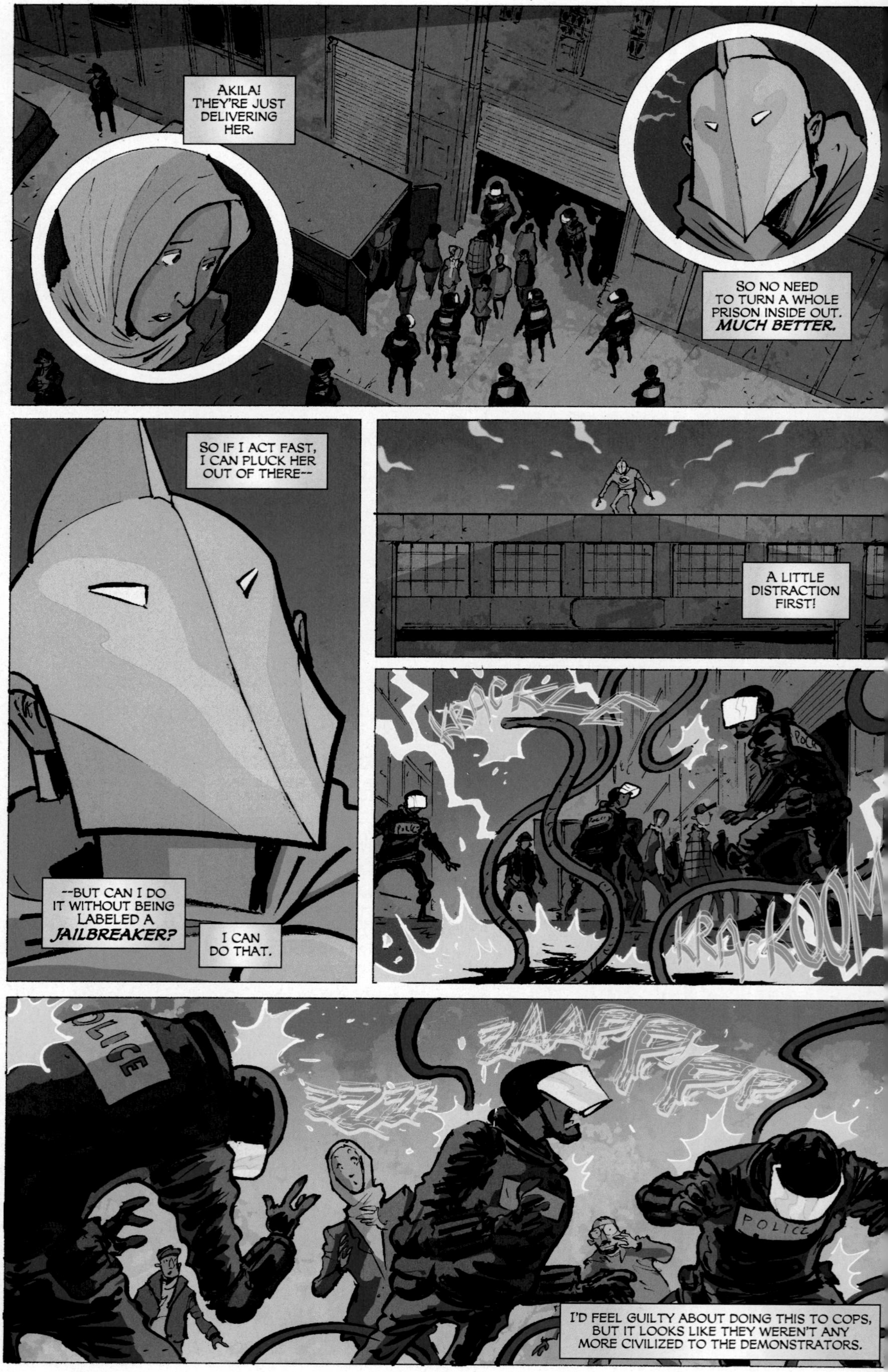
AKILA! THEY'RE JUST DELIVERING HER.
SO NO NEED TO TURN A WHOLE PRISON INSIDE OUT. *MUCH BETTER.*
SO IF I ACT FAST, I CAN PLUCK HER OUT OF THERE--
--BUT CAN I DO IT WITHOUT BEING LABELED A *JAILBREAKER?*
I CAN DO THAT.
A LITTLE DISTRACTION FIRST!
KRACKLE
KRACKOOM
POLICE
ZAAPPP
I'D FEEL GUILTY ABOUT DOING THIS TO COPS, BUT IT LOOKS LIKE THEY WEREN'T ANY MORE CIVILIZED TO THE DEMONSTRATORS.

GOTTA LOVE THE NEW YORK TRADITION OF MAKING FIRE ESCAPES MULTITASK-- SUNDECKS, STOREROOMS-- AND LAUNDRY DRYING RACKS!

RIDICULOUS, BUT ANONYMOUS.

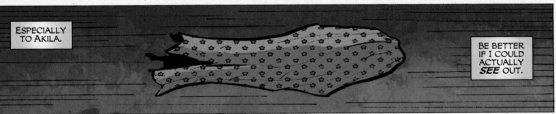

ESPECIALLY TO AKILA.

BE BETTER IF I COULD ACTUALLY *SEE* OUT.

THERE SHE IS.

WHA--?

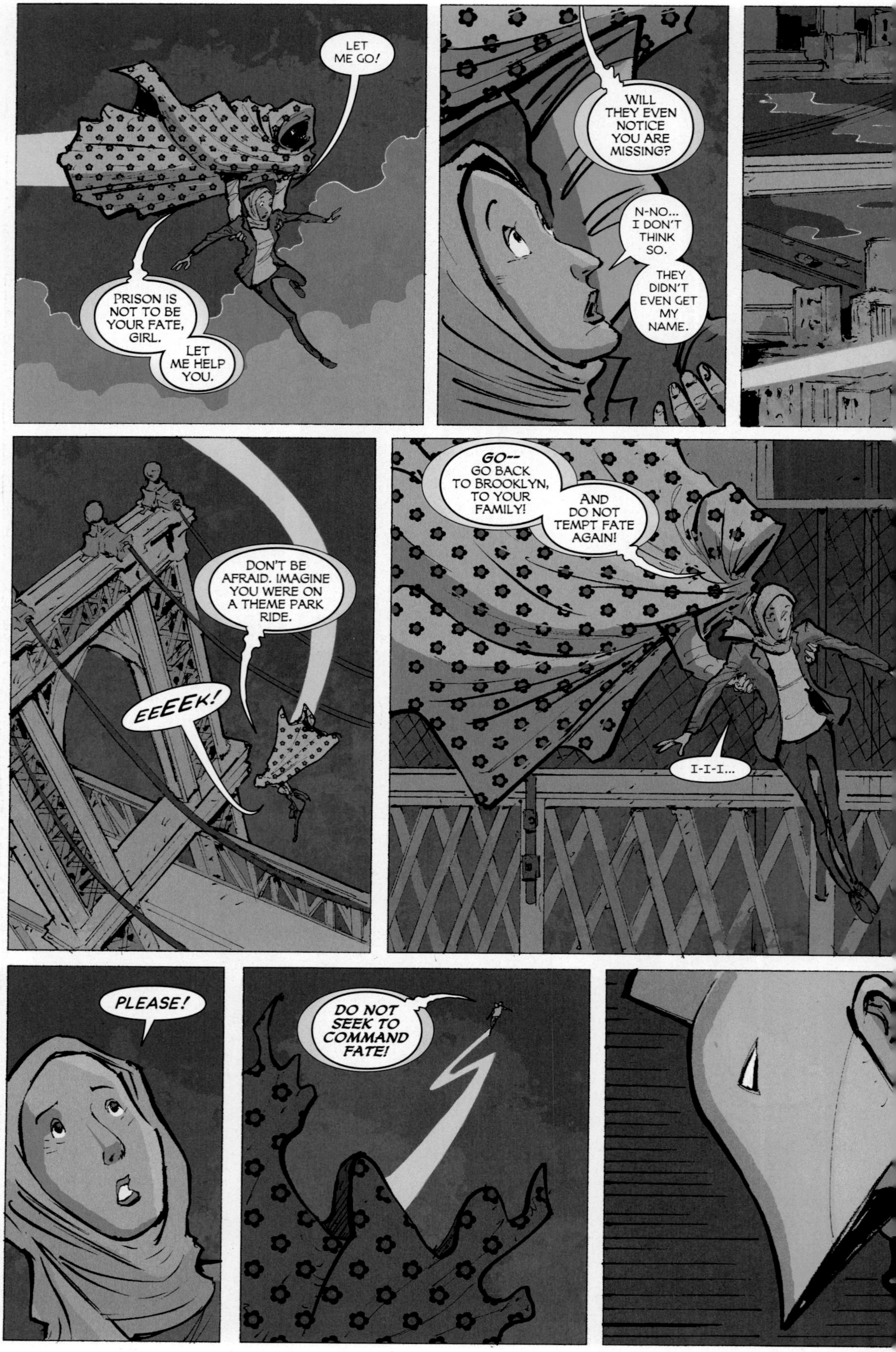
LET ME GO!
PRISON IS NOT TO BE YOUR FATE, GIRL.
LET ME HELP YOU.
WILL THEY EVEN NOTICE YOU ARE MISSING?
N-NO... I DON'T THINK SO.
THEY DIDN'T EVEN GET MY NAME.
DON'T BE AFRAID. IMAGINE YOU WERE ON A THEME PARK RIDE.
EEEEK!
GO-- GO BACK TO BROOKLYN, TO YOUR FAMILY!
AND DO NOT TEMPT FATE AGAIN!
I-I-I...
PLEASE!
DO NOT SEEK TO COMMAND FATE!

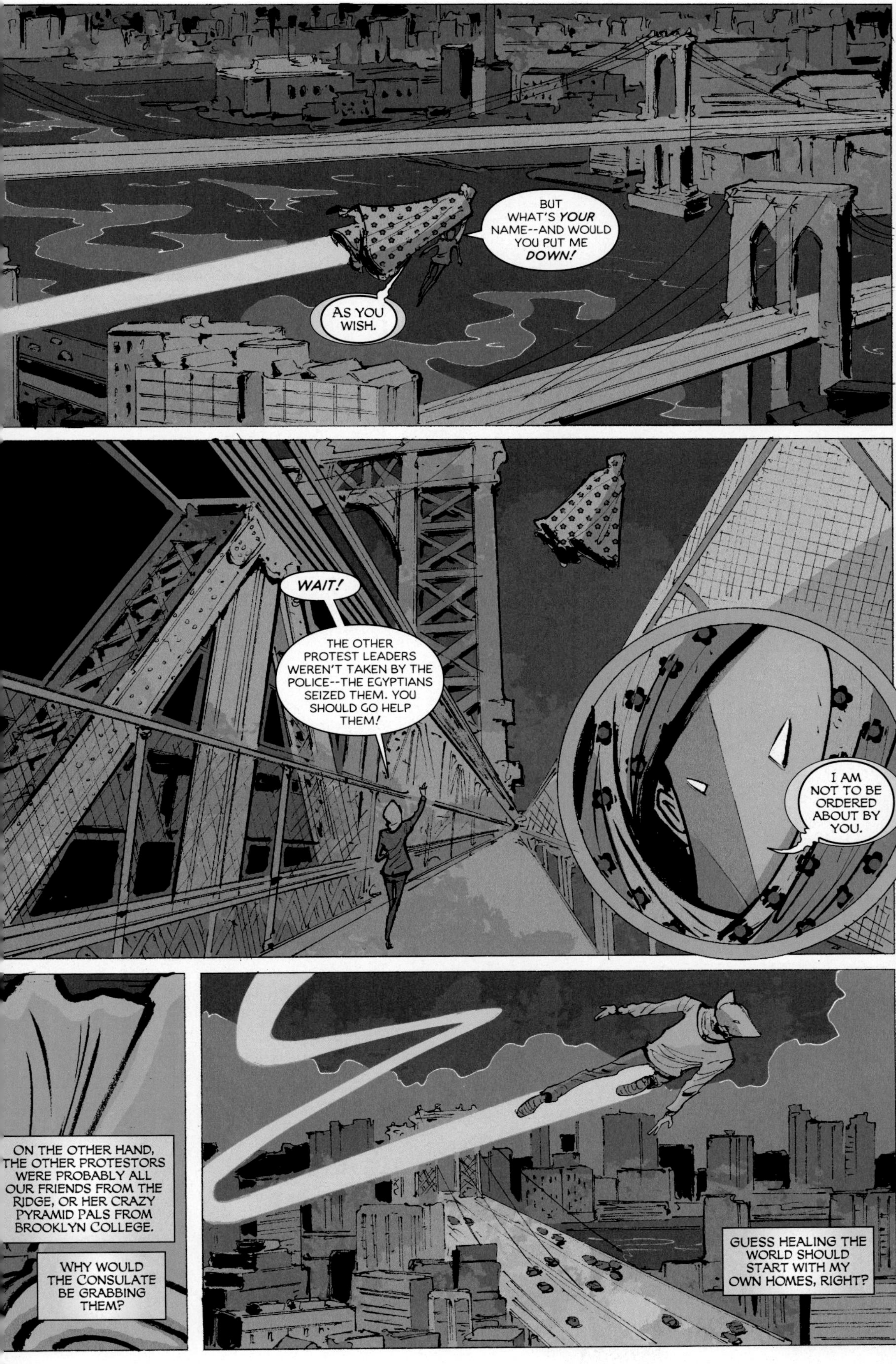
BUT WHAT'S *YOUR* NAME--AND WOULD YOU PUT ME *DOWN!*
AS YOU WISH.
WAIT!
THE OTHER PROTEST LEADERS WEREN'T TAKEN BY THE POLICE--THE EGYPTIANS SEIZED THEM. YOU SHOULD GO HELP THEM!
I AM NOT TO BE ORDERED ABOUT BY YOU.
ON THE OTHER HAND, THE OTHER PROTESTORS WERE PROBABLY ALL OUR FRIENDS FROM THE RIDGE, OR HER CRAZY PYRAMID PALS FROM BROOKLYN COLLEGE.
WHY WOULD THE CONSULATE BE GRABBING THEM?
GUESS HEALING THE WORLD SHOULD START WITH MY OWN HOMES, RIGHT?

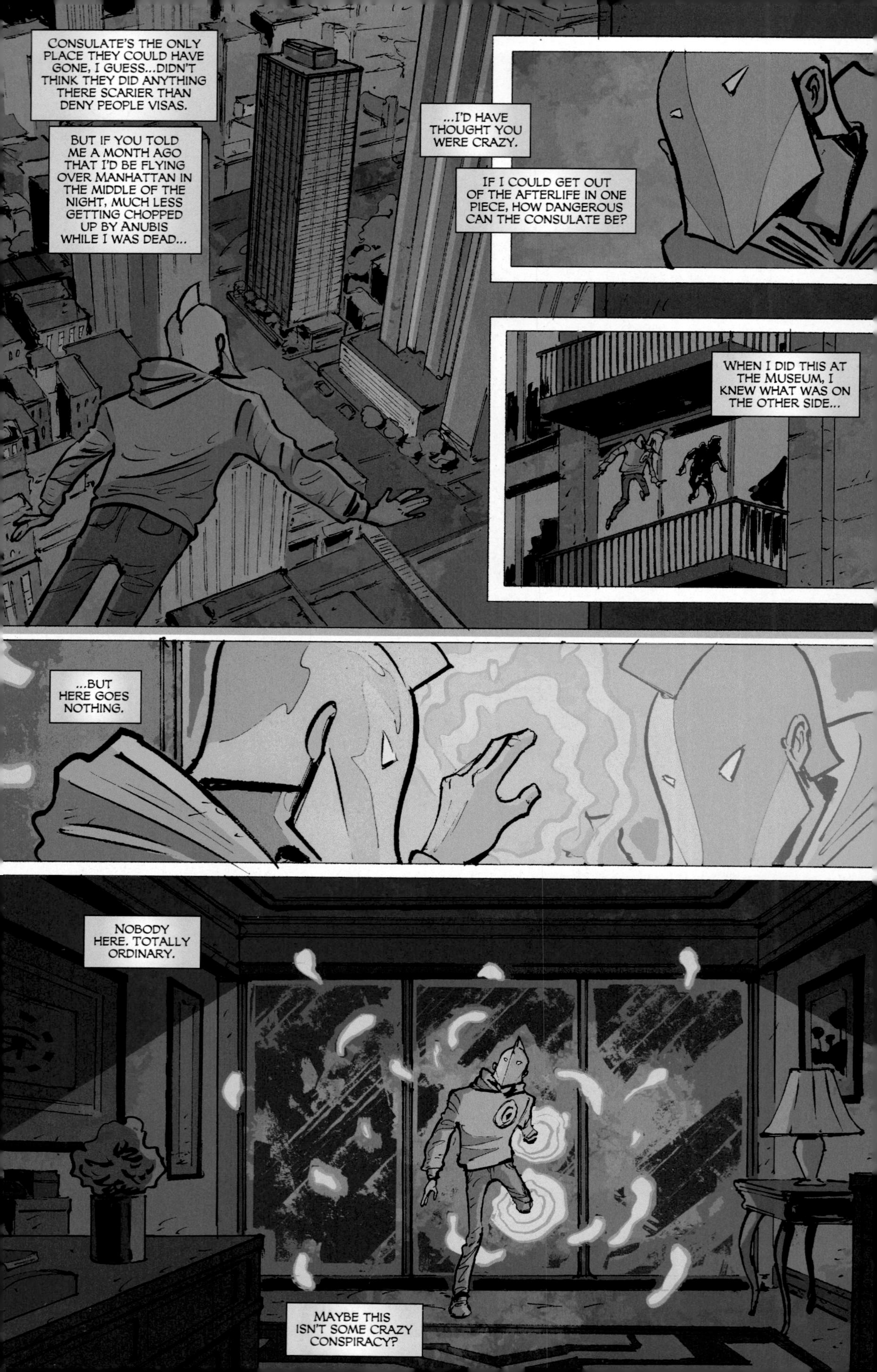
CONSULATE'S THE ONLY PLACE THEY COULD HAVE GONE, I GUESS...DIDN'T THINK THEY DID ANYTHING THERE SCARIER THAN DENY PEOPLE VISAS.
BUT IF YOU TOLD ME A MONTH AGO THAT I'D BE FLYING OVER MANHATTAN IN THE MIDDLE OF THE NIGHT, MUCH LESS GETTING CHOPPED UP BY ANUBIS WHILE I WAS DEAD...
...I'D HAVE THOUGHT YOU WERE CRAZY.
IF I COULD GET OUT OF THE AFTERLIFE IN ONE PIECE, HOW DANGEROUS CAN THE CONSULATE BE?
WHEN I DID THIS AT THE MUSEUM, I KNEW WHAT WAS ON THE OTHER SIDE...
...BUT HERE GOES NOTHING.
NOBODY HERE. TOTALLY ORDINARY.
MAYBE THIS ISN'T SOME CRAZY CONSPIRACY?

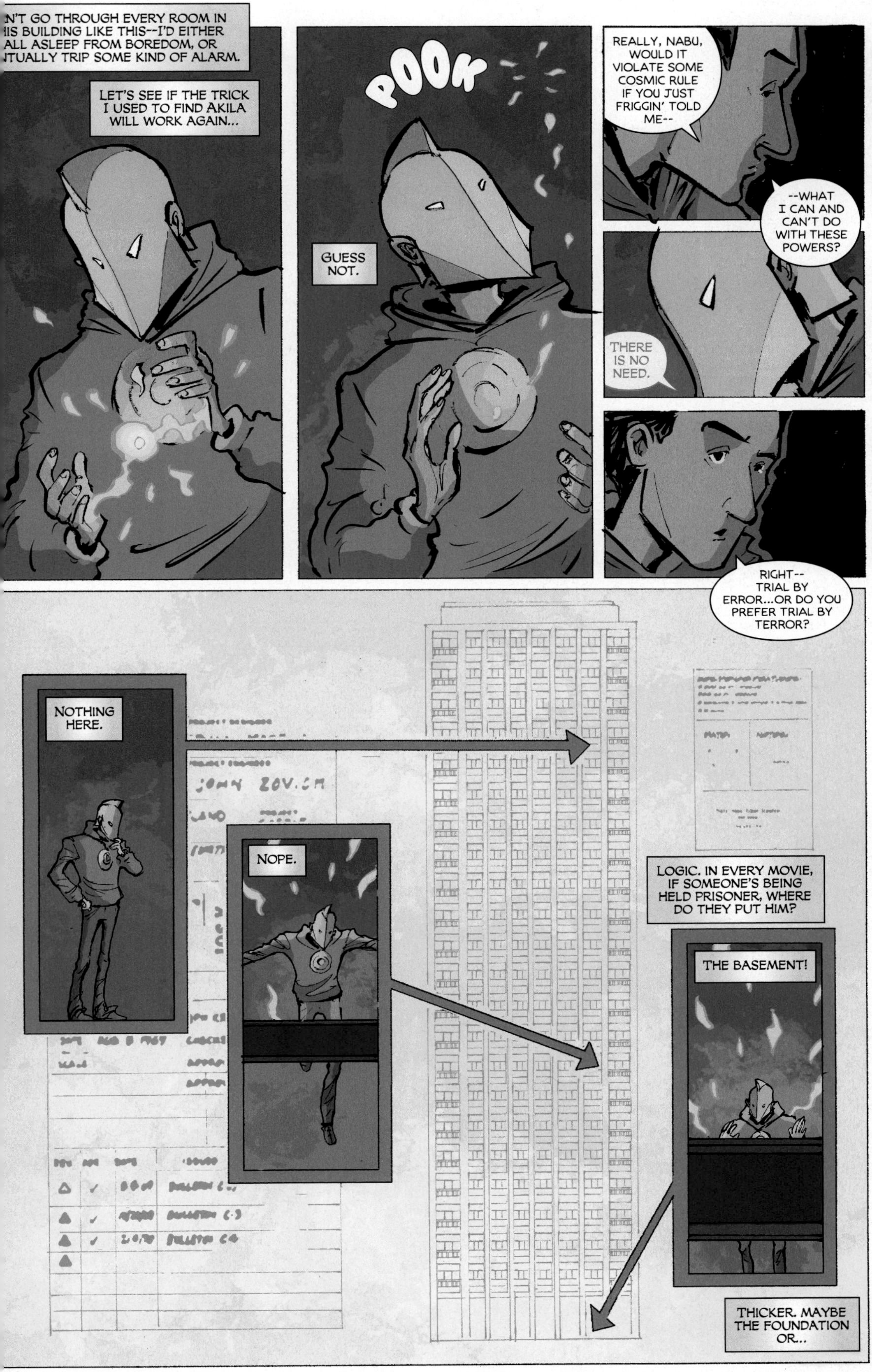
N'T GO THROUGH EVERY ROOM IN HIS BUILDING LIKE THIS--I'D EITHER ALL ASLEEP FROM BOREDOM, OR NTUALLY TRIP SOME KIND OF ALARM.
LET'S SEE IF THE TRICK I USED TO FIND AKILA WILL WORK AGAIN...
POOK
GUESS NOT.
REALLY, NABU, WOULD IT VIOLATE SOME COSMIC RULE IF YOU JUST FRIGGIN' TOLD ME--
--WHAT I CAN AND CAN'T DO WITH THESE POWERS?
THERE IS NO NEED.
RIGHT-- TRIAL BY ERROR...OR DO YOU PREFER TRIAL BY TERROR?
NOTHING HERE.
NOPE.
LOGIC. IN EVERY MOVIE, IF SOMEONE'S BEING HELD PRISONER, WHERE DO THEY PUT HIM?
THE BASEMENT!
THICKER. MAYBE THE FOUNDATION OR...

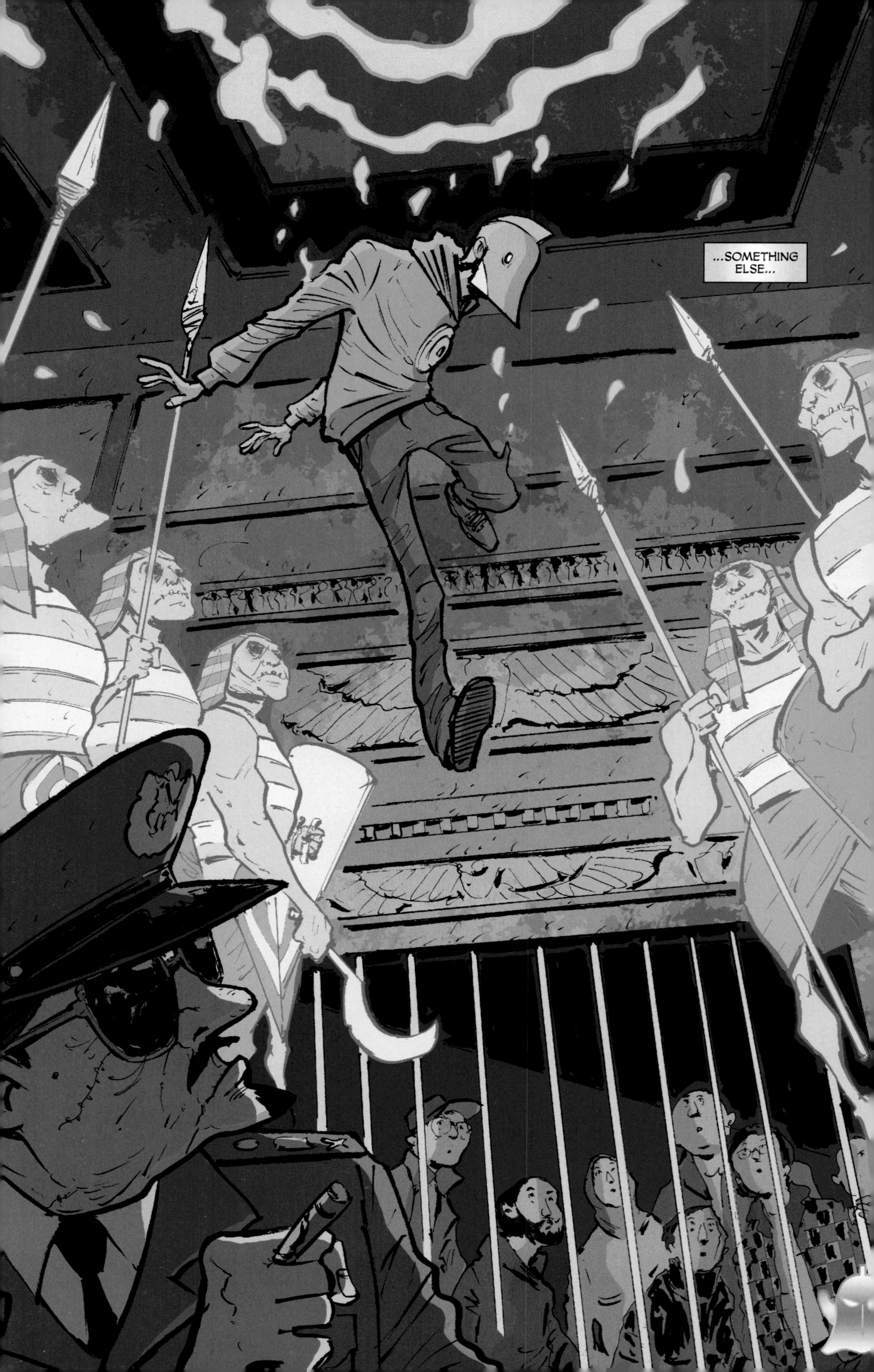
...SOMETHING ELSE...

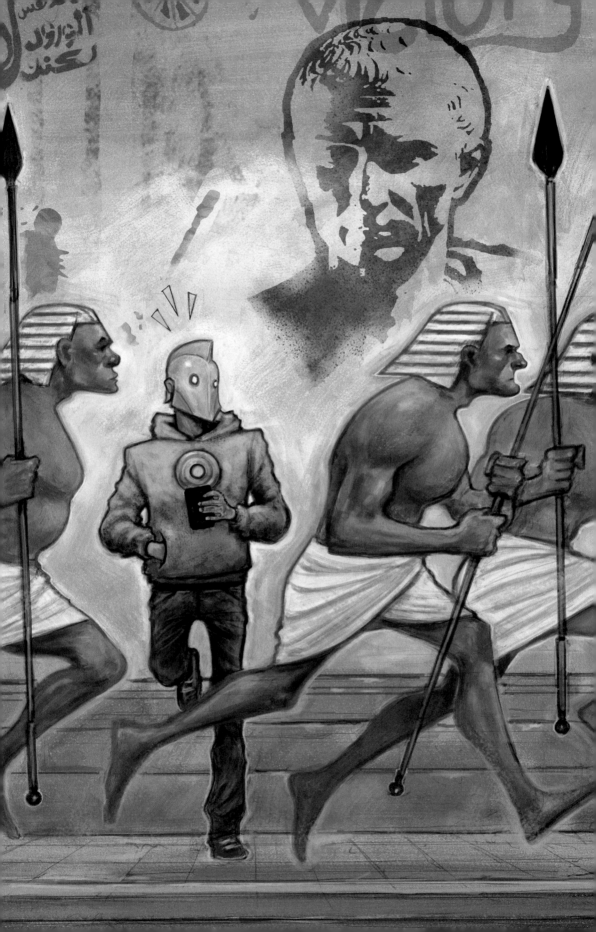

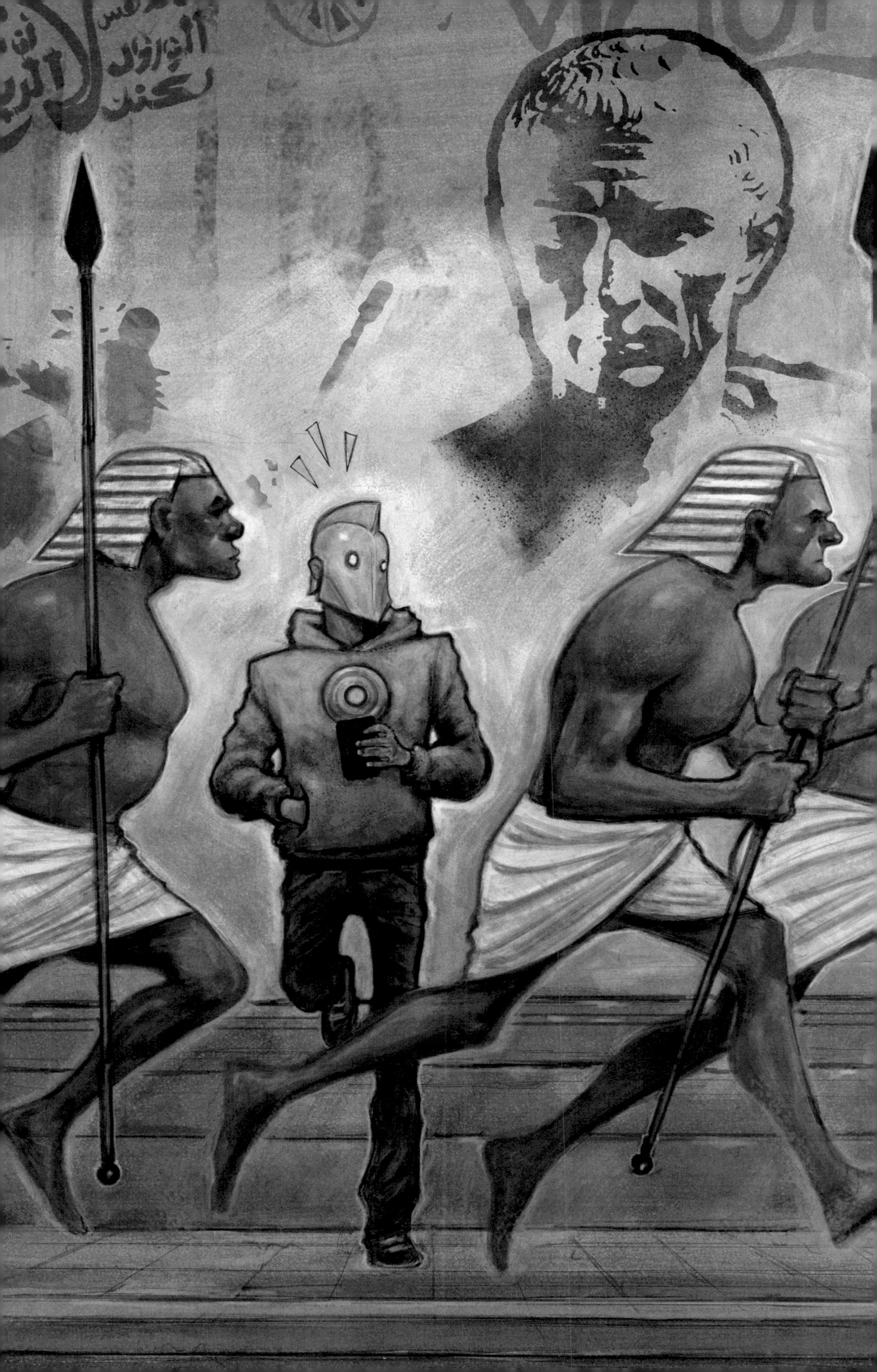

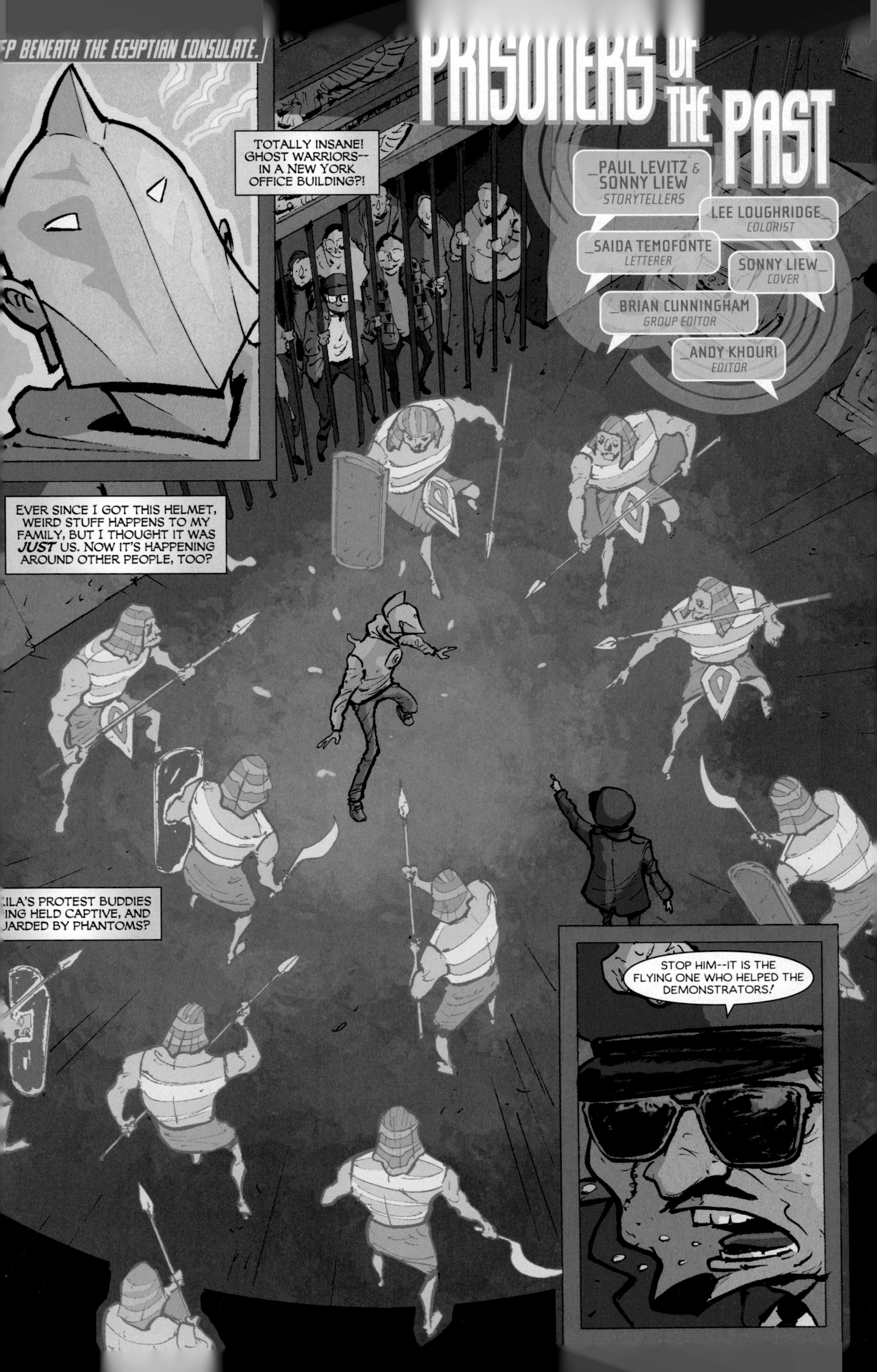

...P BENEATH THE EGYPTIAN CONSULATE.
PRISONERS OF THE PAST
PAUL LEVITZ & SONNY LIEW STORYTELLERS
LEE LOUGHRIDGE COLORIST
SAIDA TEMOFONTE LETTERER
SONNY LIEW COVER
BRIAN CUNNINGHAM GROUP EDITOR
ANDY KHOURI EDITOR
TOTALLY INSANE! GHOST WARRIORS-- IN A NEW YORK OFFICE BUILDING?!
EVER SINCE I GOT THIS HELMET, WEIRD STUFF HAPPENS TO MY FAMILY, BUT I THOUGHT IT WAS JUST US. NOW IT'S HAPPENING AROUND OTHER PEOPLE, TOO?
...ILA'S PROTEST BUDDIES ...ING HELD CAPTIVE, AND ...ARDED BY PHANTOMS?
STOP HIM--IT IS THE FLYING ONE WHO HELPED THE DEMONSTRATORS!

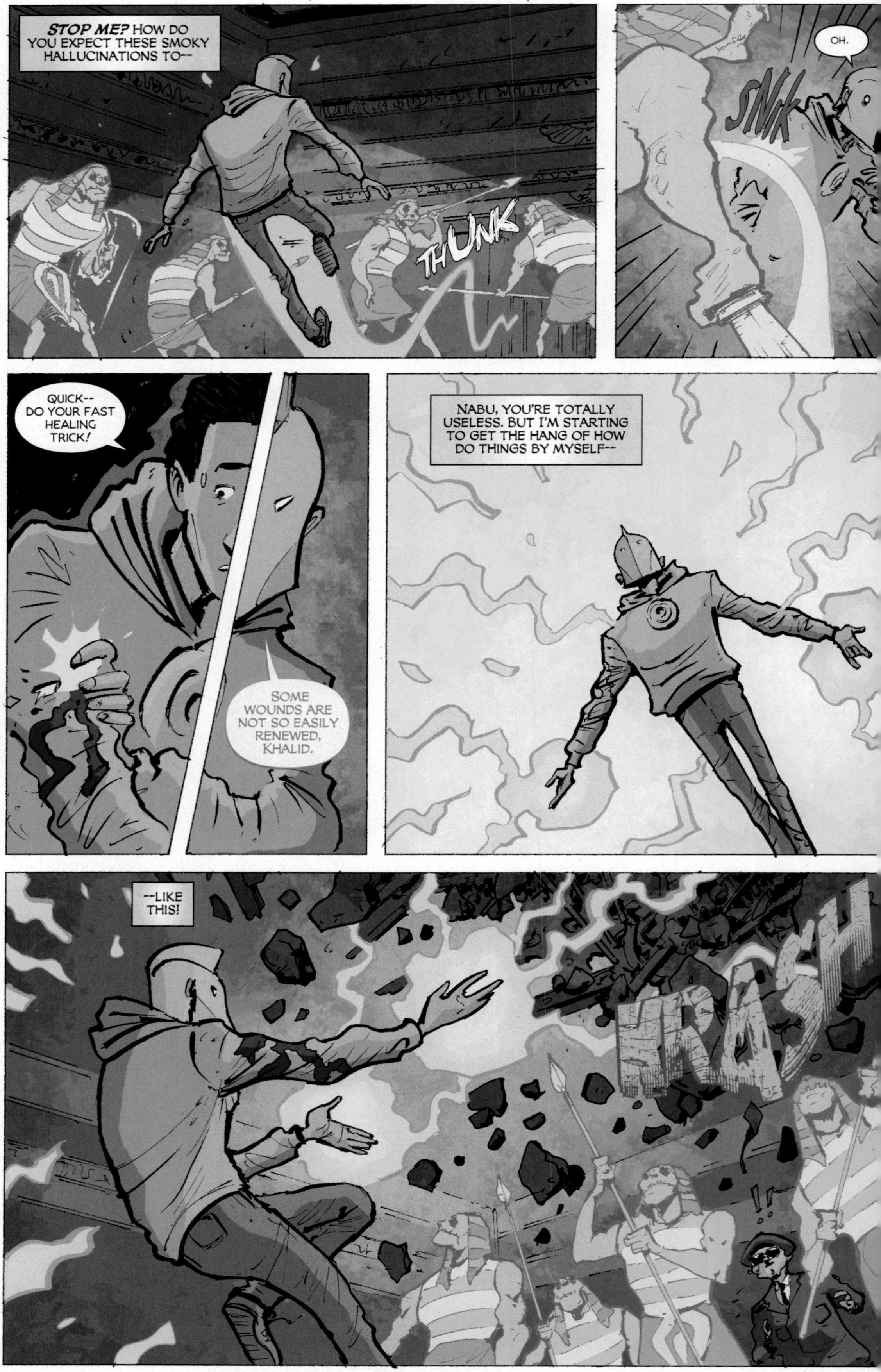
STOP ME? HOW DO YOU EXPECT THESE SMOKY HALLUCINATIONS TO--
THUNK
OH.
SNIK
QUICK-- DO YOUR FAST HEALING TRICK!
SOME WOUNDS ARE NOT SO EASILY RENEWED, KHALID.
NABU, YOU'RE TOTALLY USELESS. BUT I'M STARTING TO GET THE HANG OF HOW DO THINGS BY MYSELF--
--LIKE THIS!
!!

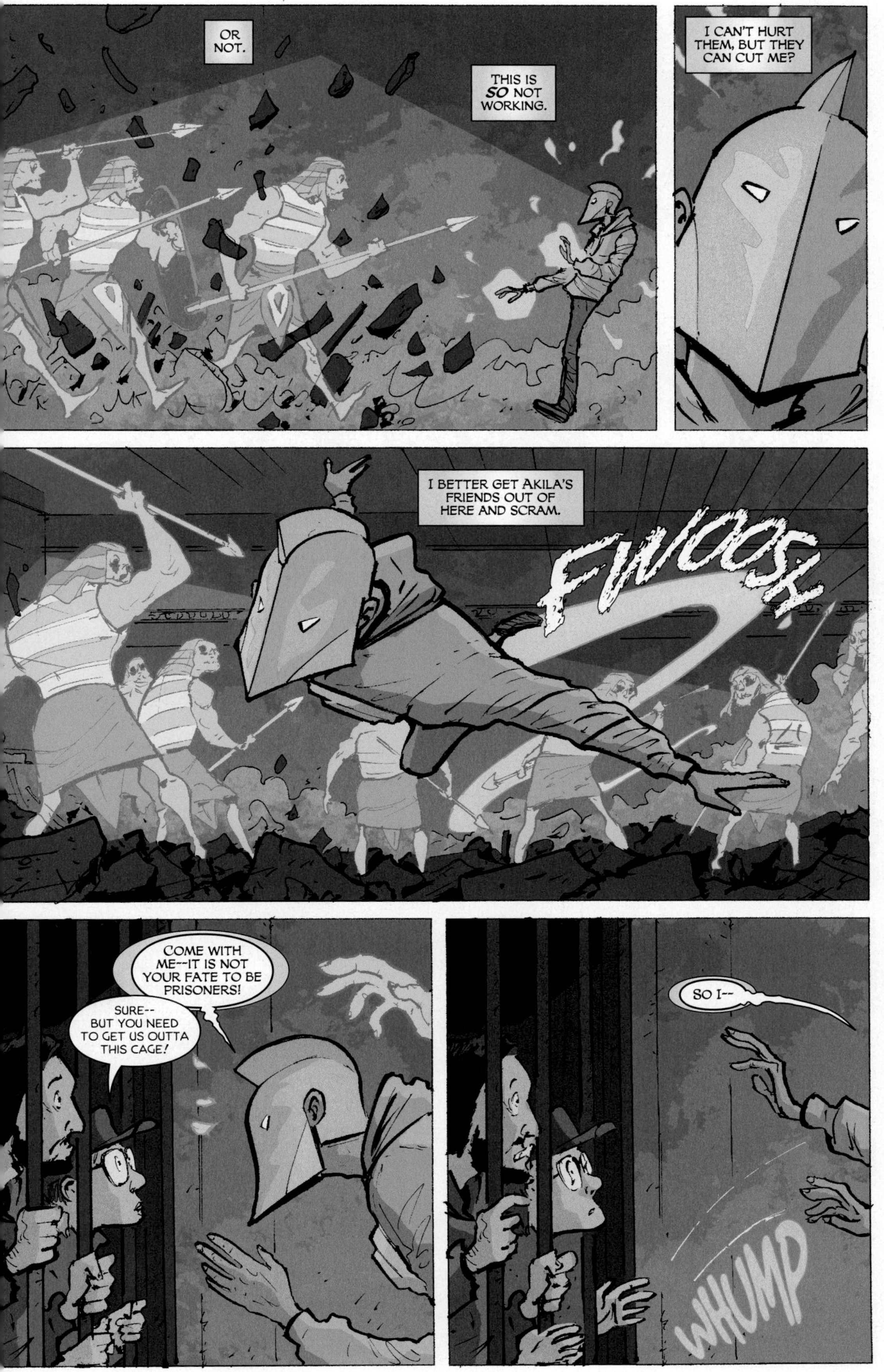

OR NOT.
THIS IS SO NOT WORKING.
I CAN'T HURT THEM, BUT THEY CAN CUT ME?
I BETTER GET AKILA'S FRIENDS OUT OF HERE AND SCRAM.
FWOOSH
COME WITH ME--IT IS NOT YOUR FATE TO BE PRISONERS!
SURE-- BUT YOU NEED TO GET US OUTTA THIS CAGE!
SO I--
WHUMP

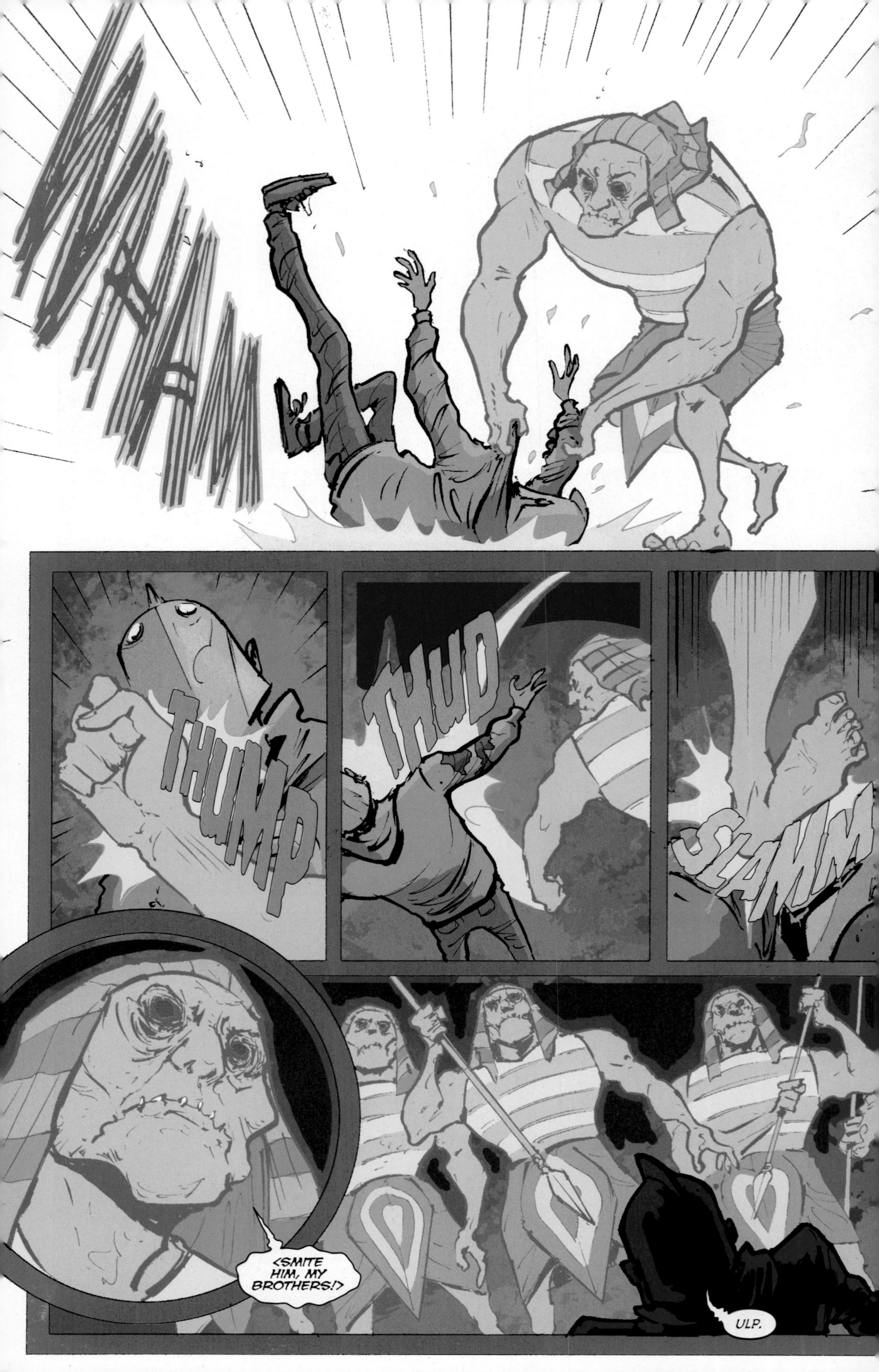
WHAM
THUMP
THUD
SLAMM
<SMITE HIM, MY BROTHERS!>
ULP.

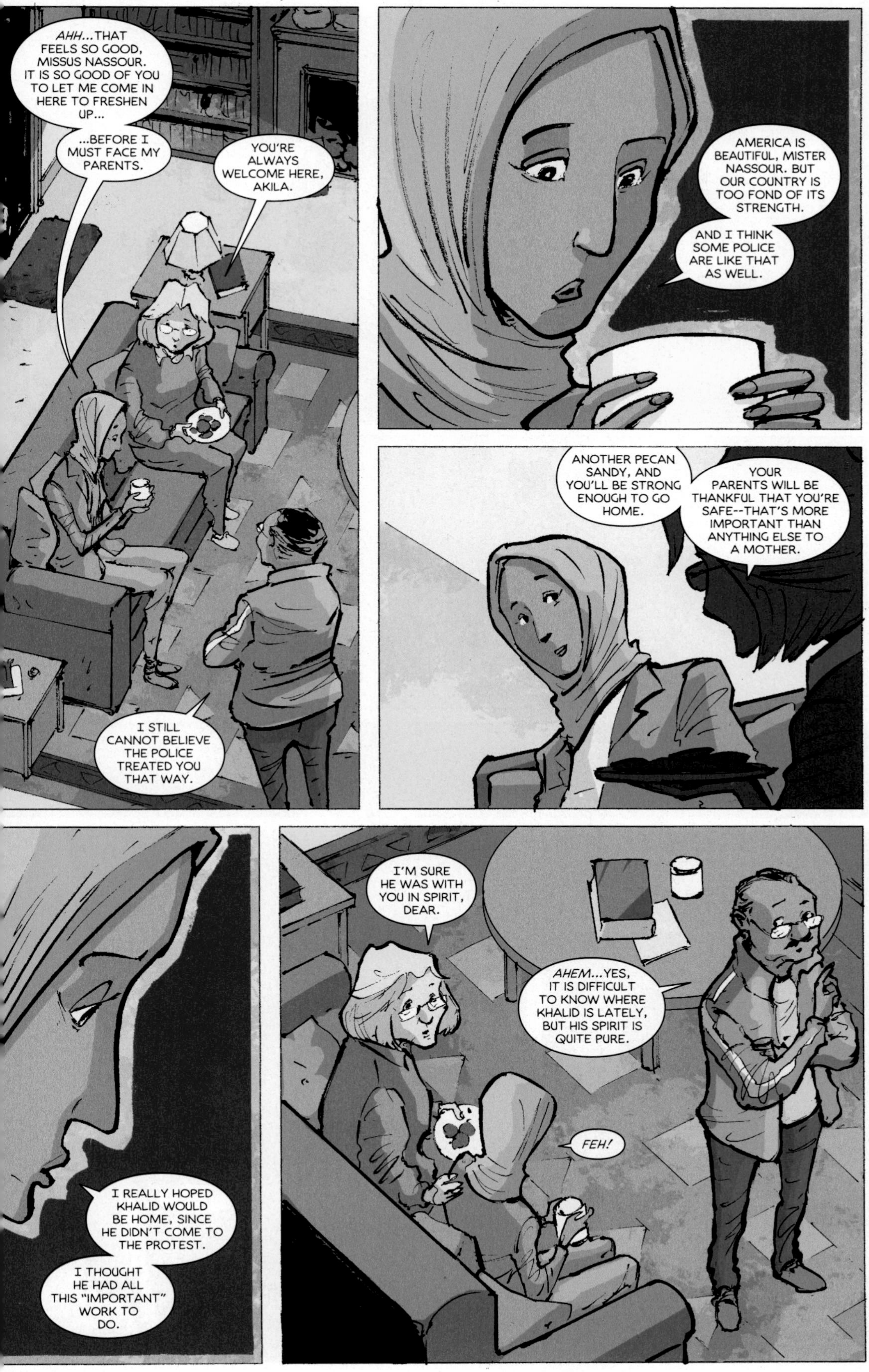
AHH...THAT FEELS SO GOOD, MISSUS NASSOUR. IT IS SO GOOD OF YOU TO LET ME COME IN HERE TO FRESHEN UP...
...BEFORE I MUST FACE MY PARENTS.
YOU'RE ALWAYS WELCOME HERE, AKILA.
I STILL CANNOT BELIEVE THE POLICE TREATED YOU THAT WAY.
AMERICA IS BEAUTIFUL, MISTER NASSOUR. BUT OUR COUNTRY IS TOO FOND OF ITS STRENGTH.
AND I THINK SOME POLICE ARE LIKE THAT AS WELL.
ANOTHER PECAN SANDY, AND YOU'LL BE STRONG ENOUGH TO GO HOME.
YOUR PARENTS WILL BE THANKFUL THAT YOU'RE SAFE--THAT'S MORE IMPORTANT THAN ANYTHING ELSE TO A MOTHER.
I REALLY HOPED KHALID WOULD BE HOME, SINCE HE DIDN'T COME TO THE PROTEST.
I THOUGHT HE HAD ALL THIS "IMPORTANT" WORK TO DO.
I'M SURE HE WAS WITH YOU IN SPIRIT, DEAR.
AHEM...YES, IT IS DIFFICULT TO KNOW WHERE KHALID IS LATELY, BUT HIS SPIRIT IS QUITE PURE.
FEH!

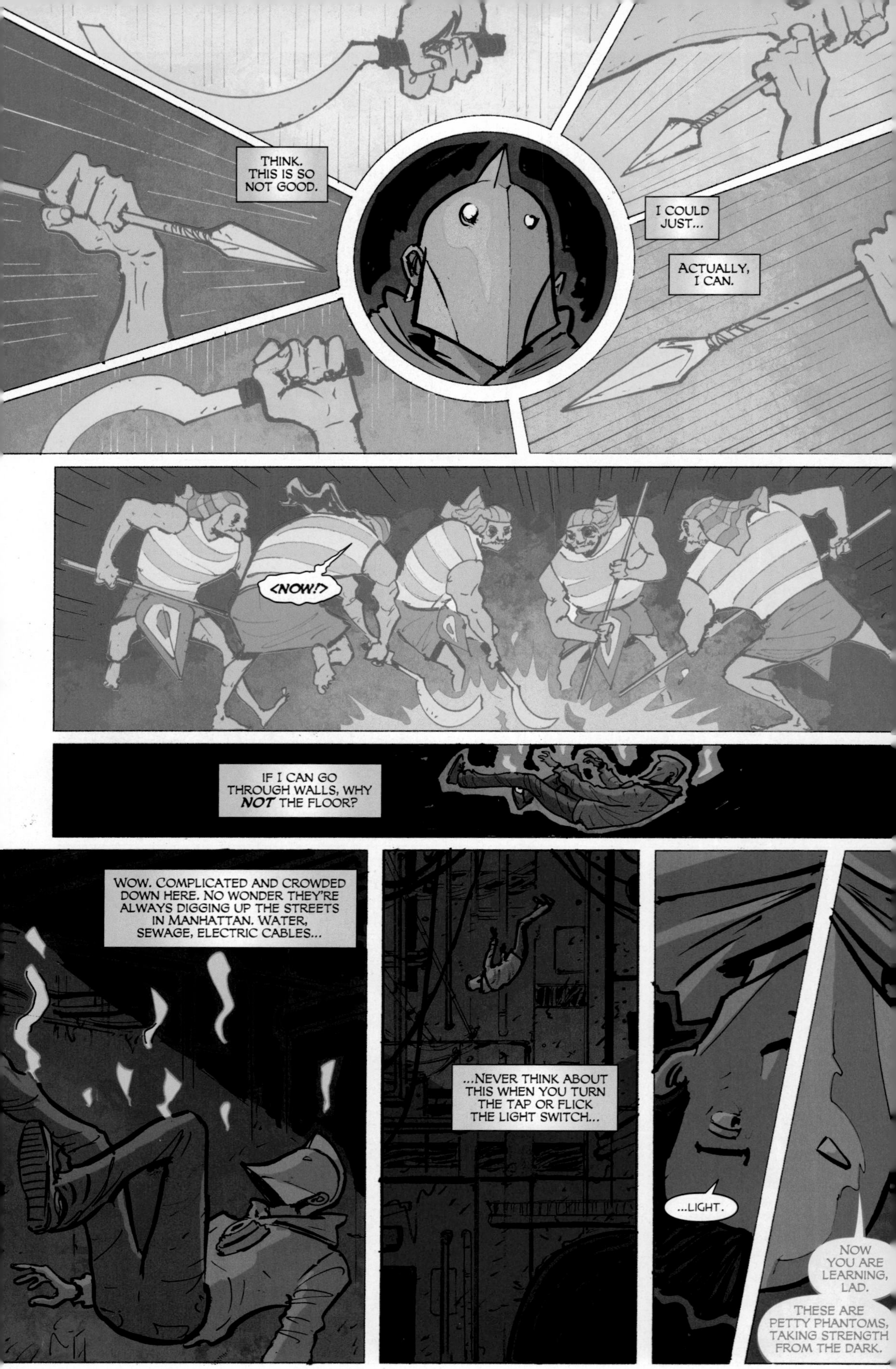
THINK. THIS IS SO NOT GOOD.
I COULD JUST...
ACTUALLY, I CAN.
<NOW!>
IF I CAN GO THROUGH WALLS, WHY NOT THE FLOOR?
WOW. COMPLICATED AND CROWDED DOWN HERE. NO WONDER THEY'RE ALWAYS DIGGING UP THE STREETS IN MANHATTAN. WATER, SEWAGE, ELECTRIC CABLES...
...NEVER THINK ABOUT THIS WHEN YOU TURN THE TAP OR FLICK THE LIGHT SWITCH...
...LIGHT.
NOW YOU ARE LEARNING, LAD.
THESE ARE PETTY PHANTOMS, TAKING STRENGTH FROM THE DARK.

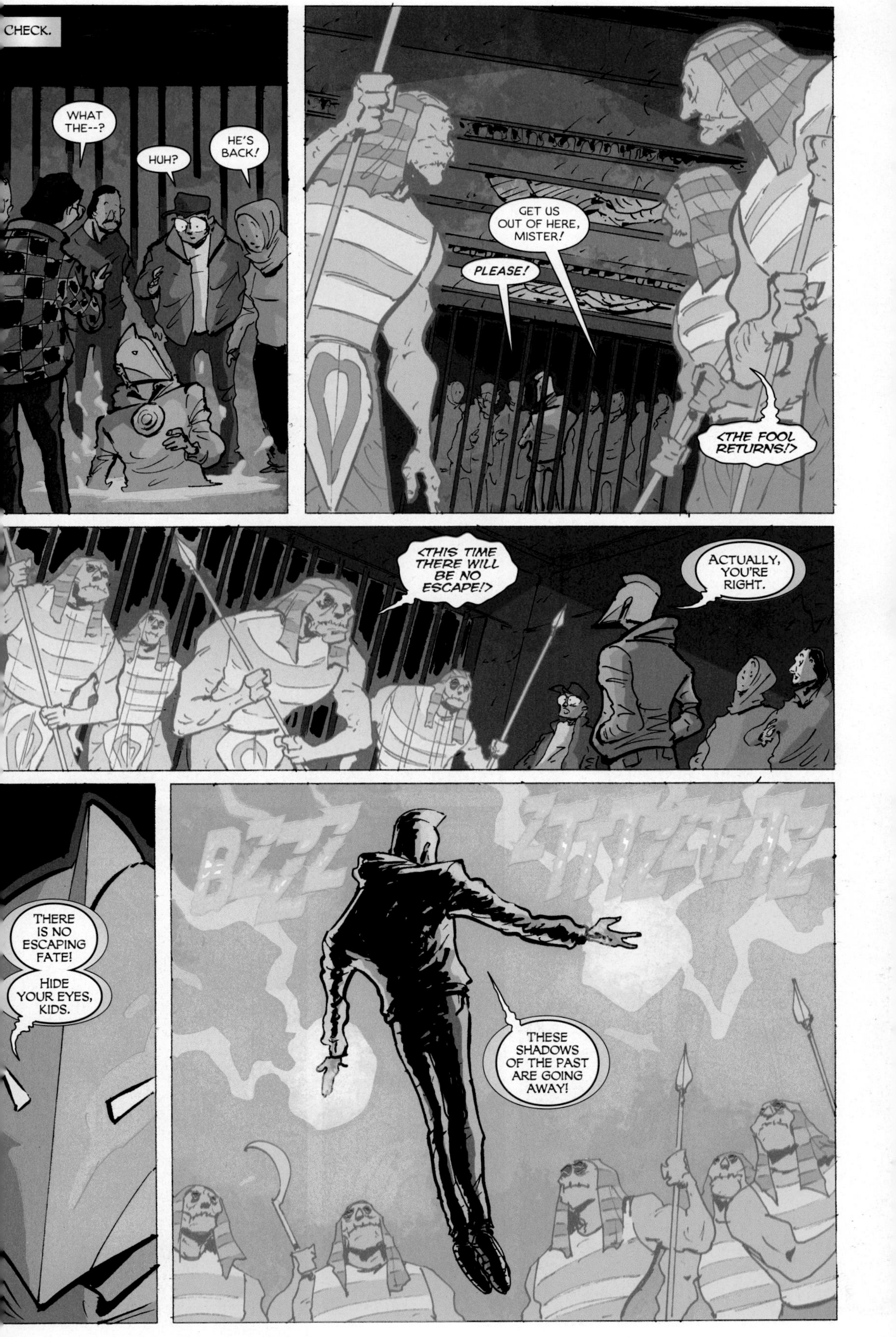
CHECK.
WHAT THE--?
HUH?
HE'S BACK!
GET US OUT OF HERE, MISTER!
PLEASE!
<THE FOOL RETURNS!>
<THIS TIME THERE WILL BE NO ESCAPE!>
ACTUALLY, YOU'RE RIGHT.
THERE IS NO ESCAPING FATE!
HIDE YOUR EYES, KIDS.
THESE SHADOWS OF THE PAST ARE GOING AWAY!

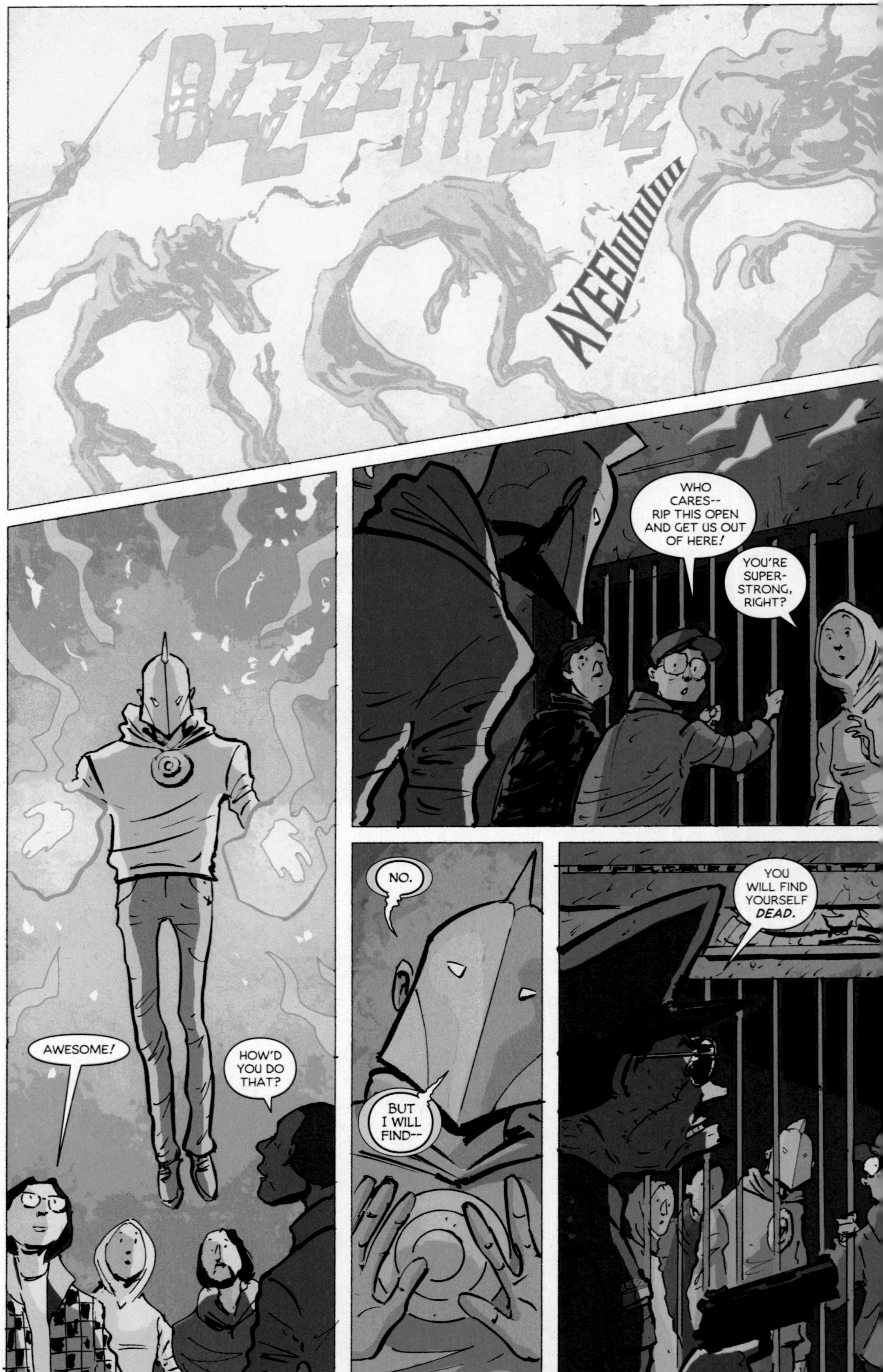
BZZZTTZZTZ
AYEEIIIIIIIIII
WHO CARES-- RIP THIS OPEN AND GET US OUT OF HERE!
YOU'RE SUPER-STRONG, RIGHT?
AWESOME!
HOW'D YOU DO THAT?
NO.
BUT I WILL FIND--
YOU WILL FIND YOURSELF DEAD.

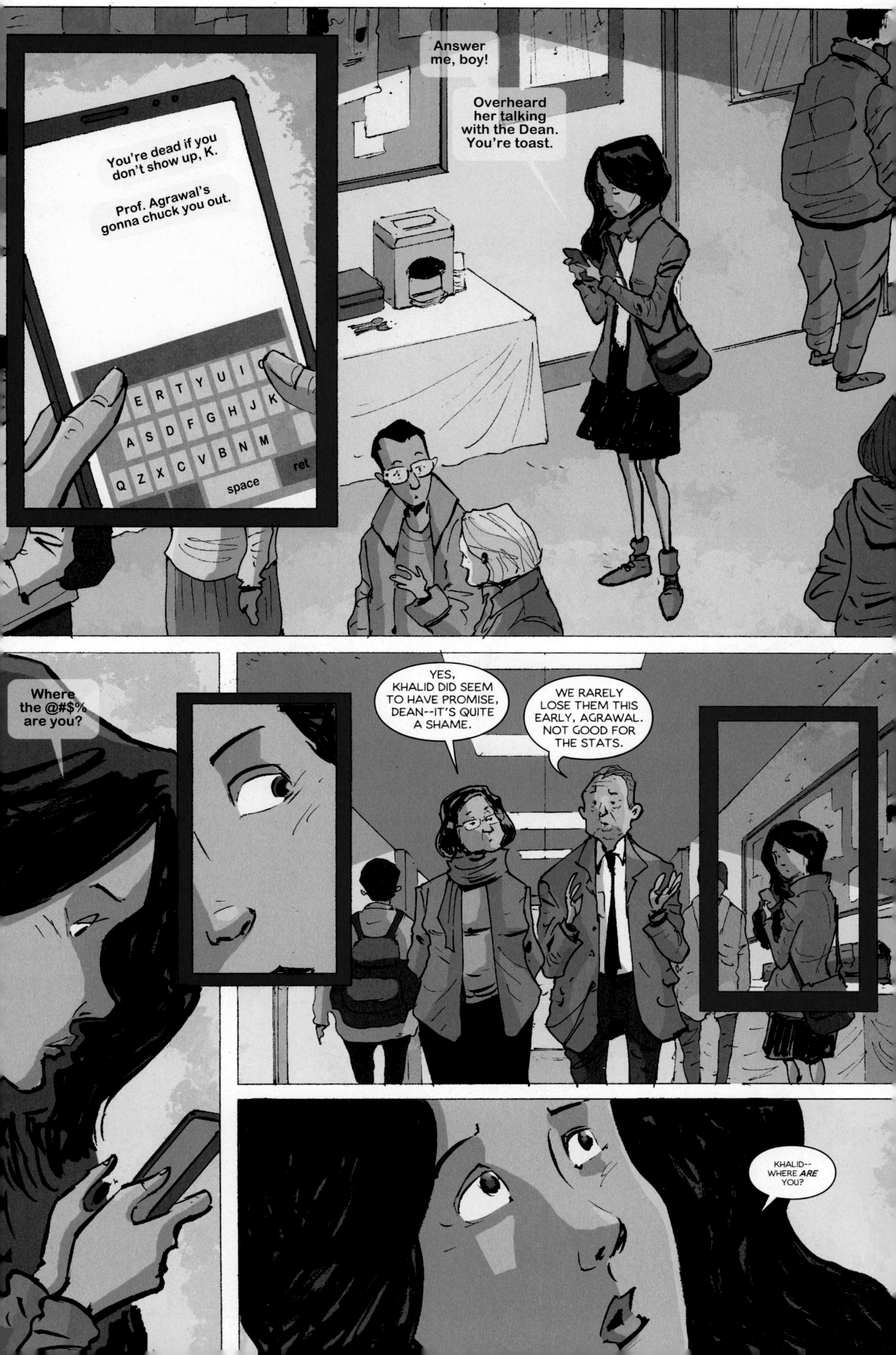
You're dead if you don't show up, K.
Prof. Agrawal's gonna chuck you out.
Answer me, boy!
Overheard her talking with the Dean. You're toast.
Where the @#$% are you?
YES, KHALID DID SEEM TO HAVE PROMISE, DEAN--IT'S QUITE A SHAME.
WE RARELY LOSE THEM THIS EARLY, AGRAWAL. NOT GOOD FOR THE STATS.
KHALID-- WHERE ARE YOU?

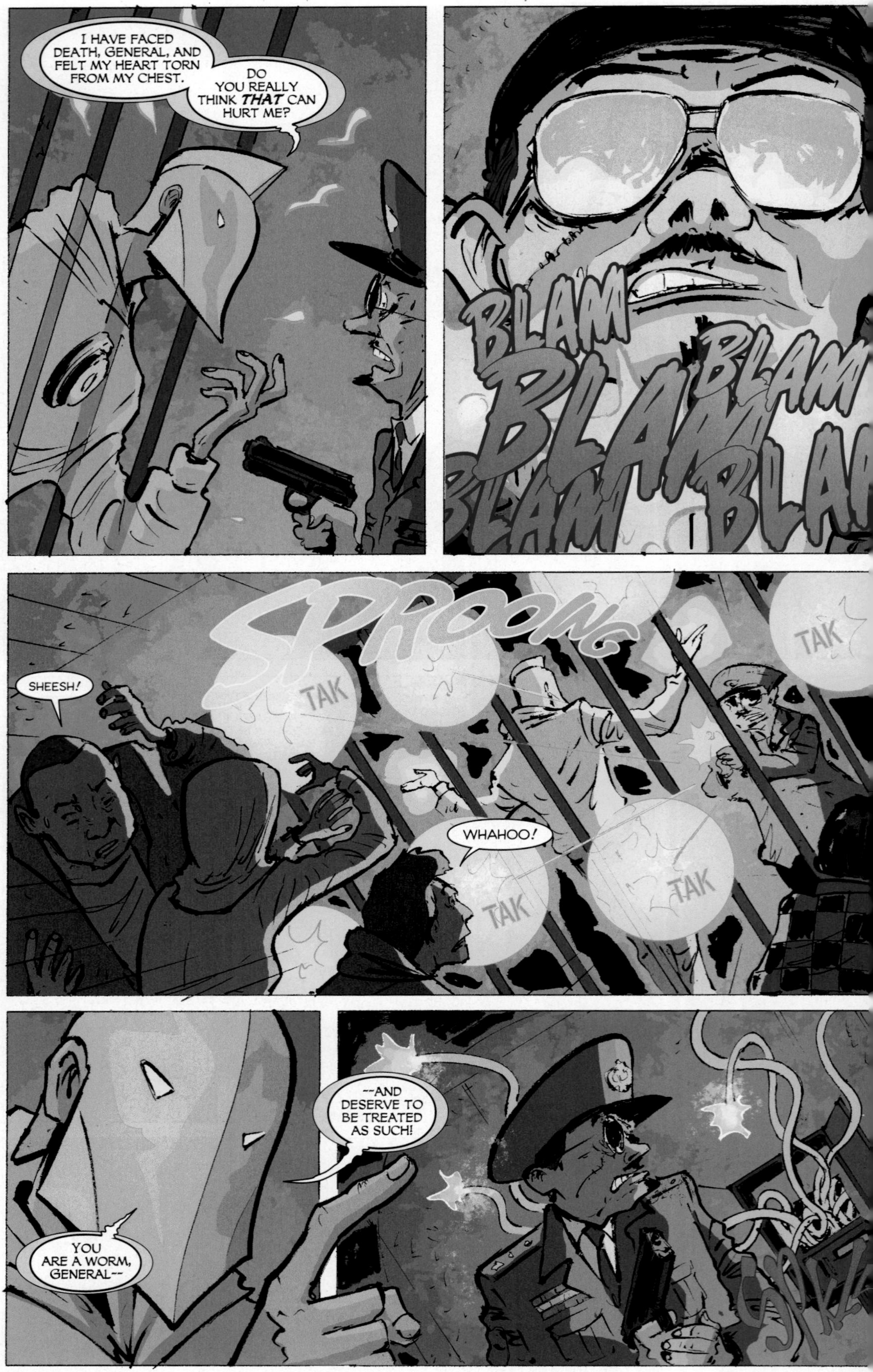
I HAVE FACED DEATH, GENERAL, AND FELT MY HEART TORN FROM MY CHEST.
DO YOU REALLY THINK *THAT* CAN HURT ME?
BLAM BLAM BLAM BLAM BLAM BLAM
SPROOING
SHEESH!
TAK
TAK
WHAHOO!
TAK
TAK
YOU ARE A WORM, GENERAL--
--AND DESERVE TO BE TREATED AS SUCH!

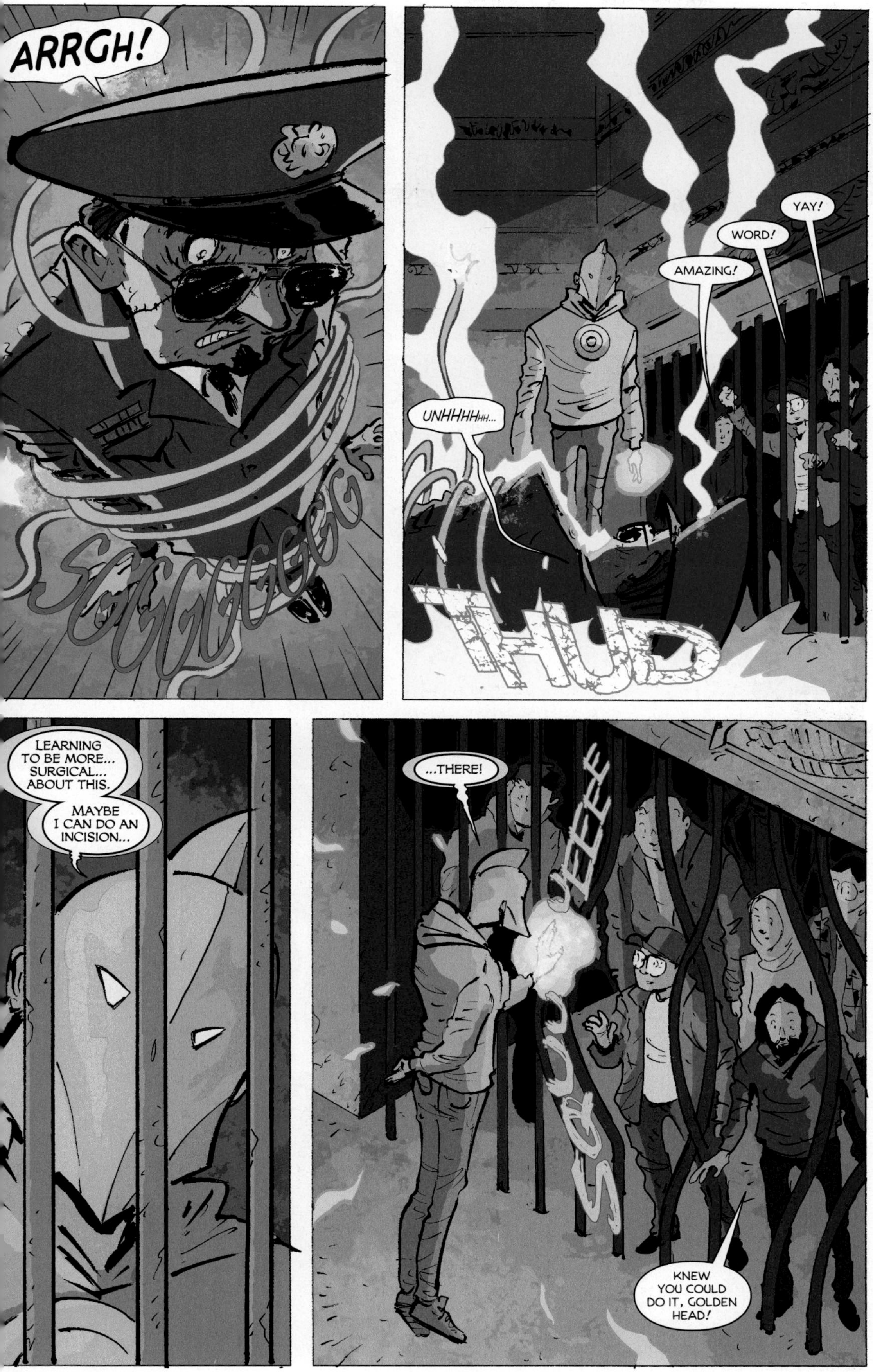
ARRGH!
SCCCCCCCG
UNHHHHhh...
AMAZING!
WORD!
YAY!
THUD
LEARNING TO BE MORE... SURGICAL... ABOUT THIS.
MAYBE I CAN DO AN INCISION...
...THERE!
KNEW YOU COULD DO IT, GOLDEN HEAD!

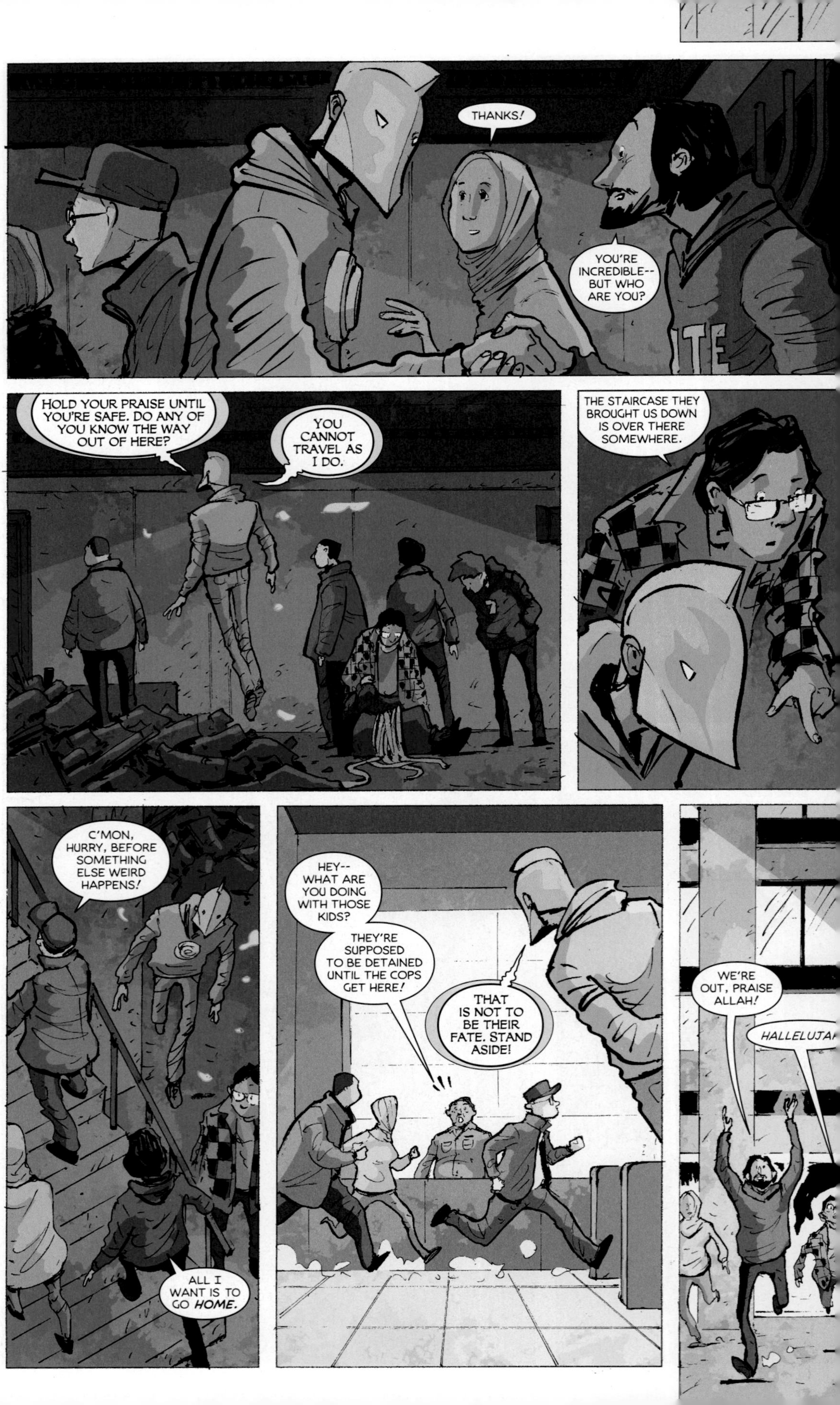
THANKS!
YOU'RE INCREDIBLE-- BUT WHO ARE YOU?
HOLD YOUR PRAISE UNTIL YOU'RE SAFE. DO ANY OF YOU KNOW THE WAY OUT OF HERE?
YOU CANNOT TRAVEL AS I DO.
THE STAIRCASE THEY BROUGHT US DOWN IS OVER THERE SOMEWHERE.
C'MON, HURRY, BEFORE SOMETHING ELSE WEIRD HAPPENS!
ALL I WANT IS TO GO HOME.
HEY-- WHAT ARE YOU DOING WITH THOSE KIDS?
THEY'RE SUPPOSED TO BE DETAINED UNTIL THE COPS GET HERE!
THAT IS NOT TO BE THEIR FATE. STAND ASIDE!
WE'RE OUT, PRAISE ALLAH!
HALLELUJA

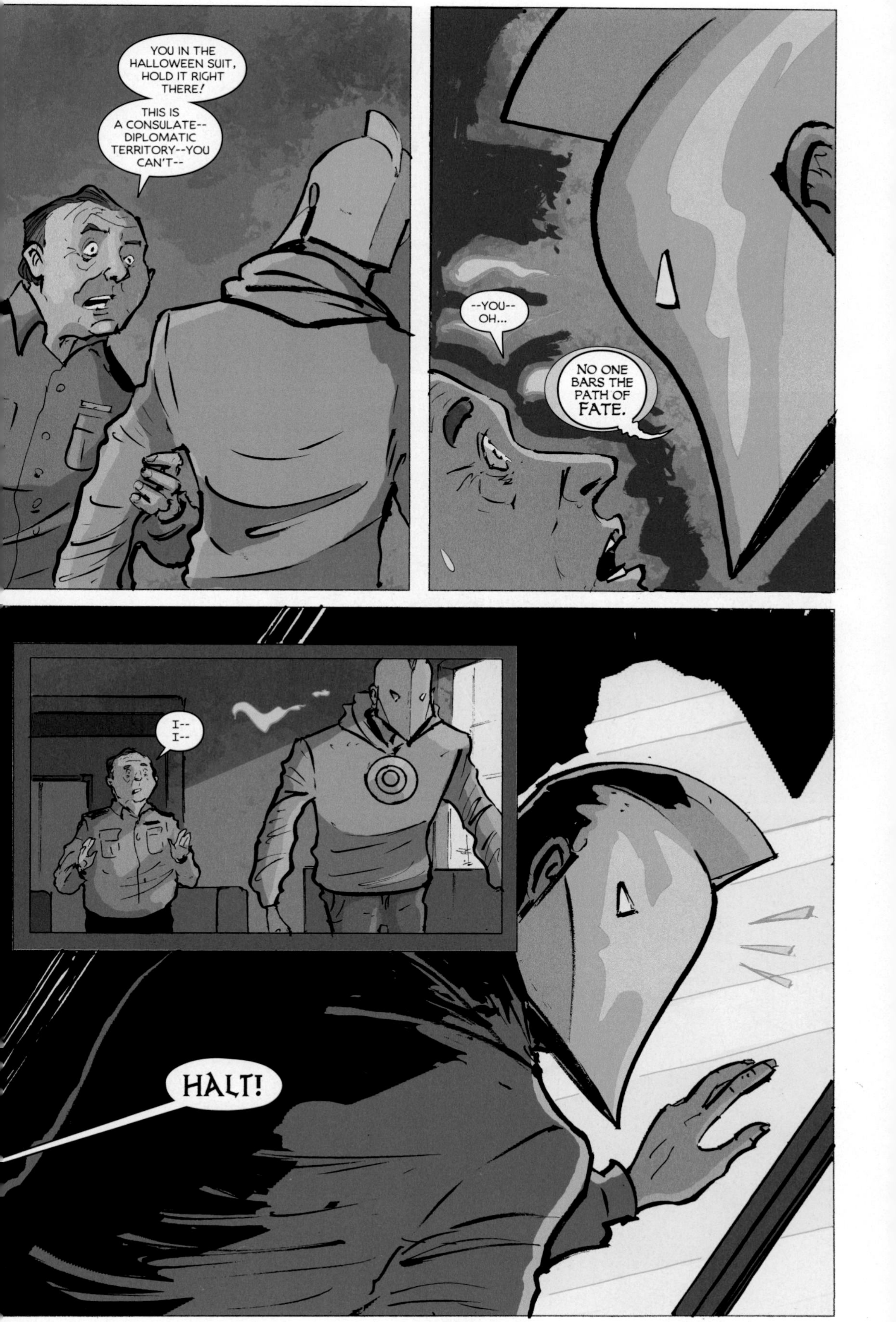
YOU IN THE HALLOWEEN SUIT, HOLD IT RIGHT THERE!
THIS IS A CONSULATE--DIPLOMATIC TERRITORY--YOU CAN'T--
--YOU--OH...
NO ONE BARS THE PATH OF FATE.
I--I--
HALT!

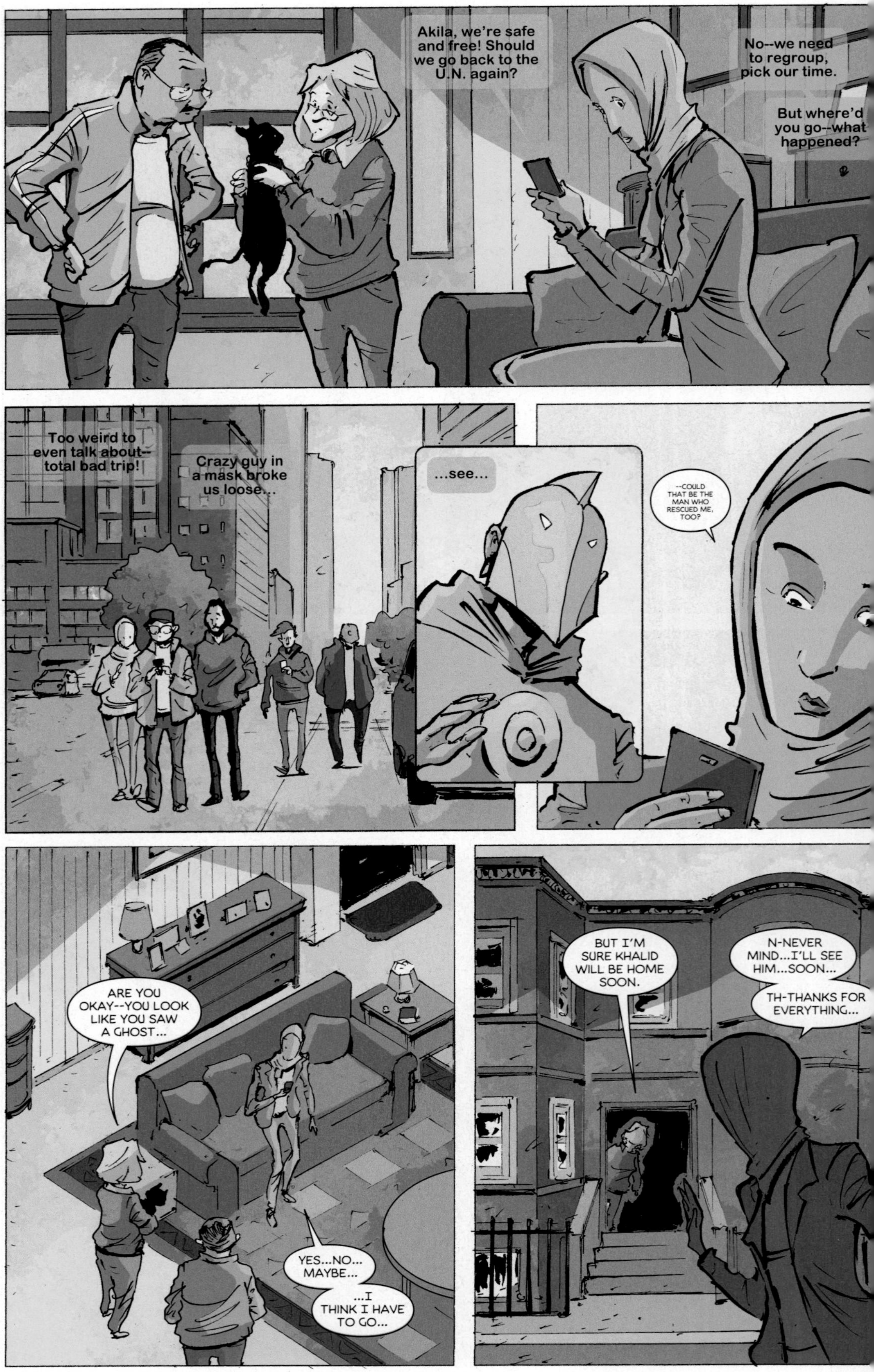
Akila, we're safe and free! Should we go back to the U.N. again?
No--we need to regroup, pick our time.
But where'd you go--what happened?
Too weird to even talk about--total bad trip!
Crazy guy in a mask broke us loose...
...see...
--COULD THAT BE THE MAN WHO RESCUED ME, TOO?
ARE YOU OKAY--YOU LOOK LIKE YOU SAW A GHOST...
YES...NO... MAYBE...
...I THINK I HAVE TO GO...
BUT I'M SURE KHALID WILL BE HOME SOON.
N-NEVER MIND...I'LL SEE HIM...SOON...
TH-THANKS FOR EVERYTHING...

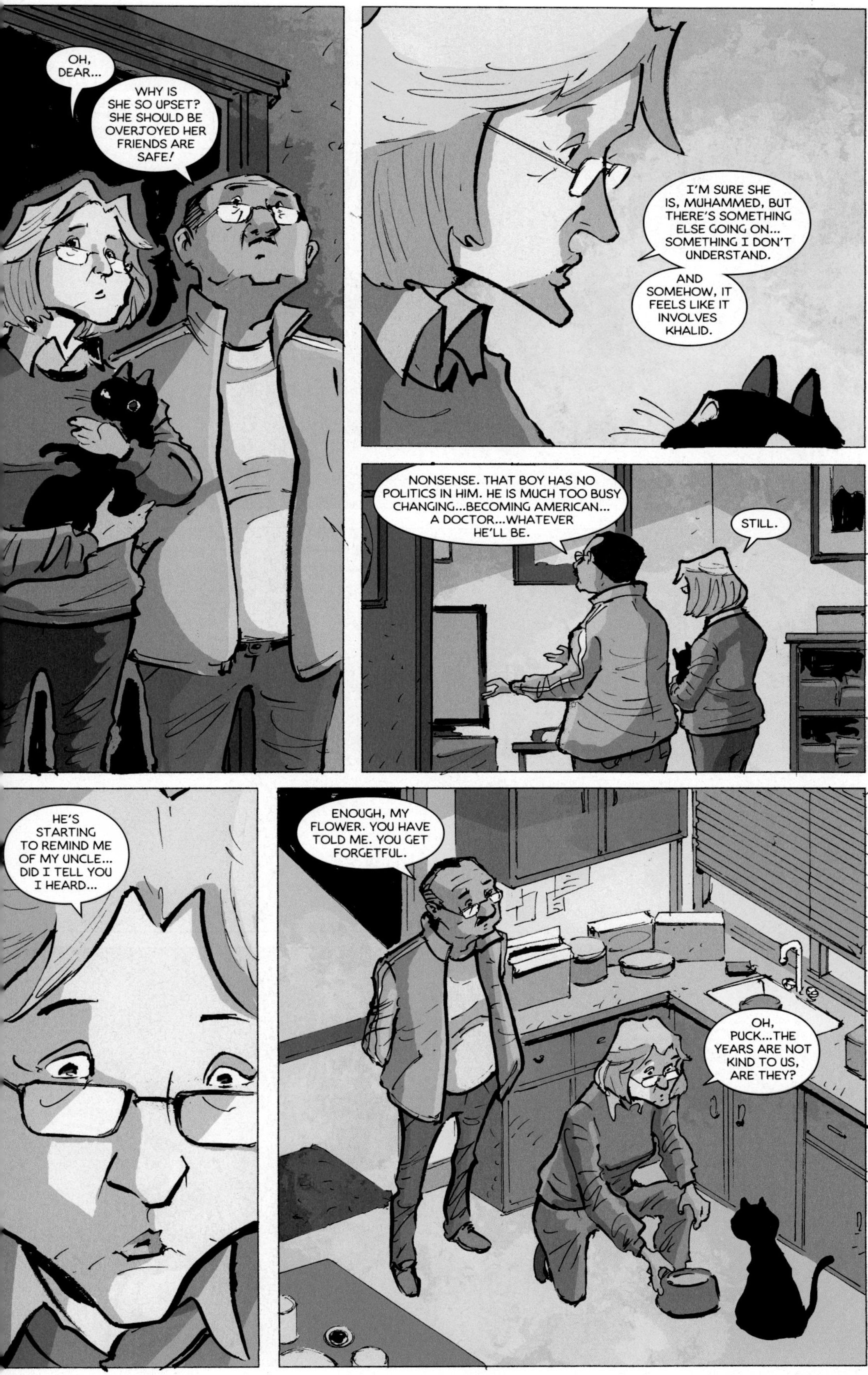
OH, DEAR...
WHY IS SHE SO UPSET? SHE SHOULD BE OVERJOYED HER FRIENDS ARE SAFE!
I'M SURE SHE IS, MUHAMMED, BUT THERE'S SOMETHING ELSE GOING ON... SOMETHING I DON'T UNDERSTAND.
AND SOMEHOW, IT FEELS LIKE IT INVOLVES KHALID.
NONSENSE. THAT BOY HAS NO POLITICS IN HIM. HE IS MUCH TOO BUSY CHANGING...BECOMING AMERICAN... A DOCTOR...WHATEVER HE'LL BE.
STILL.
HE'S STARTING TO REMIND ME OF MY UNCLE... DID I TELL YOU I HEARD...
ENOUGH, MY FLOWER. YOU HAVE TOLD ME. YOU GET FORGETFUL.
OH, PUCK...THE YEARS ARE NOT KIND TO US, ARE THEY?

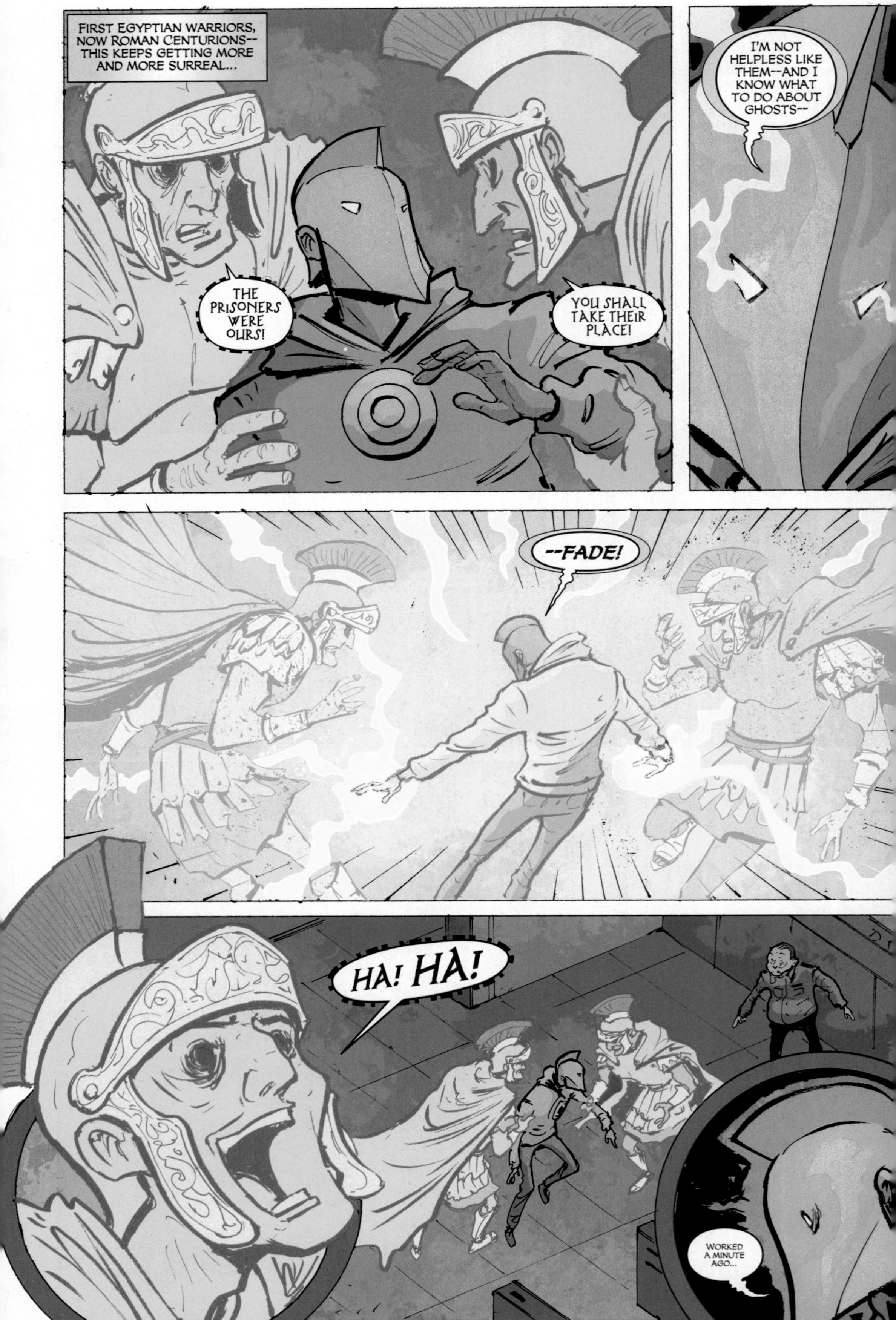
FIRST EGYPTIAN WARRIORS, NOW ROMAN CENTURIONS-- THIS KEEPS GETTING MORE AND MORE SURREAL...
THE PRISONERS WERE OURS!
YOU SHALL TAKE THEIR PLACE!
I'M NOT HELPLESS LIKE THEM--AND I KNOW WHAT TO DO ABOUT GHOSTS--
--FADE!
HA! HA!
WORKED A MINUTE AGO...

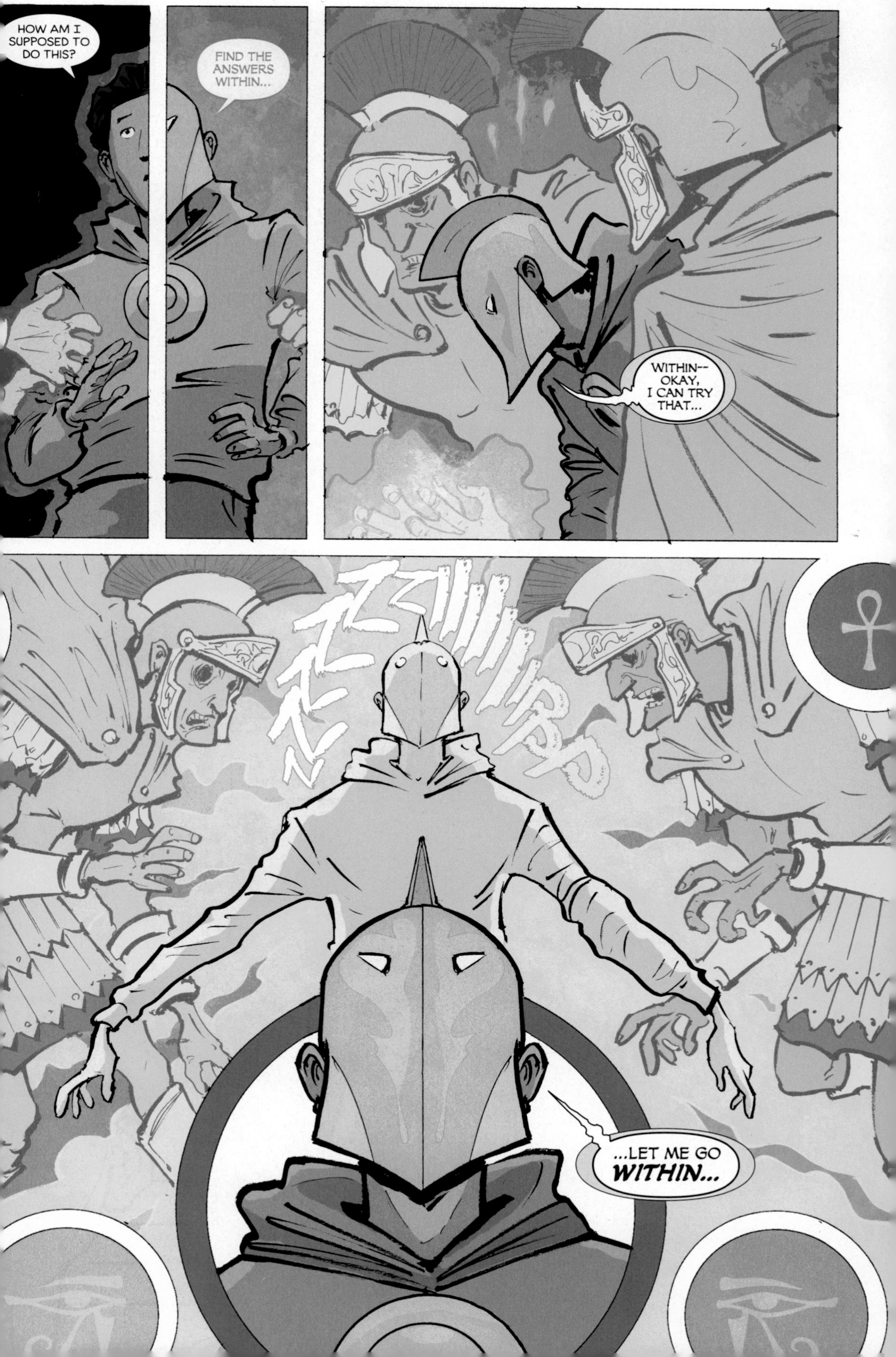
HOW AM I SUPPOSED TO DO THIS?
FIND THE ANSWERS WITHIN...
WITHIN-- OKAY, I CAN TRY THAT...
ZZZWWWAAP
...LET ME GO *WITHIN...*

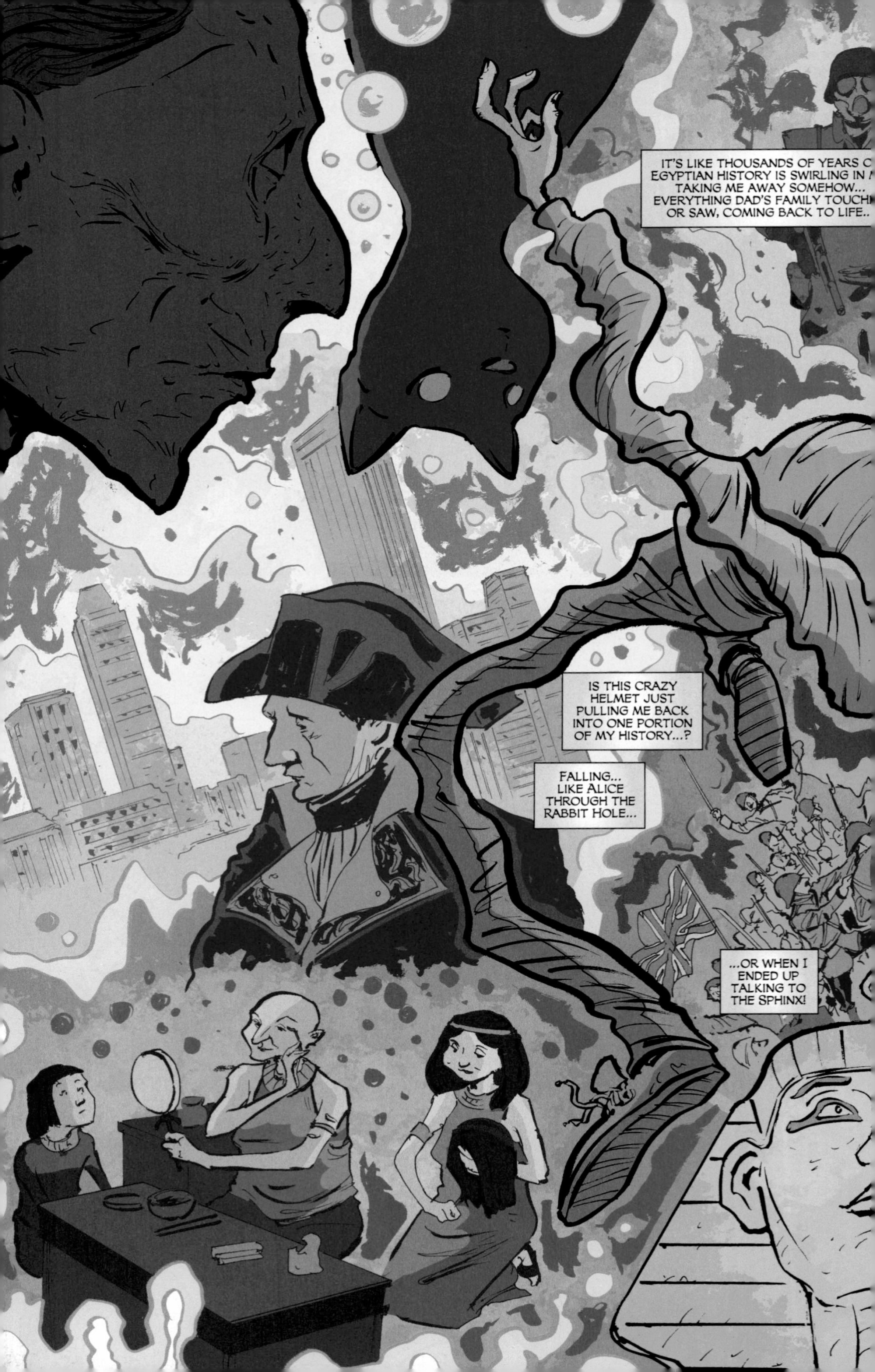

IT'S LIKE THOUSANDS OF YEARS O EGYPTIAN HISTORY IS SWIRLING IN TAKING ME AWAY SOMEHOW... EVERYTHING DAD'S FAMILY TOUCH OR SAW, COMING BACK TO LIFE..
IS THIS CRAZY HELMET JUST PULLING ME BACK INTO ONE PORTION OF MY HISTORY...?
FALLING... LIKE ALICE THROUGH THE RABBIT HOLE...
...OR WHEN I ENDED UP TALKING TO THE SPHINX!

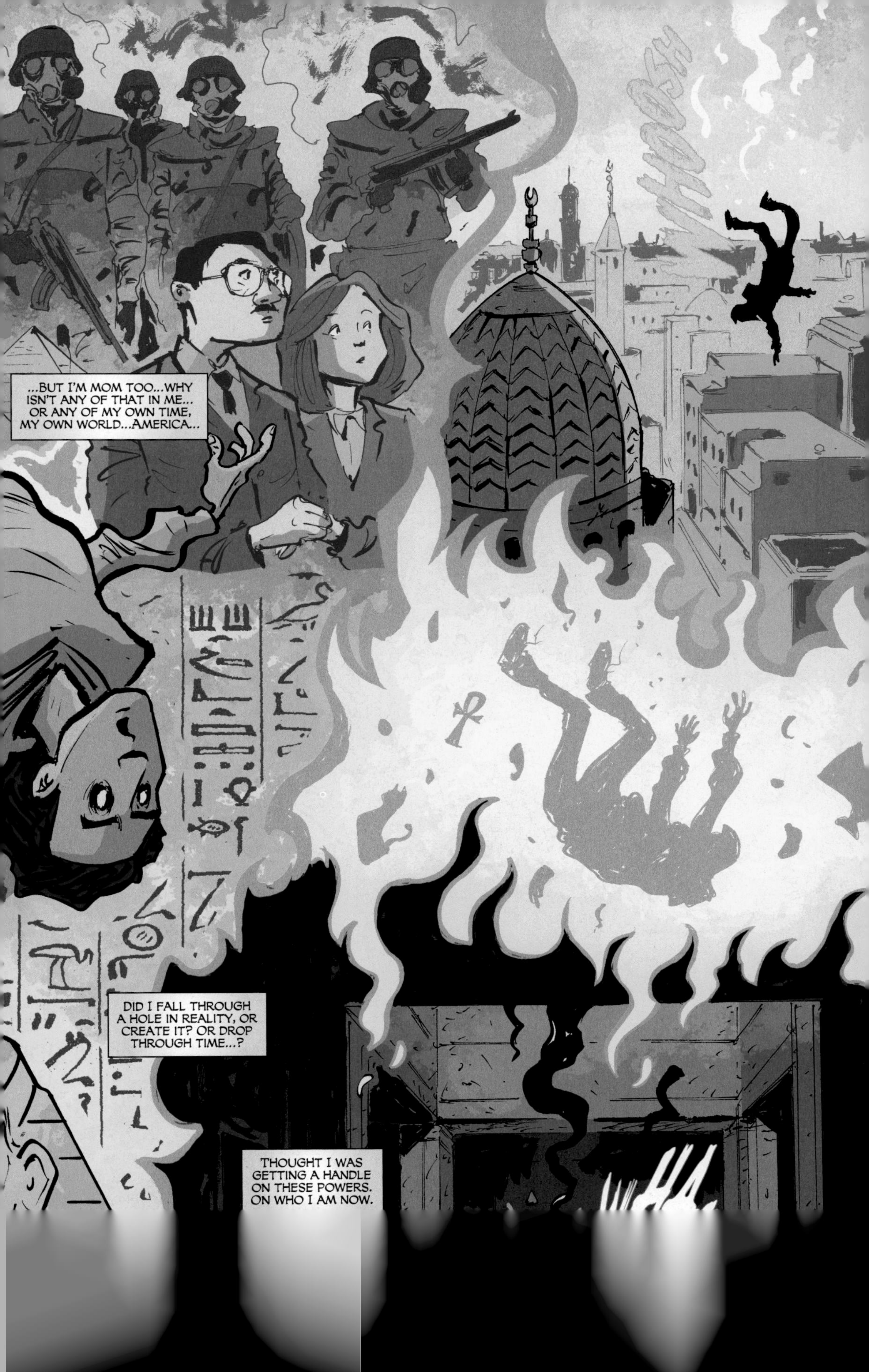
WHOOSH
...BUT I'M MOM TOO...WHY ISN'T ANY OF THAT IN ME... OR ANY OF MY OWN TIME, MY OWN WORLD...AMERICA...
DID I FALL THROUGH A HOLE IN REALITY, OR CREATE IT? OR DROP THROUGH TIME...?
THOUGHT I WAS GETTING A HANDLE ON THESE POWERS. ON WHO I AM NOW.

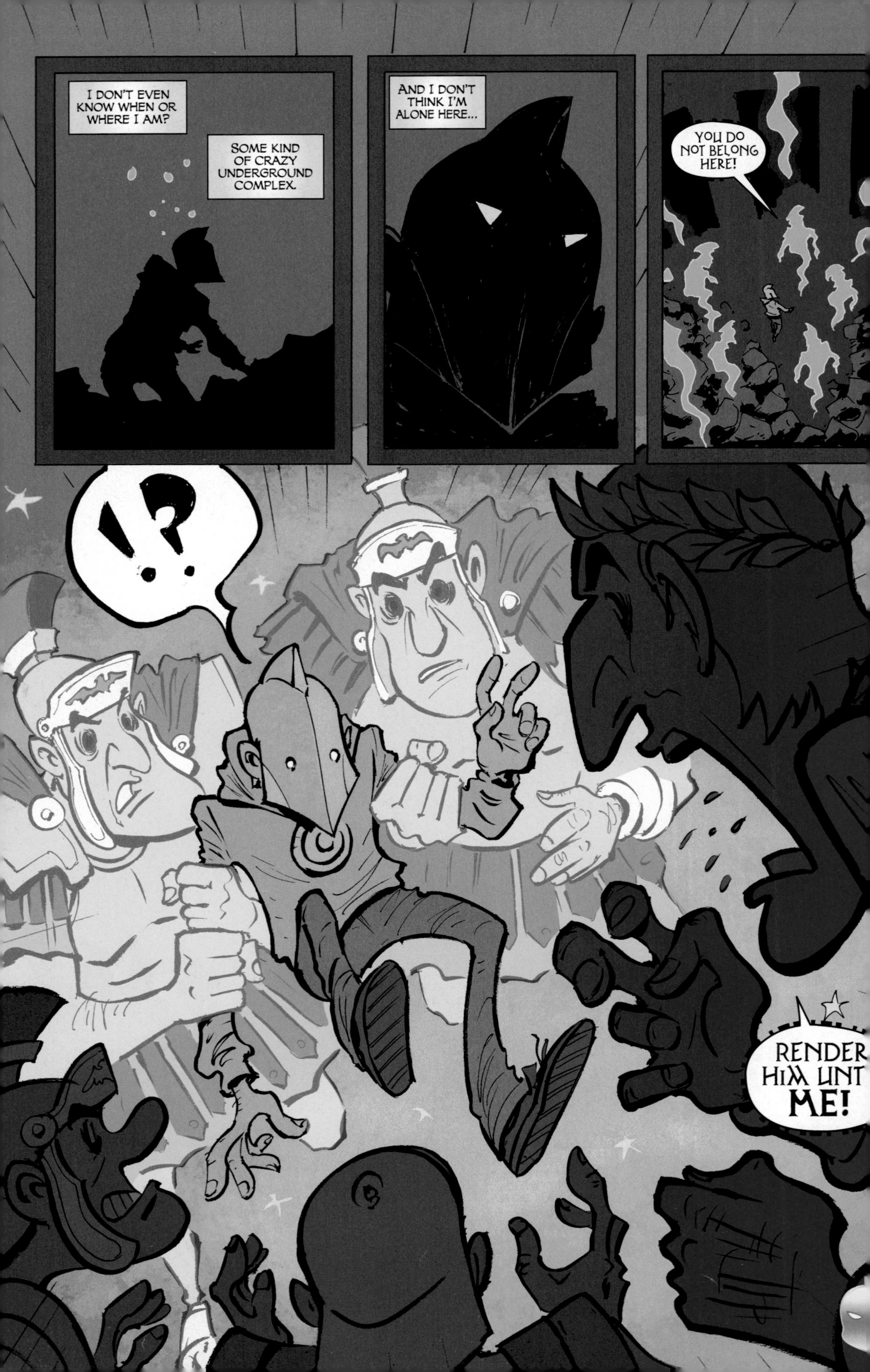
I DON'T EVEN KNOW WHEN OR WHERE I AM?
SOME KIND OF CRAZY UNDERGROUND COMPLEX.
AND I DON'T THINK I'M ALONE HERE...
YOU DO NOT BELONG HERE!
!?
RENDER HIM UNT ME!

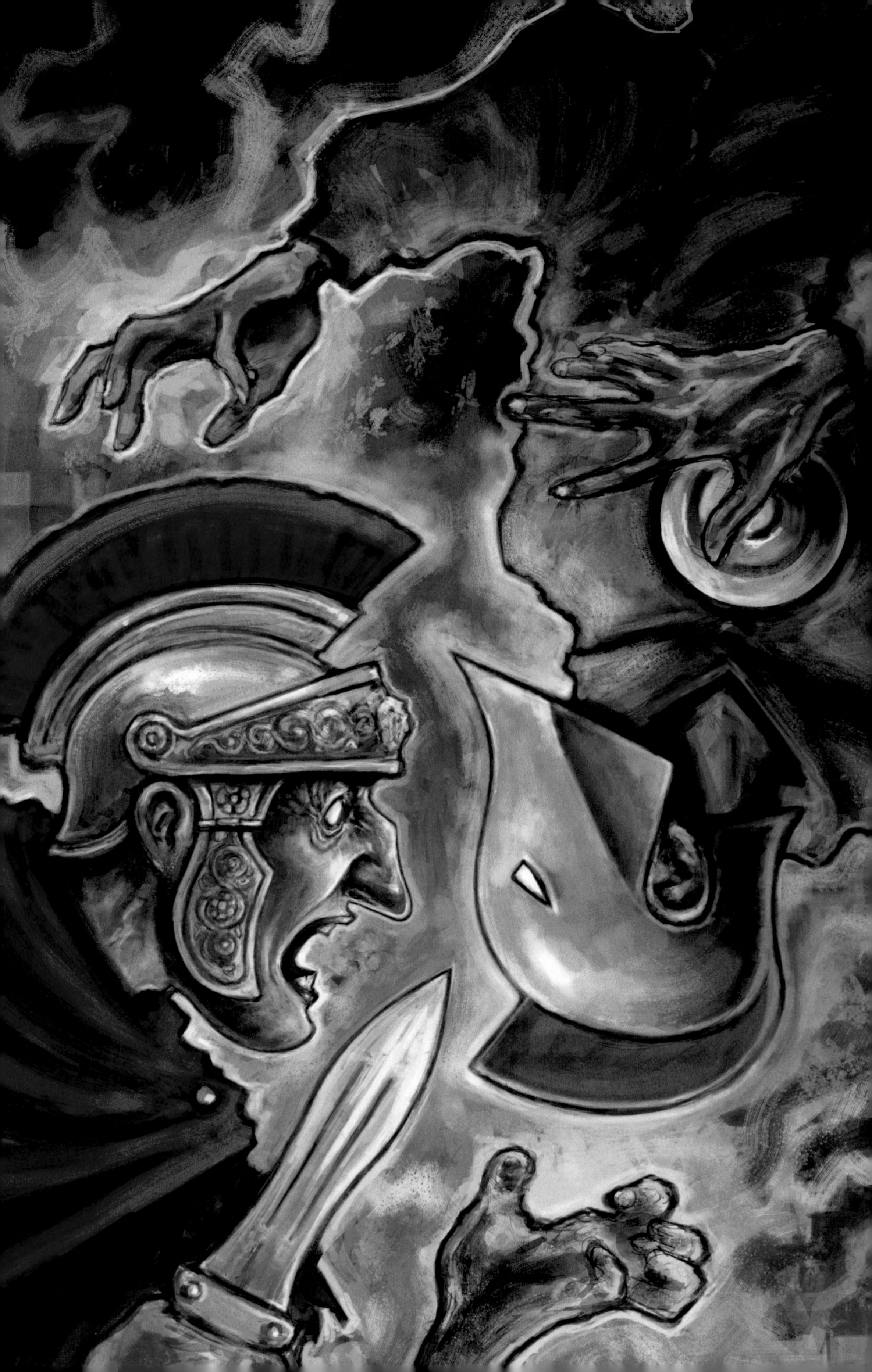

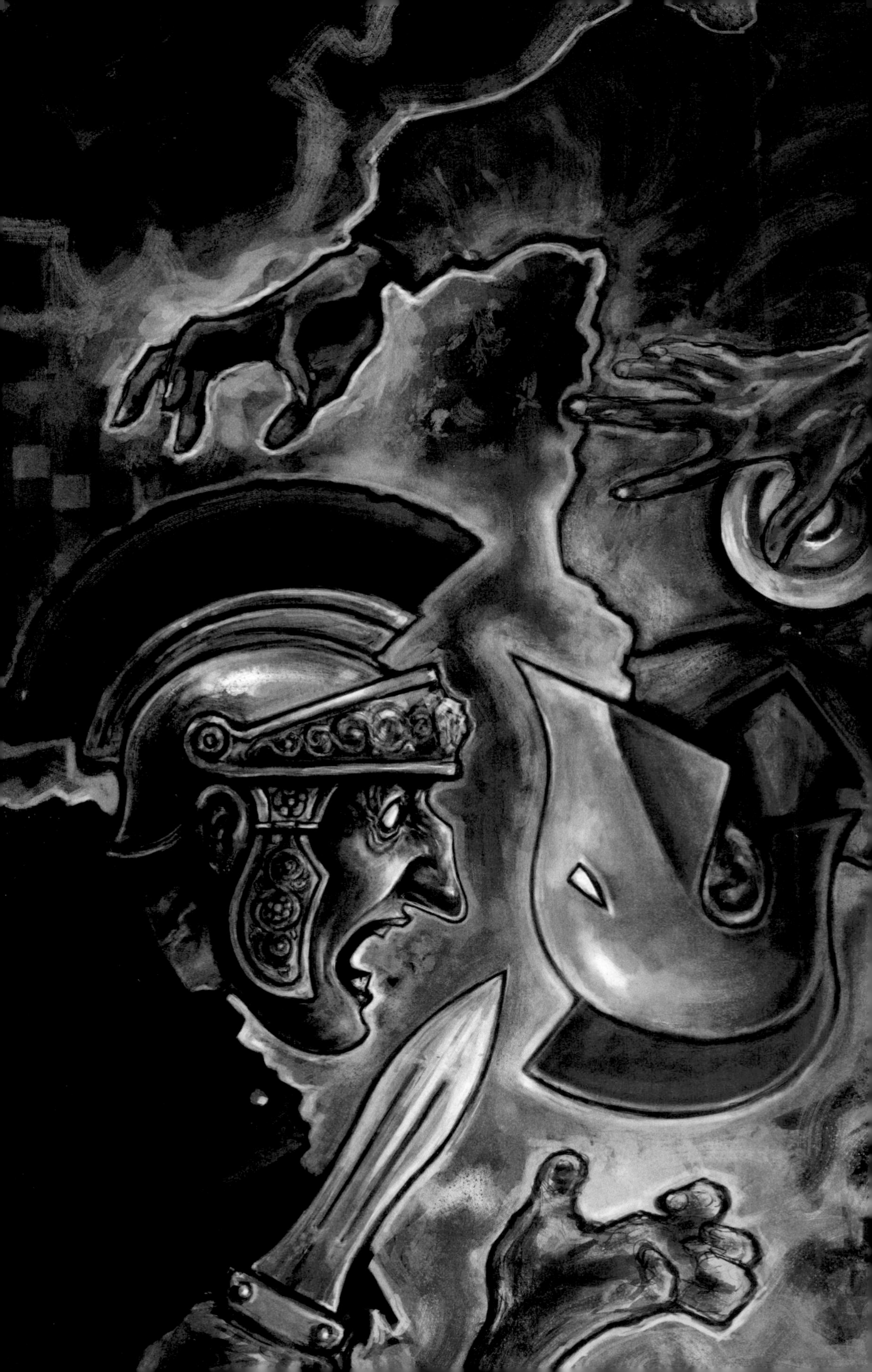

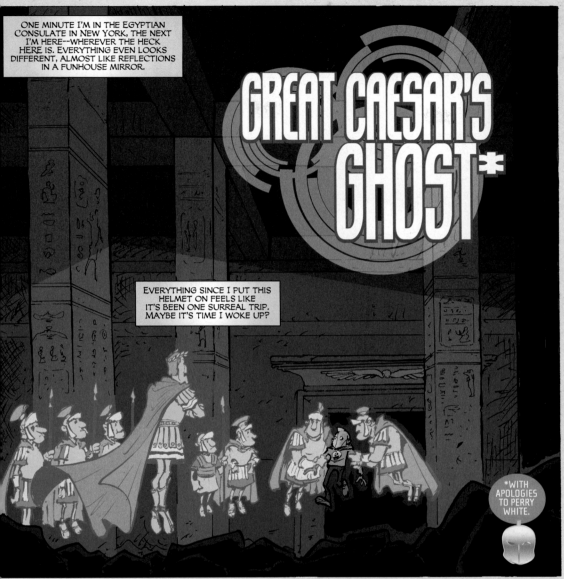

ONE MINUTE I'M IN THE EGYPTIAN CONSULATE IN NEW YORK, THE NEXT I'M HERE--WHEREVER THE HECK HERE IS. EVERYTHING EVEN LOOKS DIFFERENT, ALMOST LIKE REFLECTIONS IN A FUNHOUSE MIRROR.

GREAT CAESAR'S GHOST*

EVERYTHING SINCE I PUT THIS HELMET ON FEELS LIKE IT'S BEEN ONE SURREAL TRIP. MAYBE IT'S TIME I WOKE UP?

*WITH APOLOGIES TO PERRY WHITE.

BRING THE INTRUDER TO ME! CAESAR WISHES TO SEE WHAT MANNER OF CREATURE IT IS!

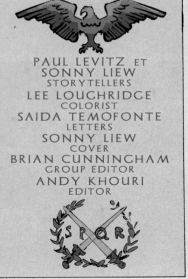

PAUL LEVITZ ET SONNY LIEW
STORYTELLERS

LEE LOUGHRIDGE
COLORIST

SAIDA TEMOFONTE
LETTERS

SONNY LIEW
COVER

BRIAN CUNNINGHAM
GROUP EDITOR

ANDY KHOURI
EDITOR

S P Q R

CAESAR?!

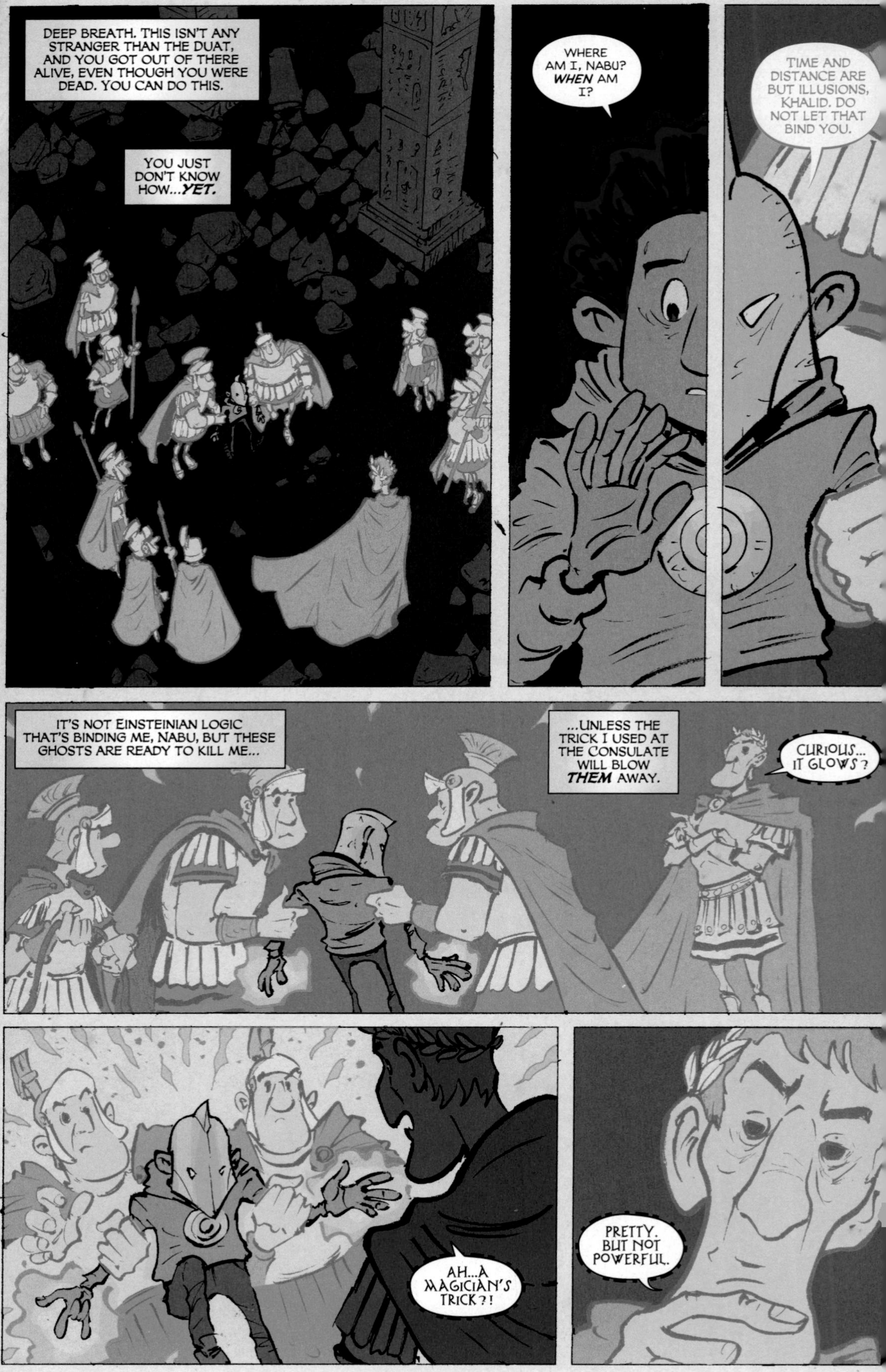
DEEP BREATH. THIS ISN'T ANY STRANGER THAN THE DUAT, AND YOU GOT OUT OF THERE ALIVE, EVEN THOUGH YOU WERE DEAD. YOU CAN DO THIS.
YOU JUST DON'T KNOW HOW...YET.
WHERE AM I, NABU? WHEN AM I?
TIME AND DISTANCE ARE BUT ILLUSIONS, KHALID. DO NOT LET THAT BIND YOU.
IT'S NOT EINSTEINIAN LOGIC THAT'S BINDING ME, NABU, BUT THESE GHOSTS ARE READY TO KILL ME...
...UNLESS THE TRICK I USED AT THE CONSULATE WILL BLOW THEM AWAY.
CURIOUS... IT GLOWS?
AH...A MAGICIAN'S TRICK?!
PRETTY. BUT NOT POWERFUL.

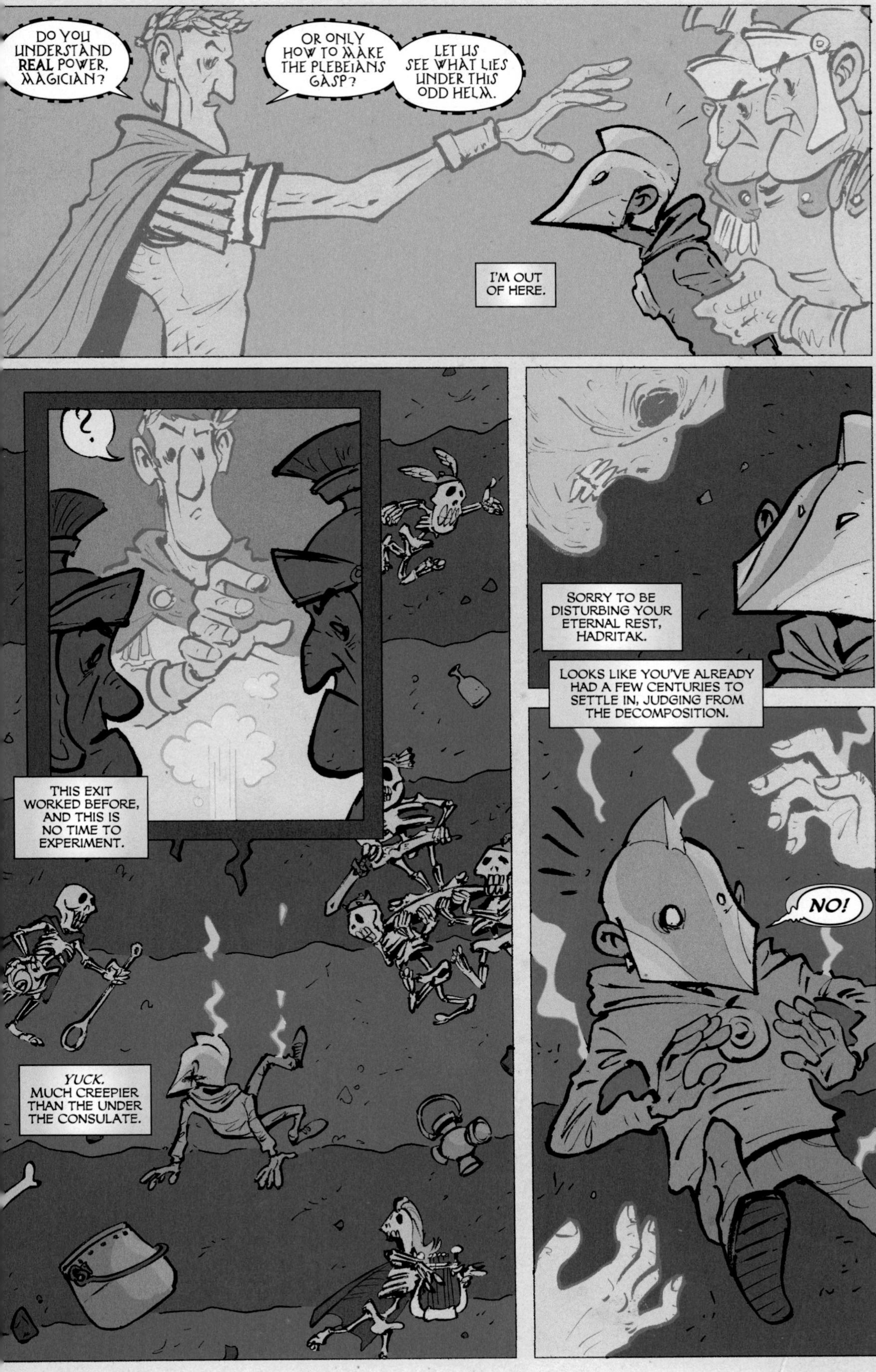
DO YOU UNDERSTAND **REAL** POWER, MAGICIAN?
OR ONLY HOW TO MAKE THE PLEBEIANS GASP?
LET US SEE WHAT LIES UNDER THIS ODD HELM.
I'M OUT OF HERE.
?
THIS EXIT WORKED BEFORE, AND THIS IS NO TIME TO EXPERIMENT.
YUCK. MUCH CREEPIER THAN THE UNDER THE CONSULATE.
SORRY TO BE DISTURBING YOUR ETERNAL REST, HADRITAK.
LOOKS LIKE YOU'VE ALREADY HAD A FEW CENTURIES TO SETTLE IN, JUDGING FROM THE DECOMPOSITION.
NO!

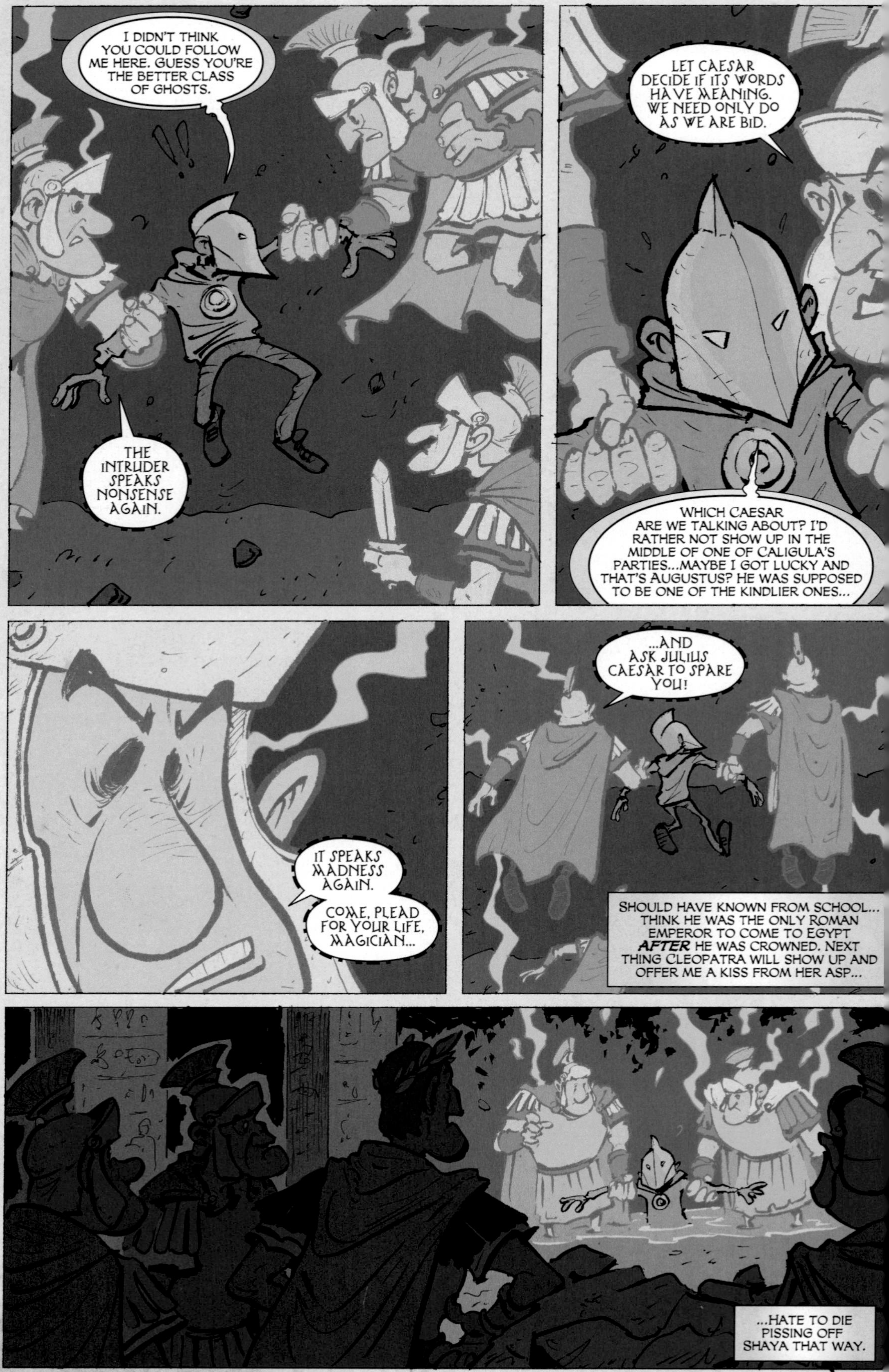
I DIDN'T THINK YOU COULD FOLLOW ME HERE. GUESS YOU'RE THE BETTER CLASS OF GHOSTS.
!!
THE INTRUDER SPEAKS NONSENSE AGAIN.
LET CAESAR DECIDE IF ITS WORDS HAVE MEANING. WE NEED ONLY DO AS WE ARE BID.
WHICH CAESAR ARE WE TALKING ABOUT? I'D RATHER NOT SHOW UP IN THE MIDDLE OF ONE OF CALIGULA'S PARTIES...MAYBE I GOT LUCKY AND THAT'S AUGUSTUS? HE WAS SUPPOSED TO BE ONE OF THE KINDLIER ONES...
IT SPEAKS MADNESS AGAIN.
COME, PLEAD FOR YOUR LIFE, MAGICIAN...
...AND ASK JULIUS CAESAR TO SPARE YOU!
SHOULD HAVE KNOWN FROM SCHOOL... THINK HE WAS THE ONLY ROMAN EMPEROR TO COME TO EGYPT ***AFTER*** HE WAS CROWNED. NEXT THING CLEOPATRA WILL SHOW UP AND OFFER ME A KISS FROM HER ASP...
...HATE TO DIE PISSING OFF SHAYA THAT WAY.

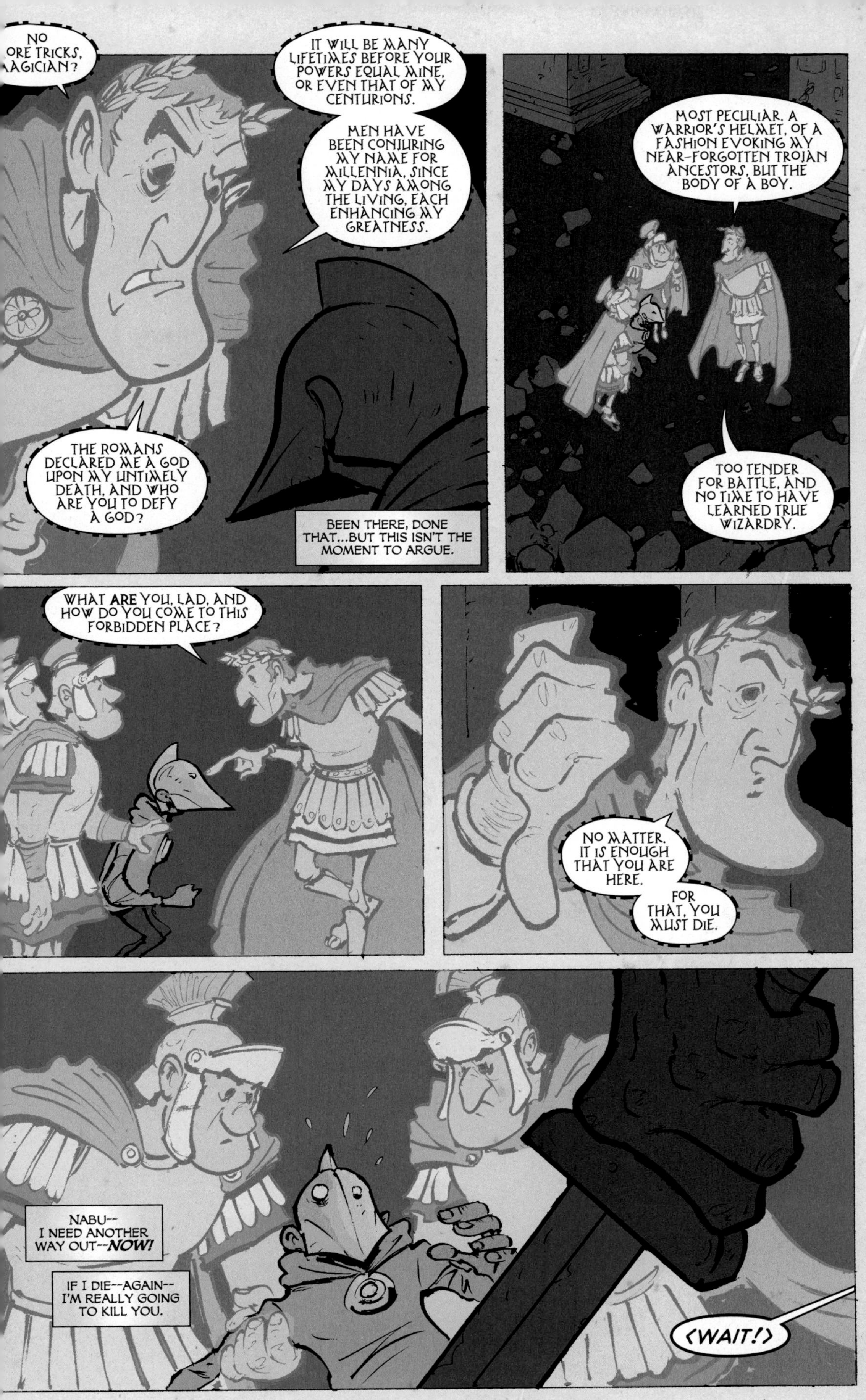
NO ORE TRICKS, AGICIAN?
IT WILL BE MANY LIFETIMES BEFORE YOUR POWERS EQUAL MINE, OR EVEN THAT OF MY CENTURIONS.
MEN HAVE BEEN CONJURING MY NAME FOR MILLENNIA, SINCE MY DAYS AMONG THE LIVING, EACH ENHANCING MY GREATNESS.
THE ROMANS DECLARED ME A GOD UPON MY UNTIMELY DEATH, AND WHO ARE YOU TO DEFY A GOD?
BEEN THERE, DONE THAT...BUT THIS ISN'T THE MOMENT TO ARGUE.
MOST PECULIAR. A WARRIOR'S HELMET, OF A FASHION EVOKING MY NEAR-FORGOTTEN TROJAN ANCESTORS, BUT THE BODY OF A BOY.
TOO TENDER FOR BATTLE, AND NO TIME TO HAVE LEARNED TRUE WIZARDRY.
WHAT **ARE** YOU, LAD, AND HOW DO YOU COME TO THIS FORBIDDEN PLACE?
NO MATTER. IT IS ENOUGH THAT YOU ARE HERE.
FOR THAT, YOU MUST DIE.
NABU-- I NEED ANOTHER WAY OUT--***NOW!***
IF I DIE--AGAIN-- I'M REALLY GOING TO KILL YOU.
<WAIT!>

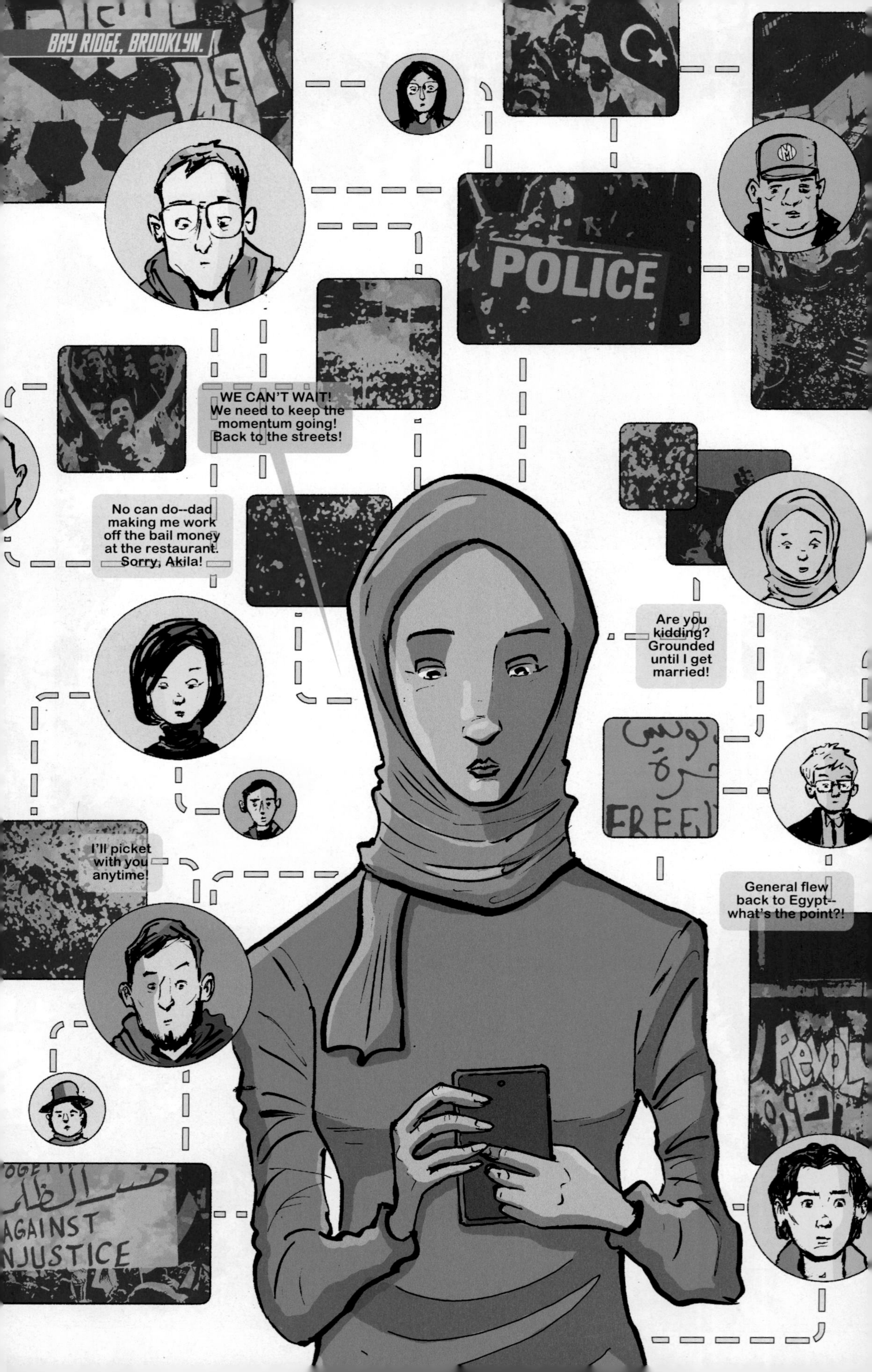
BAY RIDGE, BROOKLYN.
POLICE
WE CAN'T WAIT! We need to keep the momentum going! Back to the streets!
No can do--dad making me work off the bail money at the restaurant. Sorry, Akila!
Are you kidding? Grounded until I get married!
FREE
I'll picket with you anytime!
General flew back to Egypt--what's the point?!
AGAINST INJUSTICE

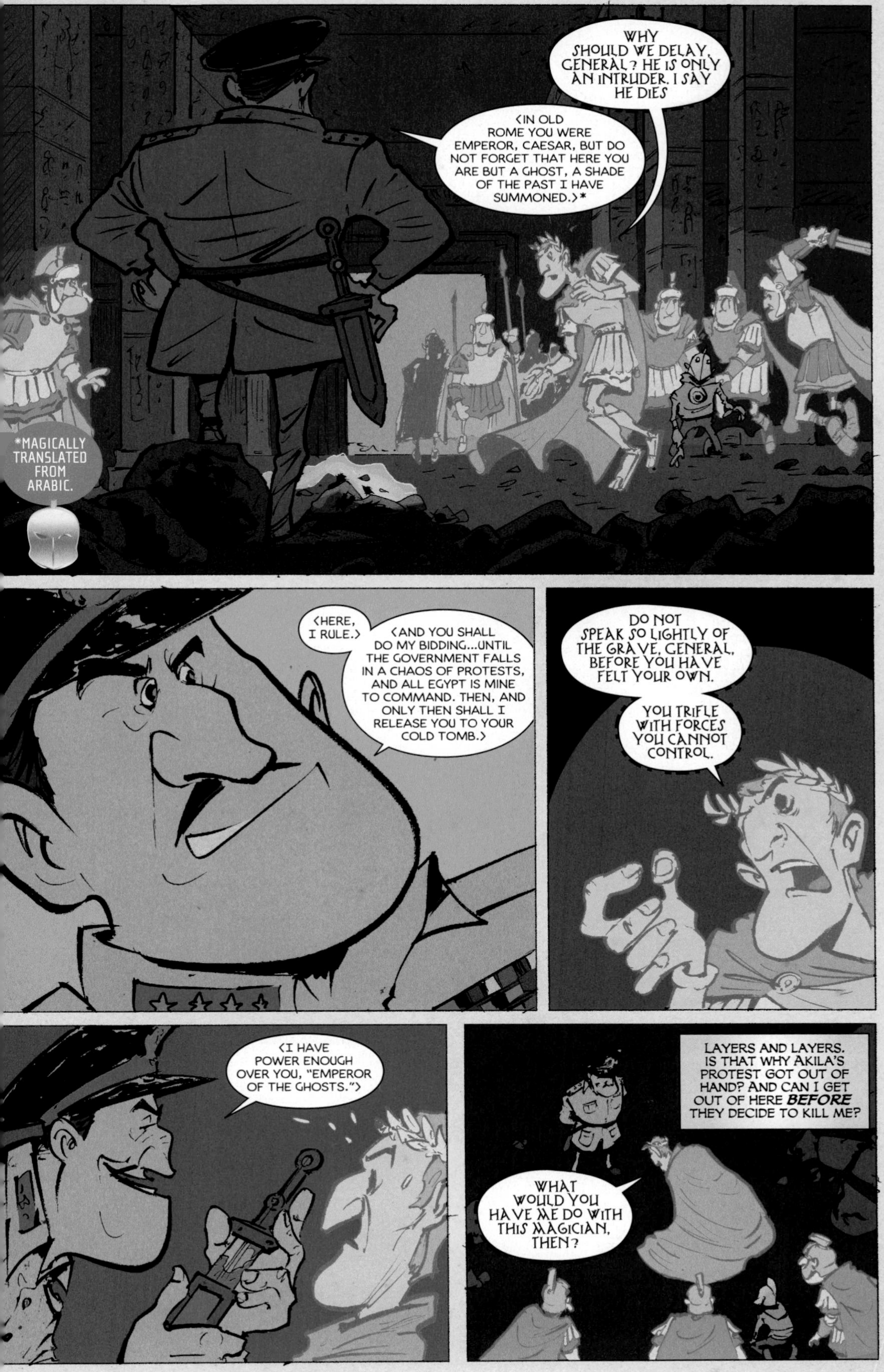

WHY SHOULD WE DELAY, GENERAL? HE IS ONLY AN INTRUDER. I SAY HE DIES
<IN OLD ROME YOU WERE EMPEROR, CAESAR, BUT DO NOT FORGET THAT HERE YOU ARE BUT A GHOST, A SHADE OF THE PAST I HAVE SUMMONED.>*
*MAGICALLY TRANSLATED FROM ARABIC.
<HERE, I RULE.>
<AND YOU SHALL DO MY BIDDING...UNTIL THE GOVERNMENT FALLS IN A CHAOS OF PROTESTS, AND ALL EGYPT IS MINE TO COMMAND. THEN, AND ONLY THEN SHALL I RELEASE YOU TO YOUR COLD TOMB.>
DO NOT SPEAK SO LIGHTLY OF THE GRAVE, GENERAL, BEFORE YOU HAVE FELT YOUR OWN.
YOU TRIFLE WITH FORCES YOU CANNOT CONTROL.
<I HAVE POWER ENOUGH OVER YOU, "EMPEROR OF THE GHOSTS.">
LAYERS AND LAYERS. IS THAT WHY AKILA'S PROTEST GOT OUT OF HAND? AND CAN I GET OUT OF HERE *BEFORE* THEY DECIDE TO KILL ME?
WHAT WOULD YOU HAVE ME DO WITH THIS MAGICIAN, THEN?

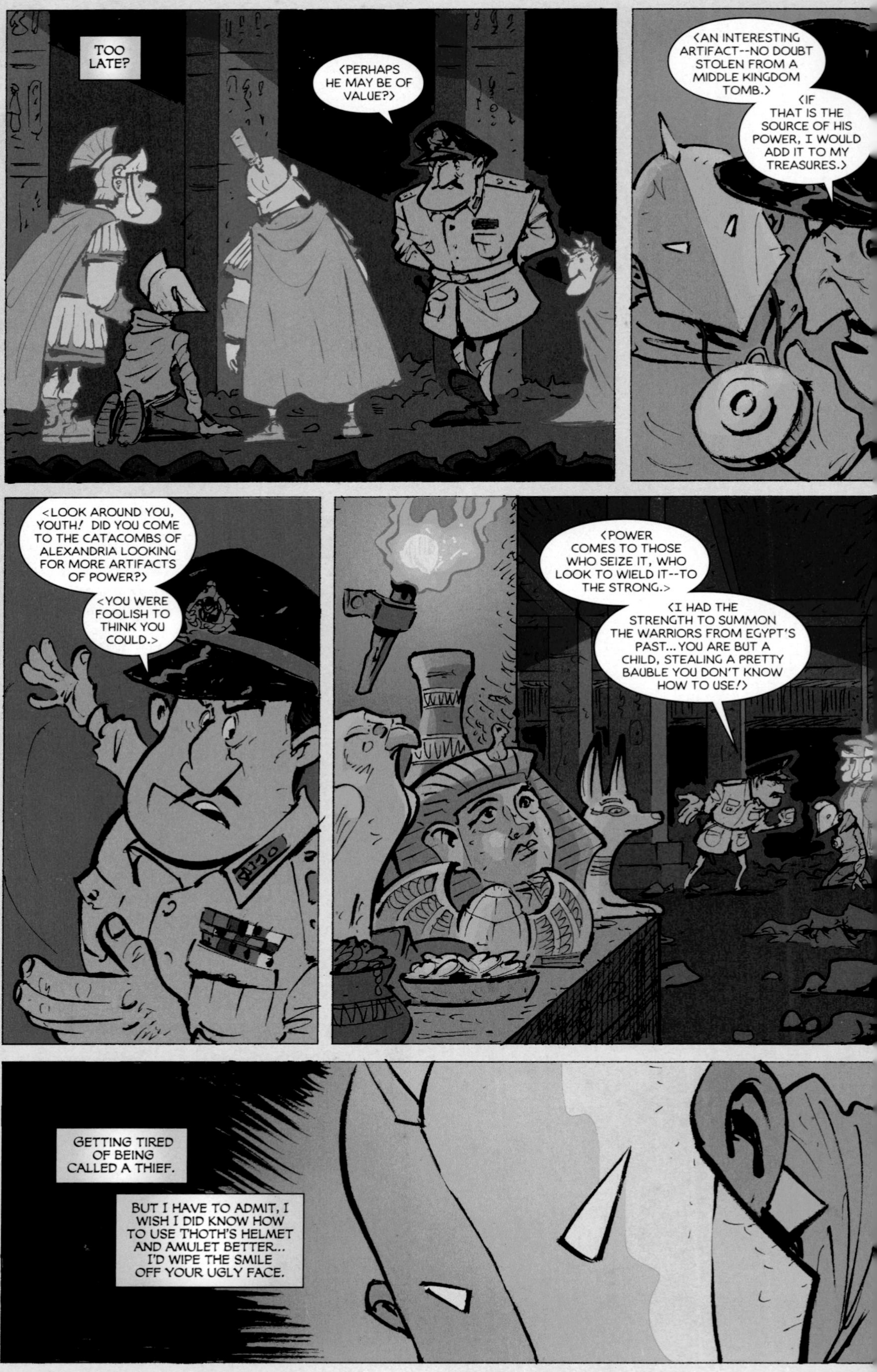
TOO LATE?
<PERHAPS HE MAY BE OF VALUE?>
<AN INTERESTING ARTIFACT--NO DOUBT STOLEN FROM A MIDDLE KINGDOM TOMB.>
<IF THAT IS THE SOURCE OF HIS POWER, I WOULD ADD IT TO MY TREASURES.>
<LOOK AROUND YOU, YOUTH! DID YOU COME TO THE CATACOMBS OF ALEXANDRIA LOOKING FOR MORE ARTIFACTS OF POWER?>
<YOU WERE FOOLISH TO THINK YOU COULD.>
<POWER COMES TO THOSE WHO SEIZE IT, WHO LOOK TO WIELD IT--TO THE STRONG.>
<I HAD THE STRENGTH TO SUMMON THE WARRIORS FROM EGYPT'S PAST... YOU ARE BUT A CHILD, STEALING A PRETTY BAUBLE YOU DON'T KNOW HOW TO USE!>
GETTING TIRED OF BEING CALLED A THIEF.
BUT I HAVE TO ADMIT, I WISH I DID KNOW HOW TO USE THOTH'S HELMET AND AMULET BETTER... I'D WIPE THE SMILE OFF YOUR UGLY FACE.

<THIS DOES NOT BELONG ON YOUR SCRAWNY NECK.>

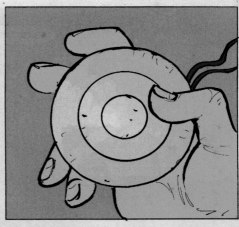

AYEEIIIIIIIIIIIIII

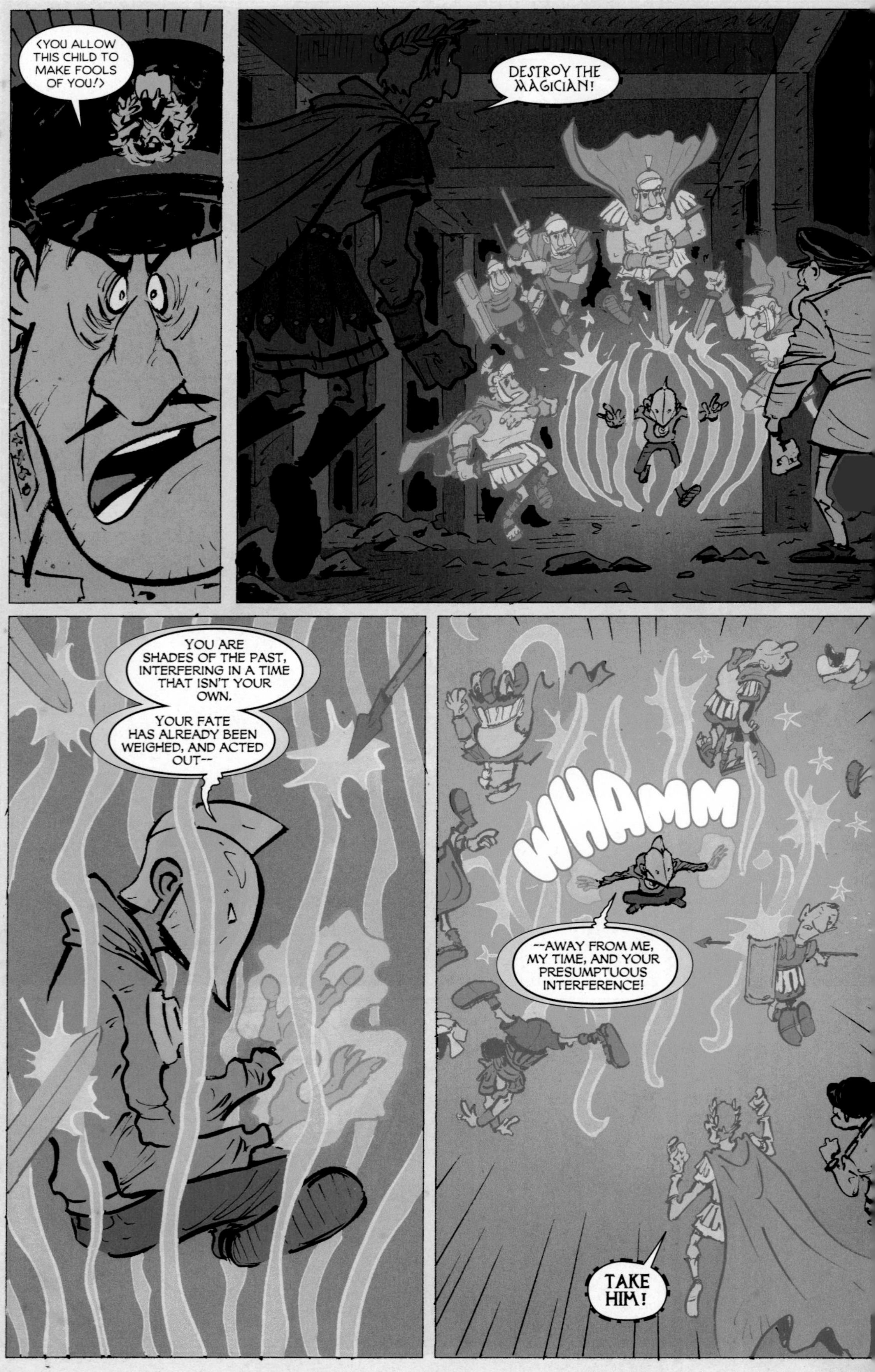
<YOU ALLOW THIS CHILD TO MAKE FOOLS OF YOU!>
DESTROY THE MAGICIAN!
YOU ARE SHADES OF THE PAST, INTERFERING IN A TIME THAT ISN'T YOUR OWN.
YOUR FATE HAS ALREADY BEEN WEIGHED, AND ACTED OUT--
WHAMM
--AWAY FROM ME, MY TIME, AND YOUR PRESUMPTUOUS INTERFERENCE!
TAKE HIM!

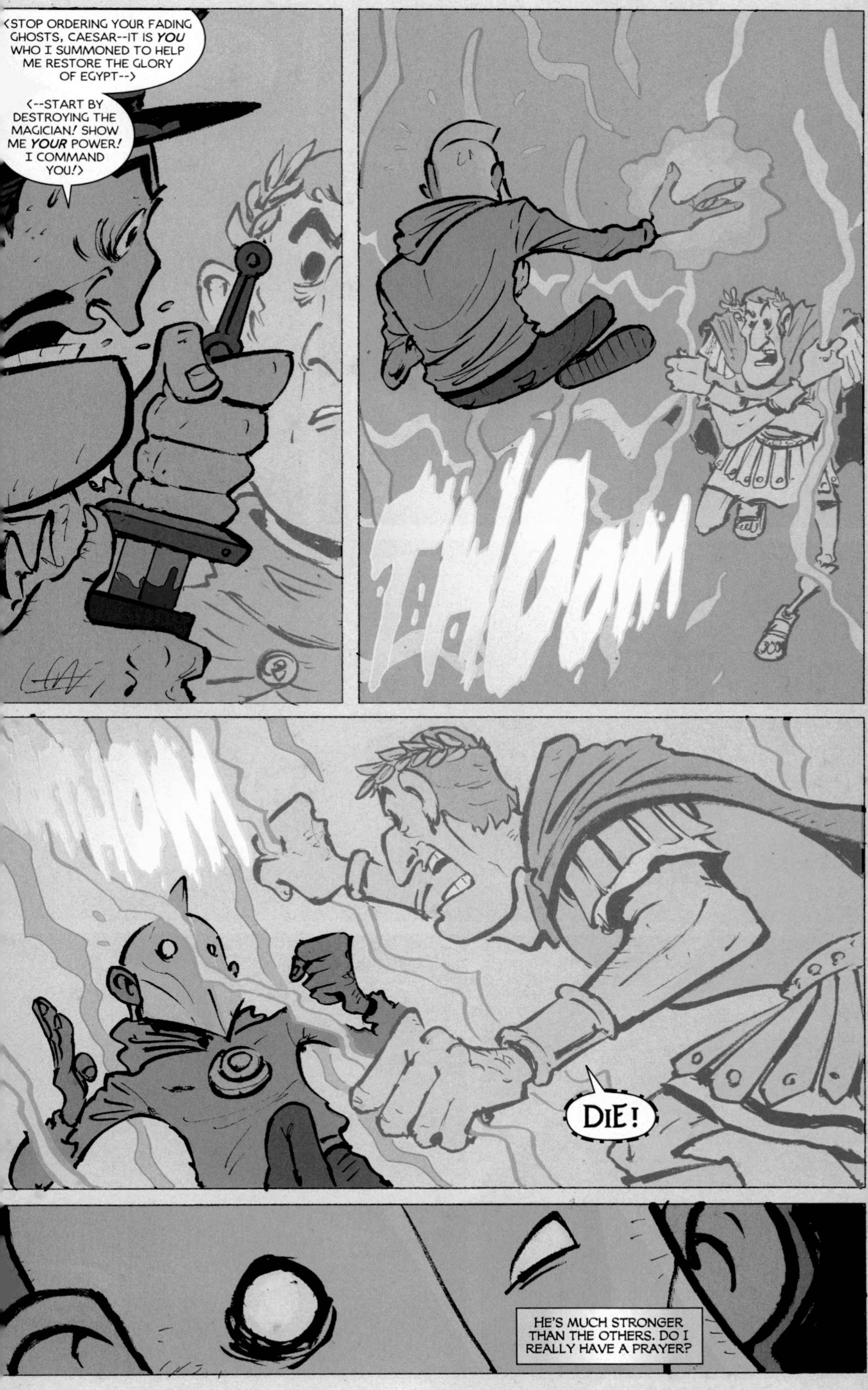
<STOP ORDERING YOUR FADING GHOSTS, CAESAR--IT IS *YOU* WHO I SUMMONED TO HELP ME RESTORE THE GLORY OF EGYPT-->
<--START BY DESTROYING THE MAGICIAN! SHOW ME ***YOUR*** POWER! I COMMAND YOU!>
THOOM
THOOM
DIE!
HE'S MUCH STRONGER THAN THE OTHERS. DO I REALLY HAVE A PRAYER?

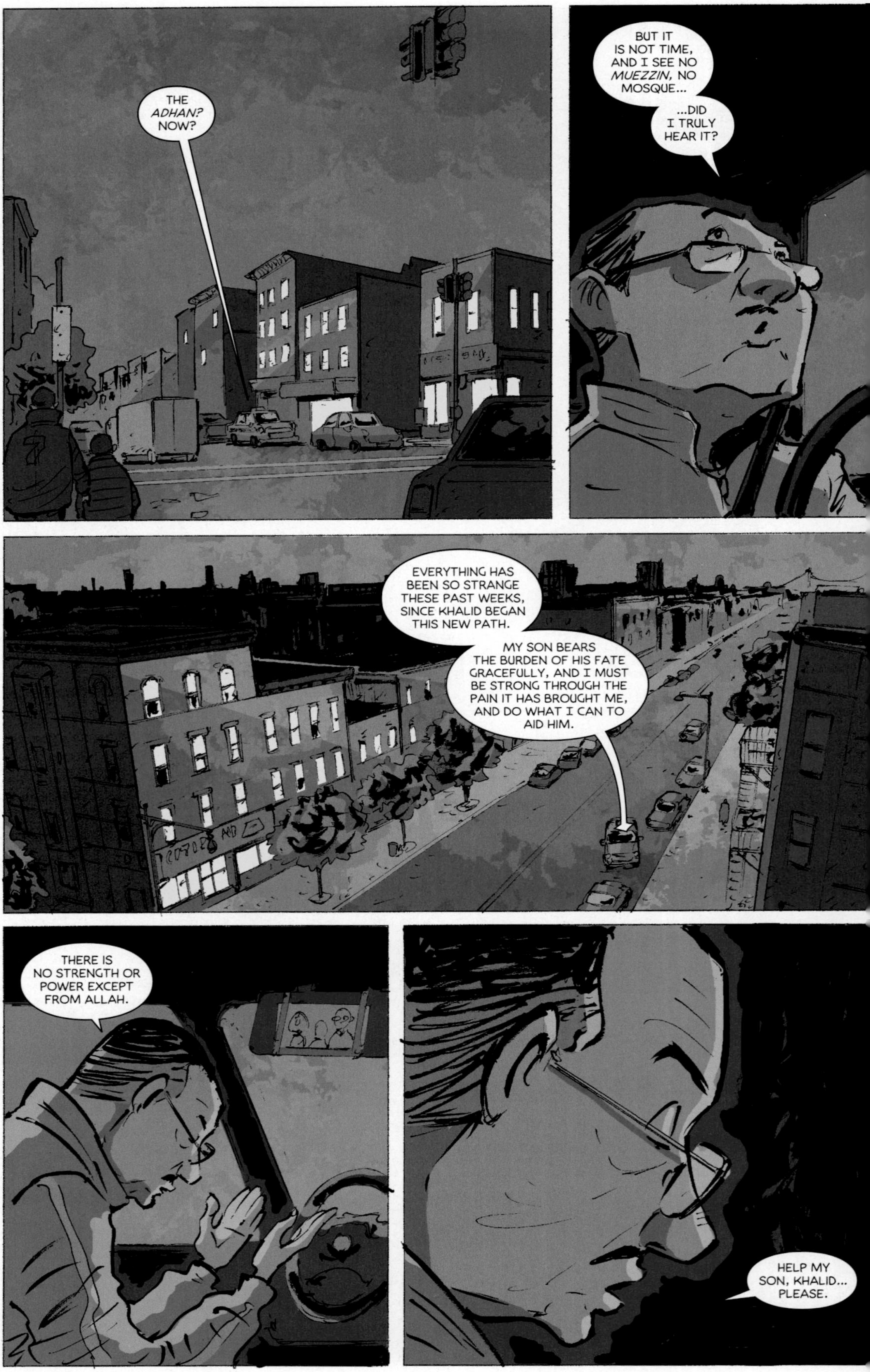
THE *ADHAN?* NOW?
BUT IT IS NOT TIME, AND I SEE NO *MUEZZIN,* NO MOSQUE...
...DID I TRULY HEAR IT?
EVERYTHING HAS BEEN SO STRANGE THESE PAST WEEKS, SINCE KHALID BEGAN THIS NEW PATH.
MY SON BEARS THE BURDEN OF HIS FATE GRACEFULLY, AND I MUST BE STRONG THROUGH THE PAIN IT HAS BROUGHT ME, AND DO WHAT I CAN TO AID HIM.
THERE IS NO STRENGTH OR POWER EXCEPT FROM ALLAH.
HELP MY SON, KHALID... PLEASE.

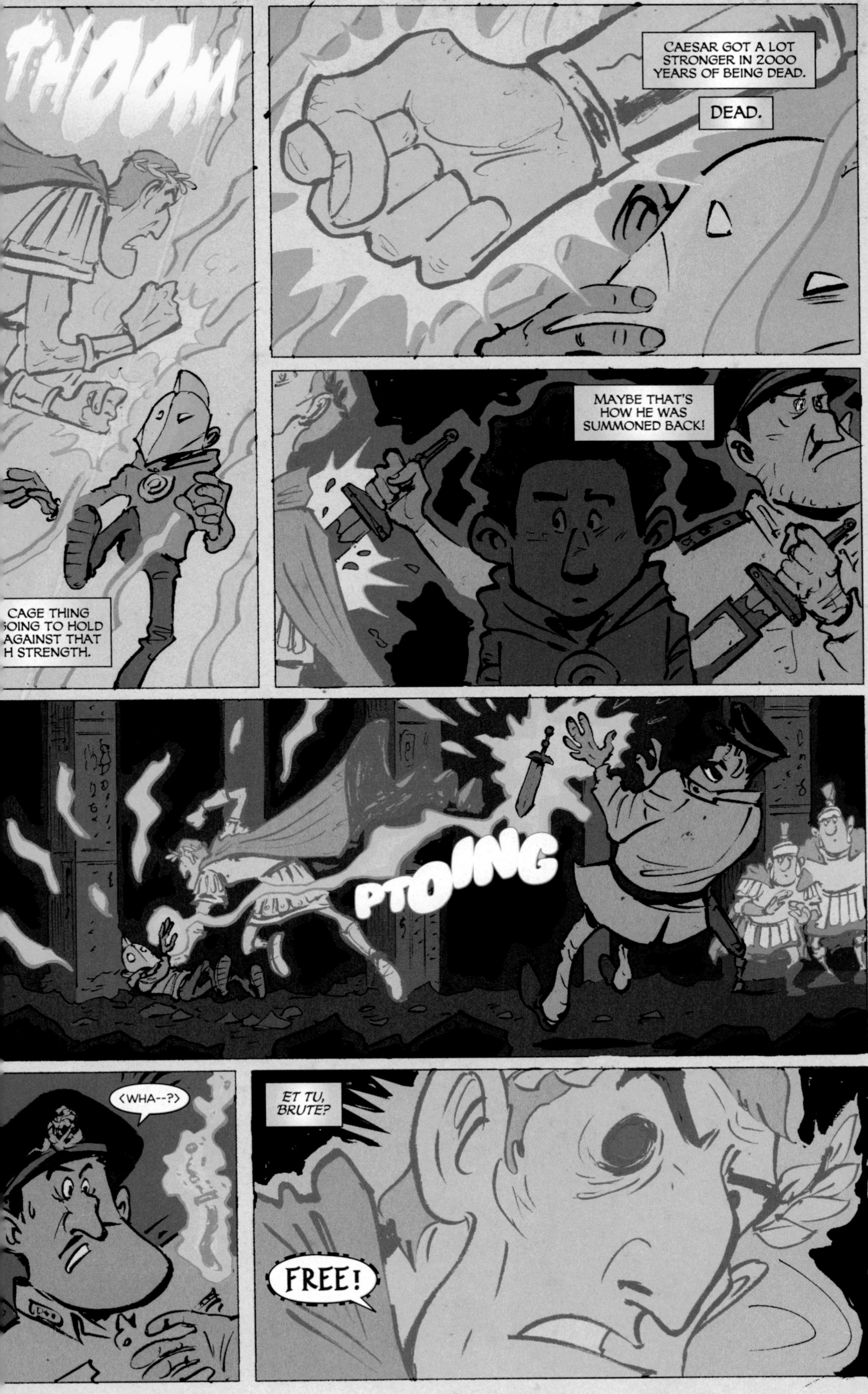
THOOM
CAGE THING
GOING TO HOLD
AGAINST THAT
H STRENGTH.
CAESAR GOT A LOT STRONGER IN 2000 YEARS OF BEING DEAD.
DEAD.
MAYBE THAT'S HOW HE WAS SUMMONED BACK!
PTOING
<WHA--?>
ET TU, BRUTE?
FREE!

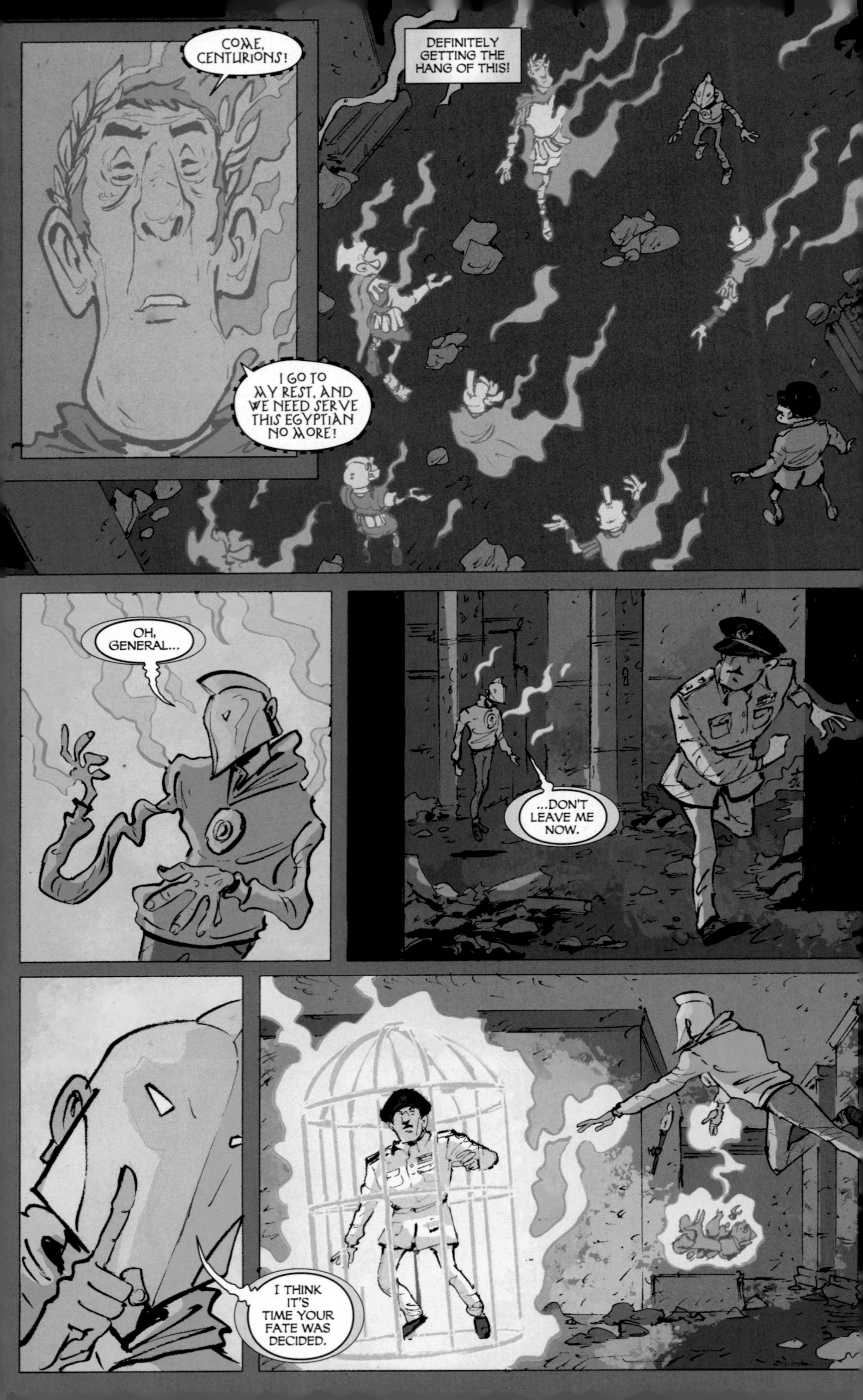
COME, CENTURIONS!
DEFINITELY GETTING THE HANG OF THIS!
I GO TO MY REST, AND WE NEED SERVE THIS EGYPTIAN NO MORE!
OH, GENERAL...
...DON'T LEAVE ME NOW.
I THINK IT'S TIME YOUR FATE WAS DECIDED.

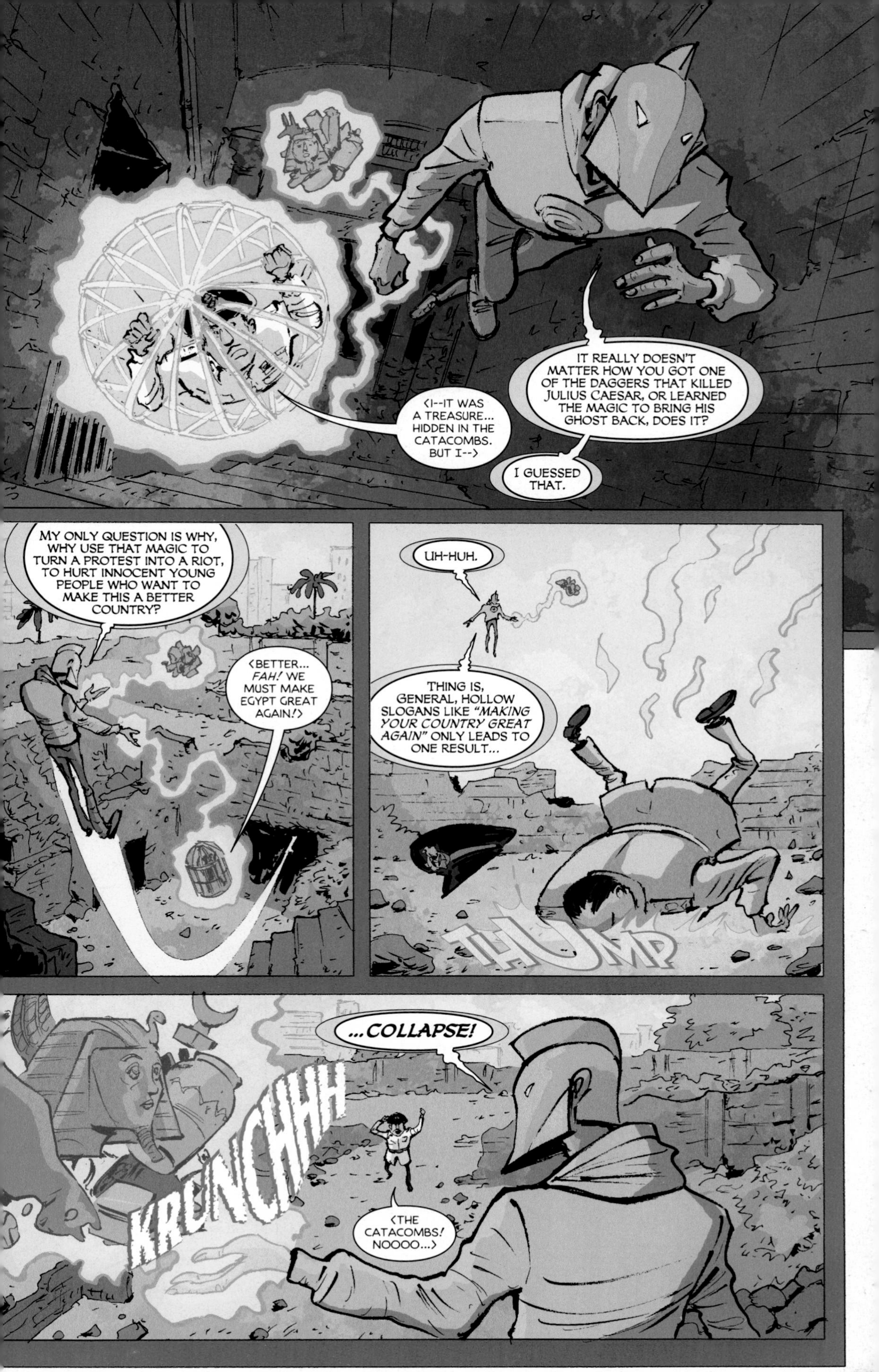
IT REALLY DOESN'T MATTER HOW YOU GOT ONE OF THE DAGGERS THAT KILLED JULIUS CAESAR, OR LEARNED THE MAGIC TO BRING HIS GHOST BACK, DOES IT?
<I--IT WAS A TREASURE... HIDDEN IN THE CATACOMBS. BUT I-->
I GUESSED THAT.
MY ONLY QUESTION IS WHY, WHY USE THAT MAGIC TO TURN A PROTEST INTO A RIOT, TO HURT INNOCENT YOUNG PEOPLE WHO WANT TO MAKE THIS A BETTER COUNTRY?
<BETTER... *FAH!* WE MUST MAKE EGYPT GREAT AGAIN!>
UH-HUH.
THING IS, GENERAL, HOLLOW SLOGANS LIKE *"MAKING YOUR COUNTRY GREAT AGAIN"* ONLY LEADS TO ONE RESULT...
THUMP
...COLLAPSE!
KRUNCHHH
<THE CATACOMBS! NOOOO...>

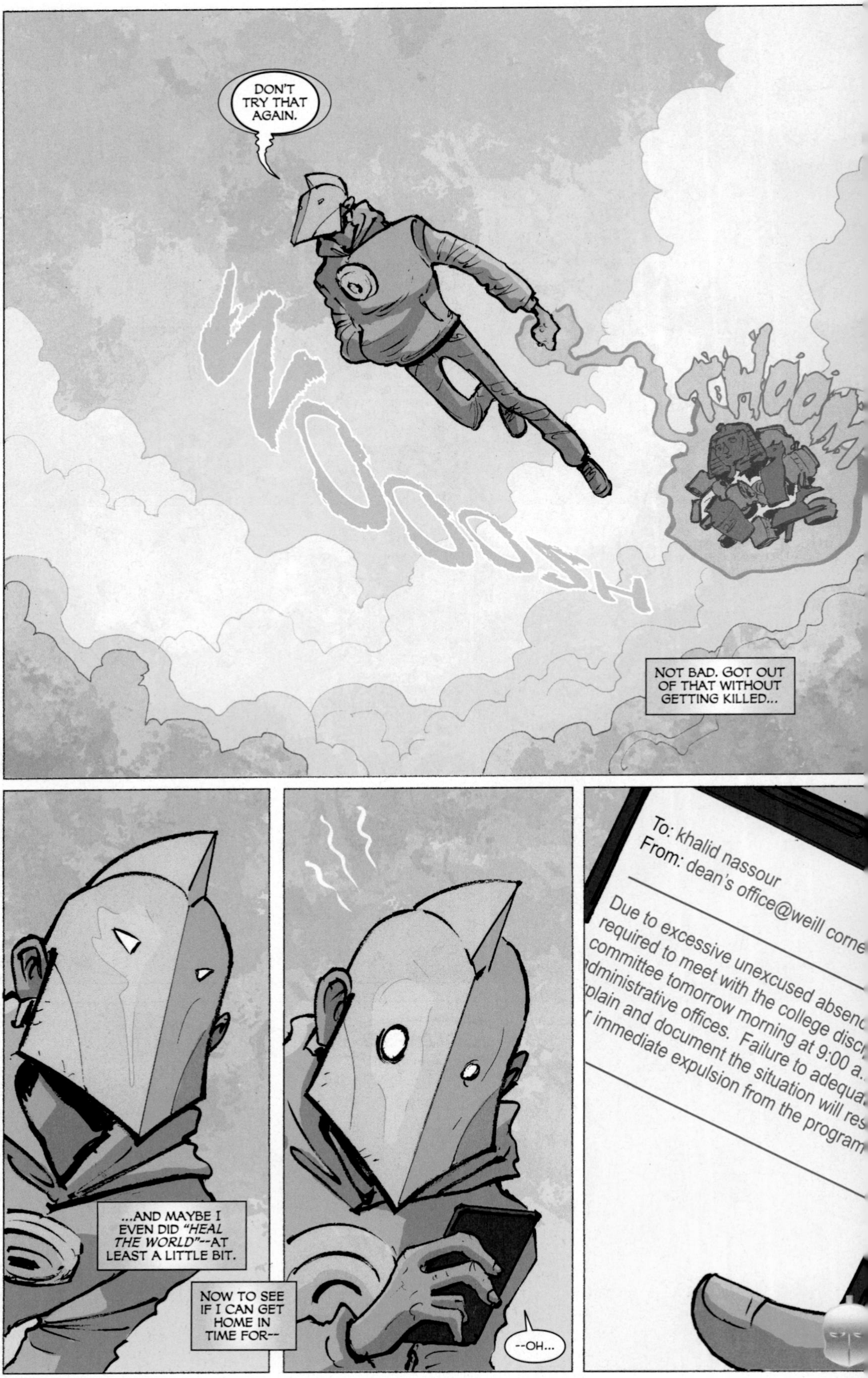
DON'T TRY THAT AGAIN.
WOOOOSH
THOOM
NOT BAD. GOT OUT OF THAT WITHOUT GETTING KILLED...
...AND MAYBE I EVEN DID "HEAL THE WORLD"--AT LEAST A LITTLE BIT.
NOW TO SEE IF I CAN GET HOME IN TIME FOR--
--OH...
To: khalid nassour
From: dean's office@weill corne
Due to excessive unexcused absenc
required to meet with the college disc
committee tomorrow morning at 9:00 a.
dministrative offices. Failure to adequa
plain and document the situation will res
r immediate expulsion from the program

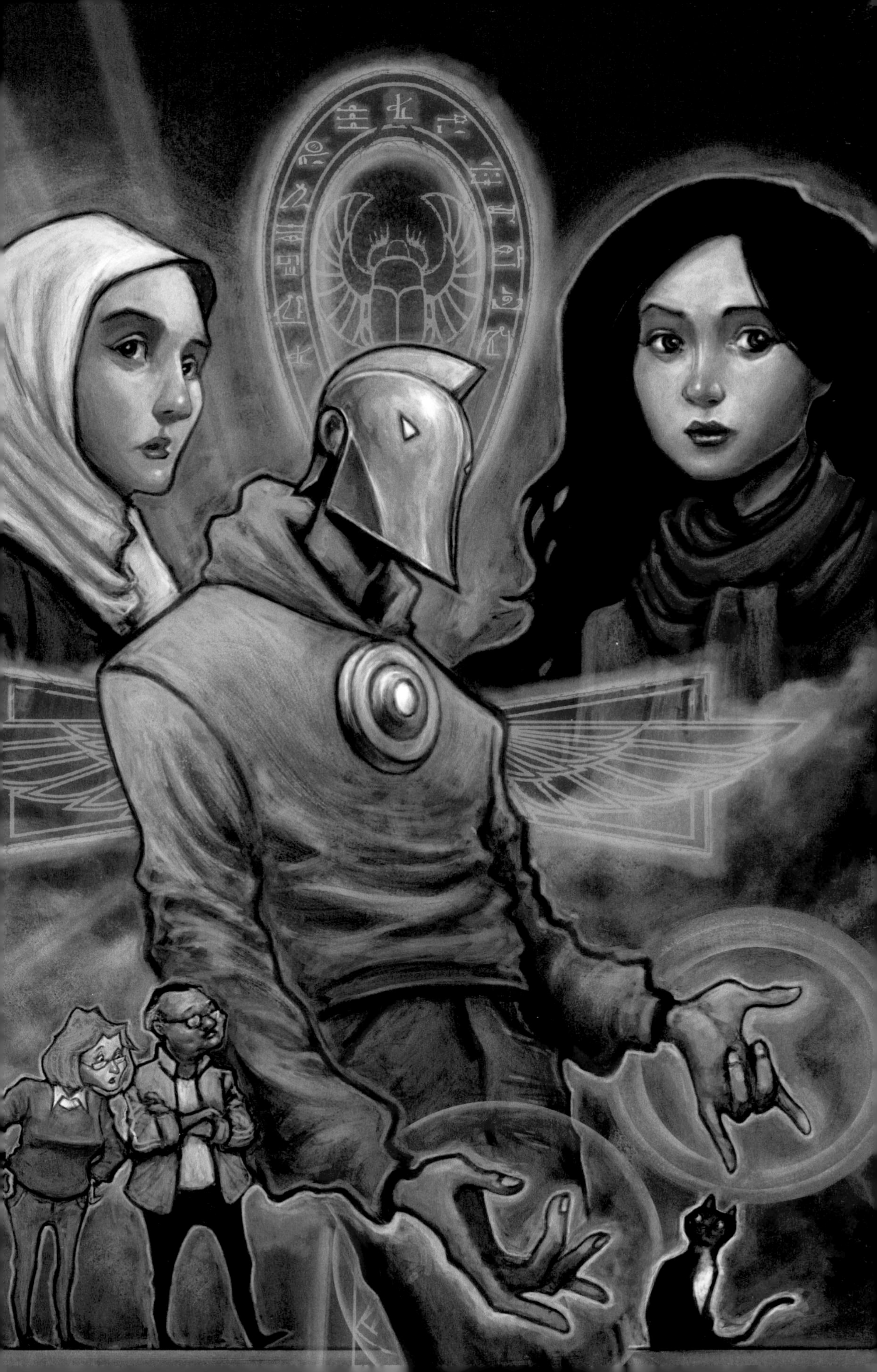

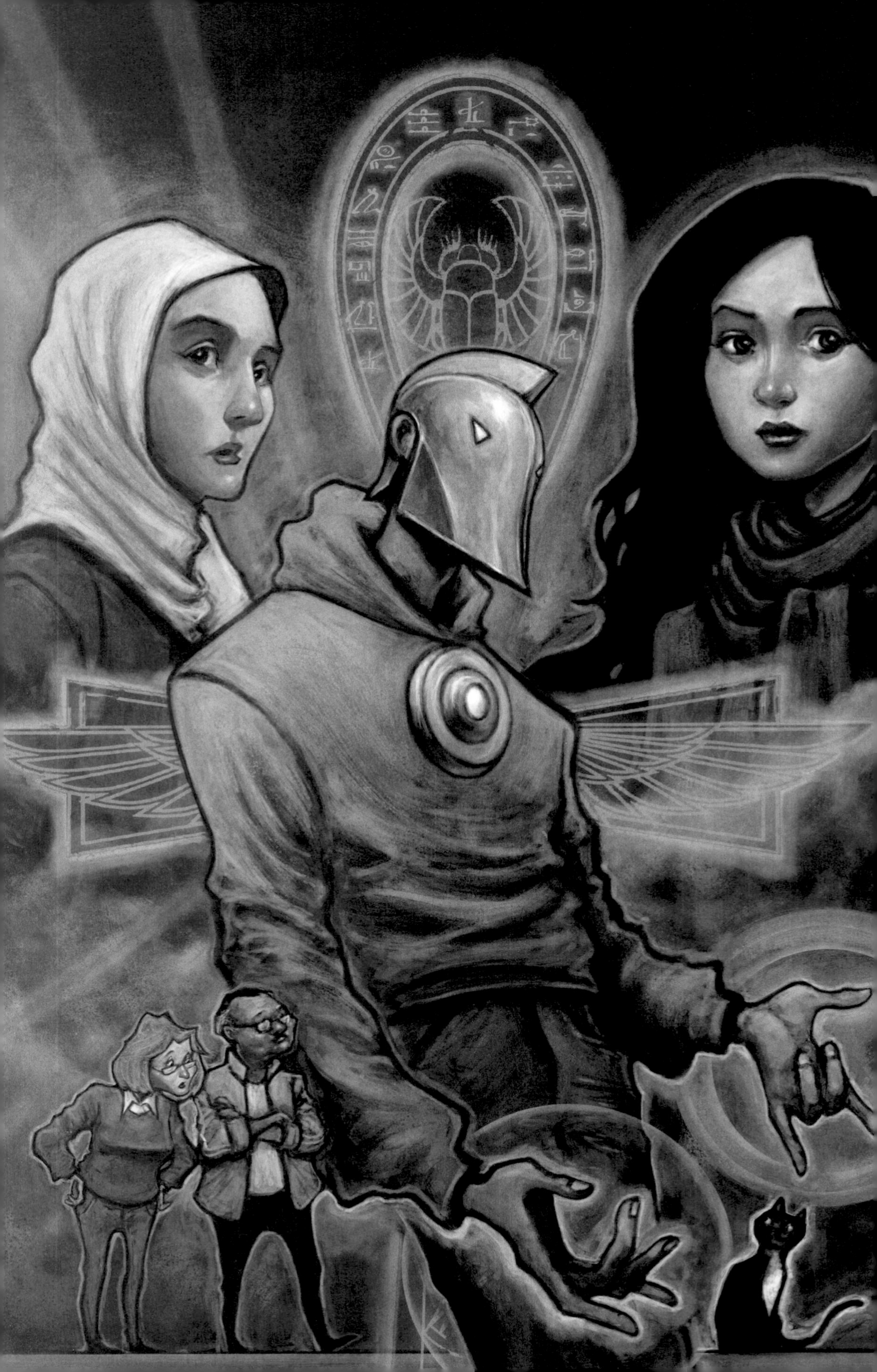

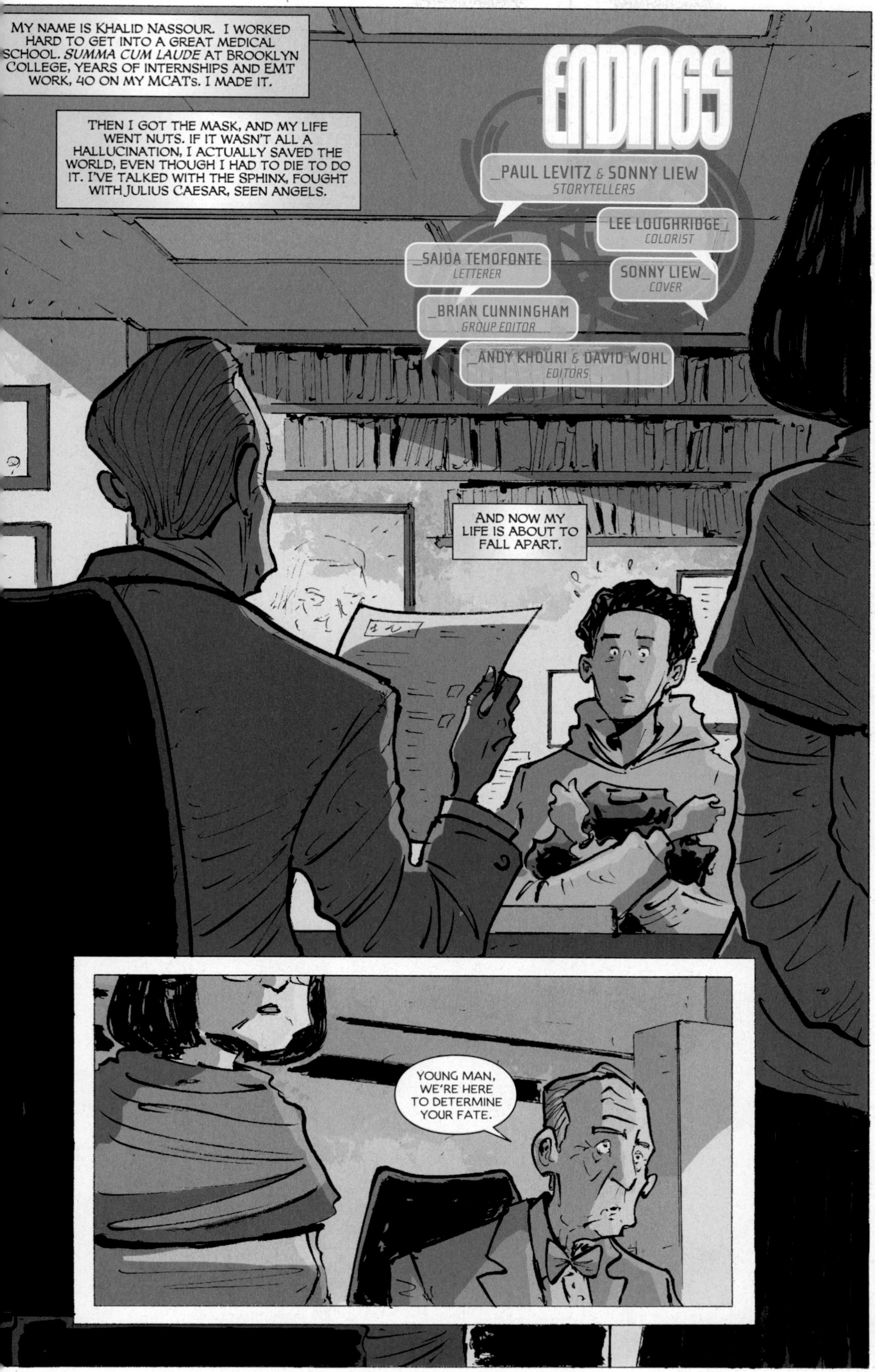
MY NAME IS KHALID NASSOUR. I WORKED HARD TO GET INTO A GREAT MEDICAL SCHOOL. *SUMMA CUM LAUDE* AT BROOKLYN COLLEGE, YEARS OF INTERNSHIPS AND EMT WORK, 40 ON MY MCATs. I MADE IT.
ENDINGS
_PAUL LEVITZ & SONNY LIEW STORYTELLERS
LEE LOUGHRIDGE_ COLORIST
_SAIDA TEMOFONTE LETTERER
SONNY LIEW_ COVER
_BRIAN CUNNINGHAM GROUP EDITOR
_ANDY KHOURI & DAVID WOHL EDITORS
THEN I GOT THE MASK, AND MY LIFE WENT NUTS. IF IT WASN'T ALL A HALLUCINATION, I ACTUALLY SAVED THE WORLD, EVEN THOUGH I HAD TO DIE TO DO IT. I'VE TALKED WITH THE SPHINX, FOUGHT WITH JULIUS CAESAR, SEEN ANGELS.
AND NOW MY LIFE IS ABOUT TO FALL APART.
YOUNG MAN, WE'RE HERE TO DETERMINE YOUR FATE.

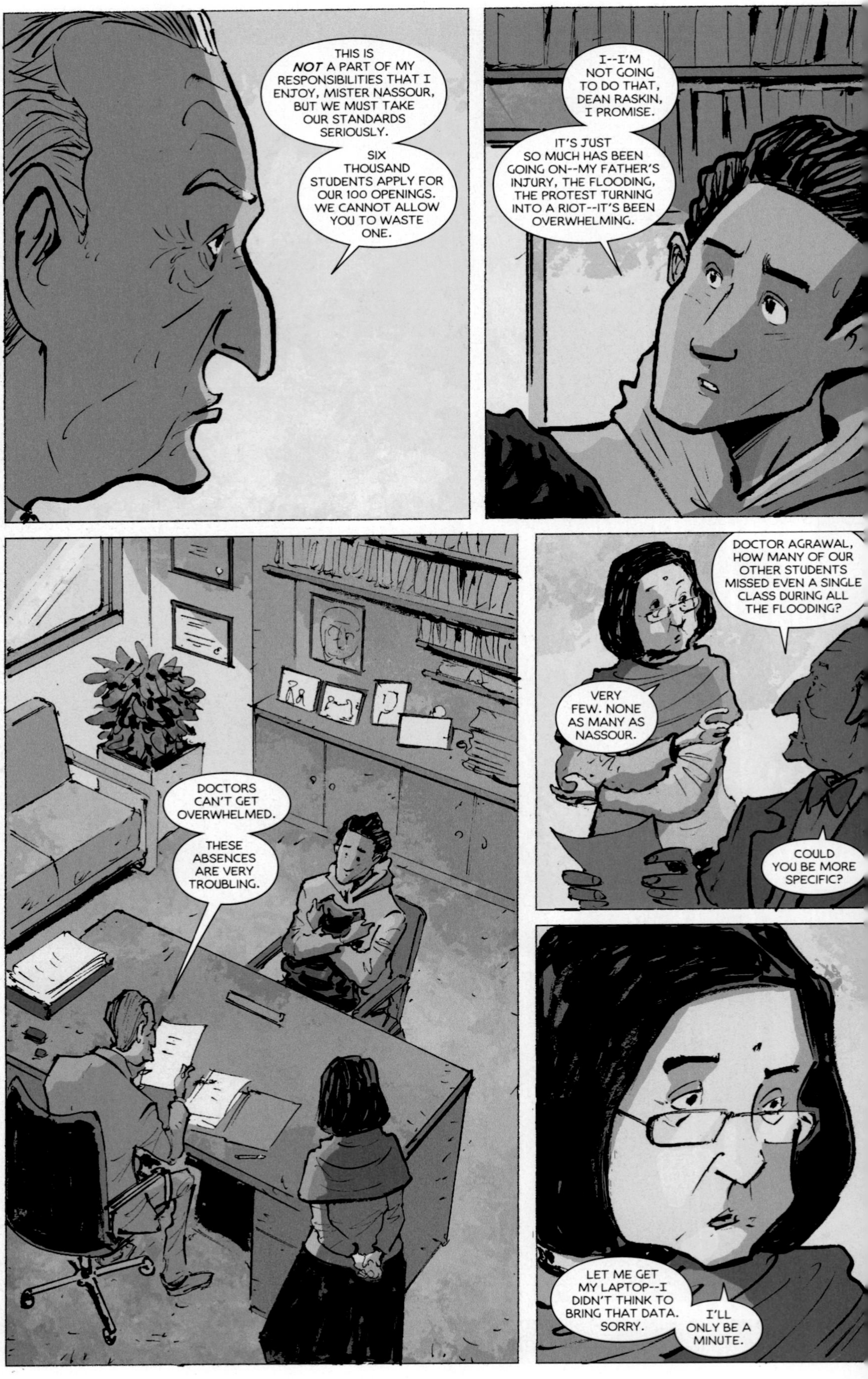
THIS IS NOT A PART OF MY RESPONSIBILITIES THAT I ENJOY, MISTER NASSOUR, BUT WE MUST TAKE OUR STANDARDS SERIOUSLY.
SIX THOUSAND STUDENTS APPLY FOR OUR 100 OPENINGS. WE CANNOT ALLOW YOU TO WASTE ONE.
I--I'M NOT GOING TO DO THAT, DEAN RASKIN, I PROMISE.
IT'S JUST SO MUCH HAS BEEN GOING ON--MY FATHER'S INJURY, THE FLOODING, THE PROTEST TURNING INTO A RIOT--IT'S BEEN OVERWHELMING.
DOCTORS CAN'T GET OVERWHELMED.
THESE ABSENCES ARE VERY TROUBLING.
DOCTOR AGRAWAL, HOW MANY OF OUR OTHER STUDENTS MISSED EVEN A SINGLE CLASS DURING ALL THE FLOODING?
VERY FEW. NONE AS MANY AS NASSOUR.
COULD YOU BE MORE SPECIFIC?
LET ME GET MY LAPTOP--I DIDN'T THINK TO BRING THAT DATA. SORRY.
I'LL ONLY BE A MINUTE.

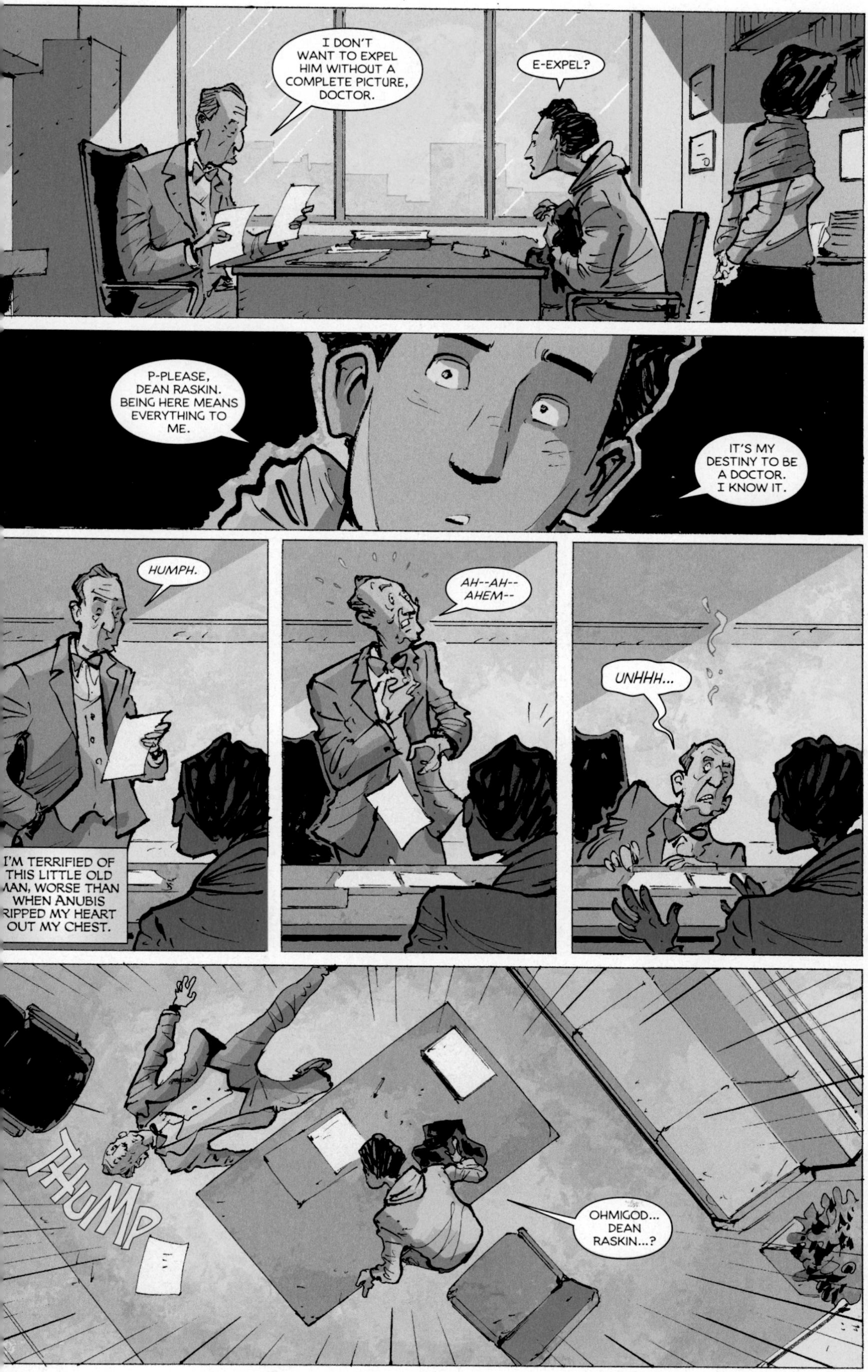
I DON'T WANT TO EXPEL HIM WITHOUT A COMPLETE PICTURE, DOCTOR.
E-EXPEL?
P-PLEASE, DEAN RASKIN. BEING HERE MEANS EVERYTHING TO ME.
IT'S MY DESTINY TO BE A DOCTOR. I KNOW IT.
HUMPH.
I'M TERRIFIED OF THIS LITTLE OLD MAN, WORSE THAN WHEN ANUBIS RIPPED MY HEART OUT MY CHEST.
AH--AH--AHEM--
UNHHH...
THUMP
OHMIGOD... DEAN RASKIN...?

ANOTHER DAY, ANOTHER HEART ATTACK RUN, EH, MOHAMMED?

AMERICA IS NOT AS EASY A PLACE FOR US AS WE DREAMED, JALAL.

WHEEOOOOO

BEATS BACK HOME. ROADS ARE SMOOTHER, TOO.

HEY, HOW'S KHALID DOING? I THOUGHT HE ONLY VOLUNTEERED BECAUSE THIS WAS AN APPROVED-OF WAY TO GO DRAG RACING.

HAH.

MY SON... I THOUGHT SERVING AS AN EMT WOULD HELP HIM GET INTO MEDICAL COLLEGE, SO HE COULD CARRY ON THE TRADITION I HAD TO ABANDON.

BUT NOW...NOW I DO NOT KNOW...

...HE HAS DONE MANY THINGS...BRAVE THINGS...

...BUT IT SEEMS THERE IS A HIGH PRICE FOR IT ALL.

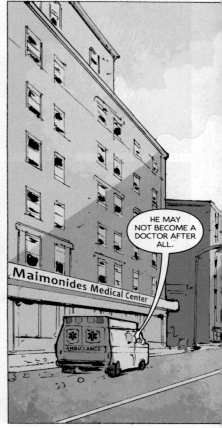

HE MAY NOT BECOME A DOCTOR AFTER ALL.

Maimonides Medical Center

AMBULANCE

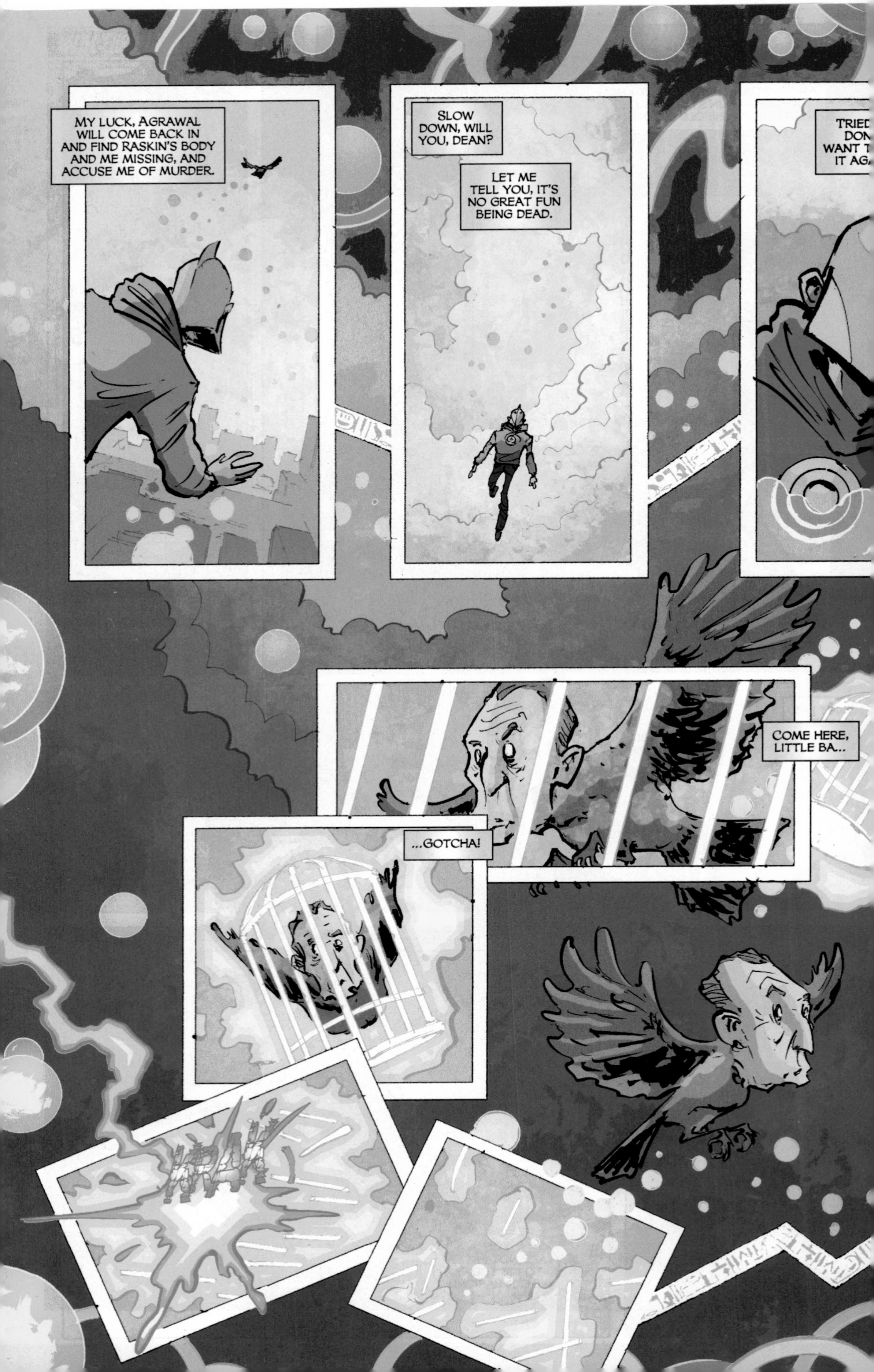
MY LUCK, AGRAWAL WILL COME BACK IN AND FIND RASKIN'S BODY AND ME MISSING, AND ACCUSE ME OF MURDER.
SLOW DOWN, WILL YOU, DEAN?
LET ME TELL YOU, IT'S NO GREAT FUN BEING DEAD.
COME HERE, LITTLE BA...
...GOTCHA!

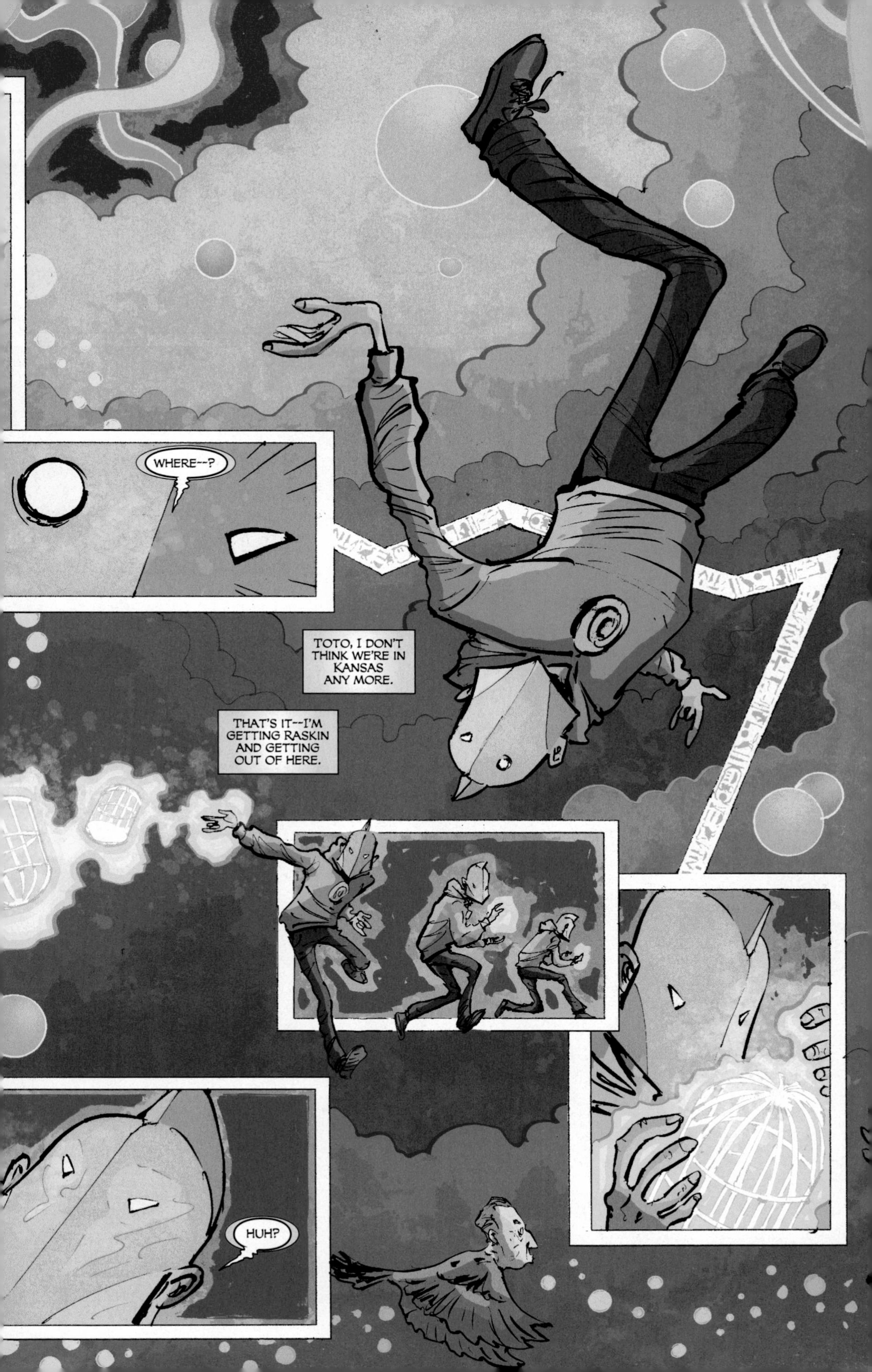
WHERE--?
TOTO, I DON'T THINK WE'RE IN KANSAS ANY MORE.
THAT'S IT--I'M GETTING RASKIN AND GETTING OUT OF HERE.
HUH?

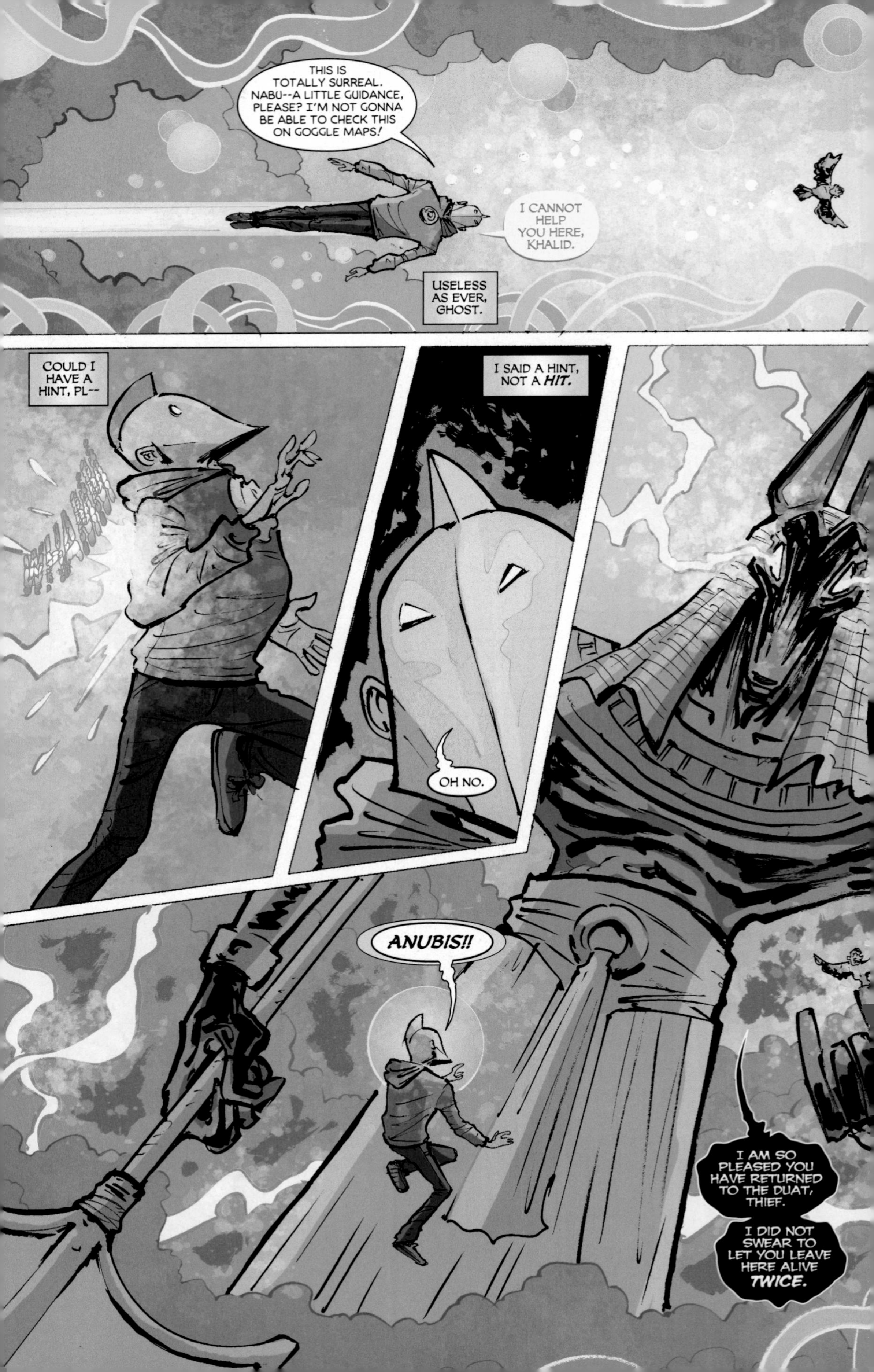
THIS IS TOTALLY SURREAL. NABU--A LITTLE GUIDANCE, PLEASE? I'M NOT GONNA BE ABLE TO CHECK THIS ON GOGGLE MAPS!
I CANNOT HELP YOU HERE, KHALID.
USELESS AS EVER, GHOST.
COULD I HAVE A HINT, PL--
I SAID A HINT, NOT A HIT.
OH NO.
ANUBIS!!
I AM SO PLEASED YOU HAVE RETURNED TO THE DUAT, THIEF.
I DID NOT SWEAR TO LET YOU LEAVE HERE ALIVE TWICE.

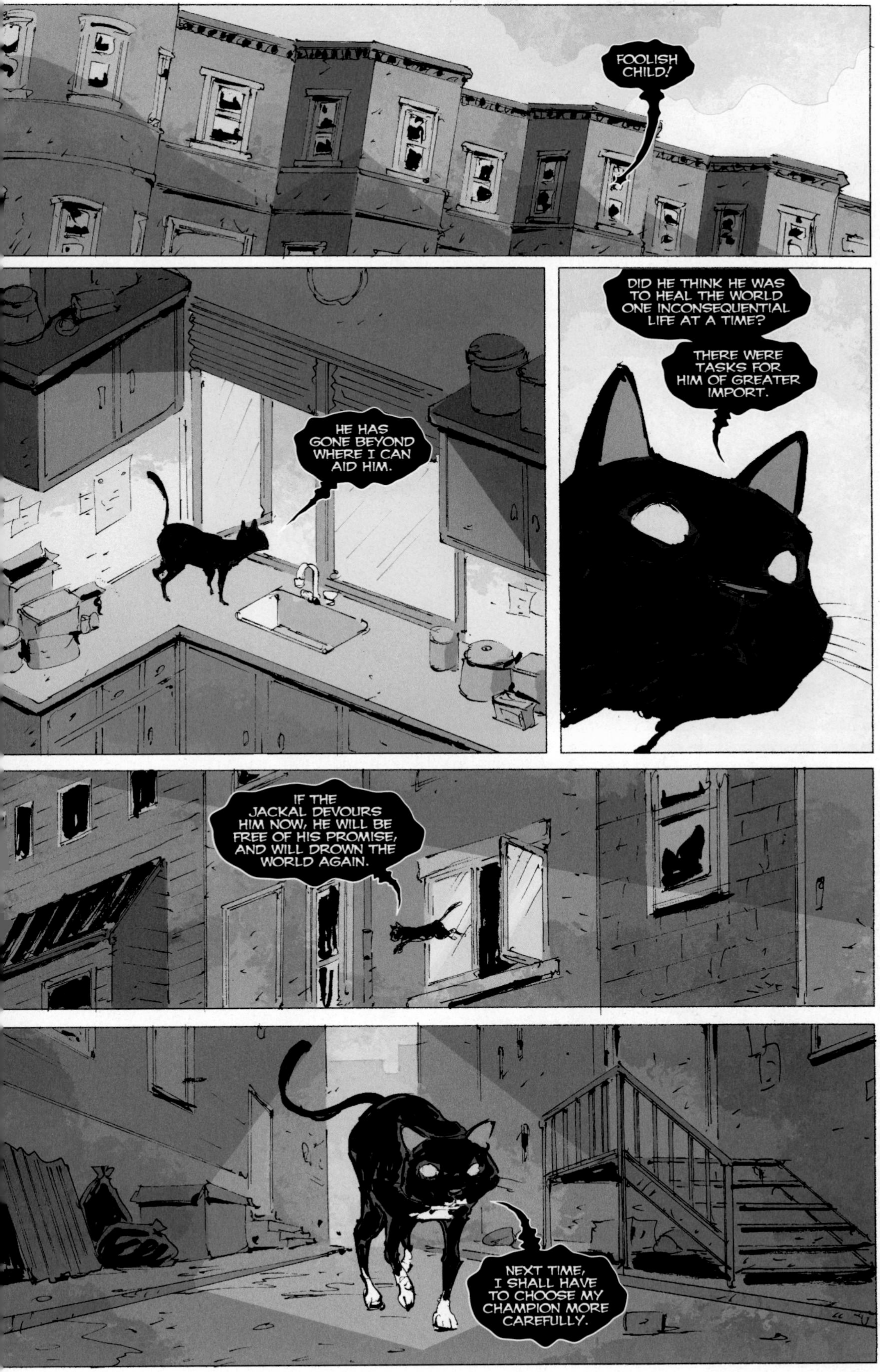
FOOLISH CHILD!
HE HAS GONE BEYOND WHERE I CAN AID HIM.
DID HE THINK HE WAS TO HEAL THE WORLD ONE INCONSEQUENTIAL LIFE AT A TIME?
THERE WERE TASKS FOR HIM OF GREATER IMPORT.
IF THE JACKAL DEVOURS HIM NOW, HE WILL BE FREE OF HIS PROMISE, AND WILL DROWN THE WORLD AGAIN.
NEXT TIME, I SHALL HAVE TO CHOOSE MY CHAMPION MORE CAREFULLY.

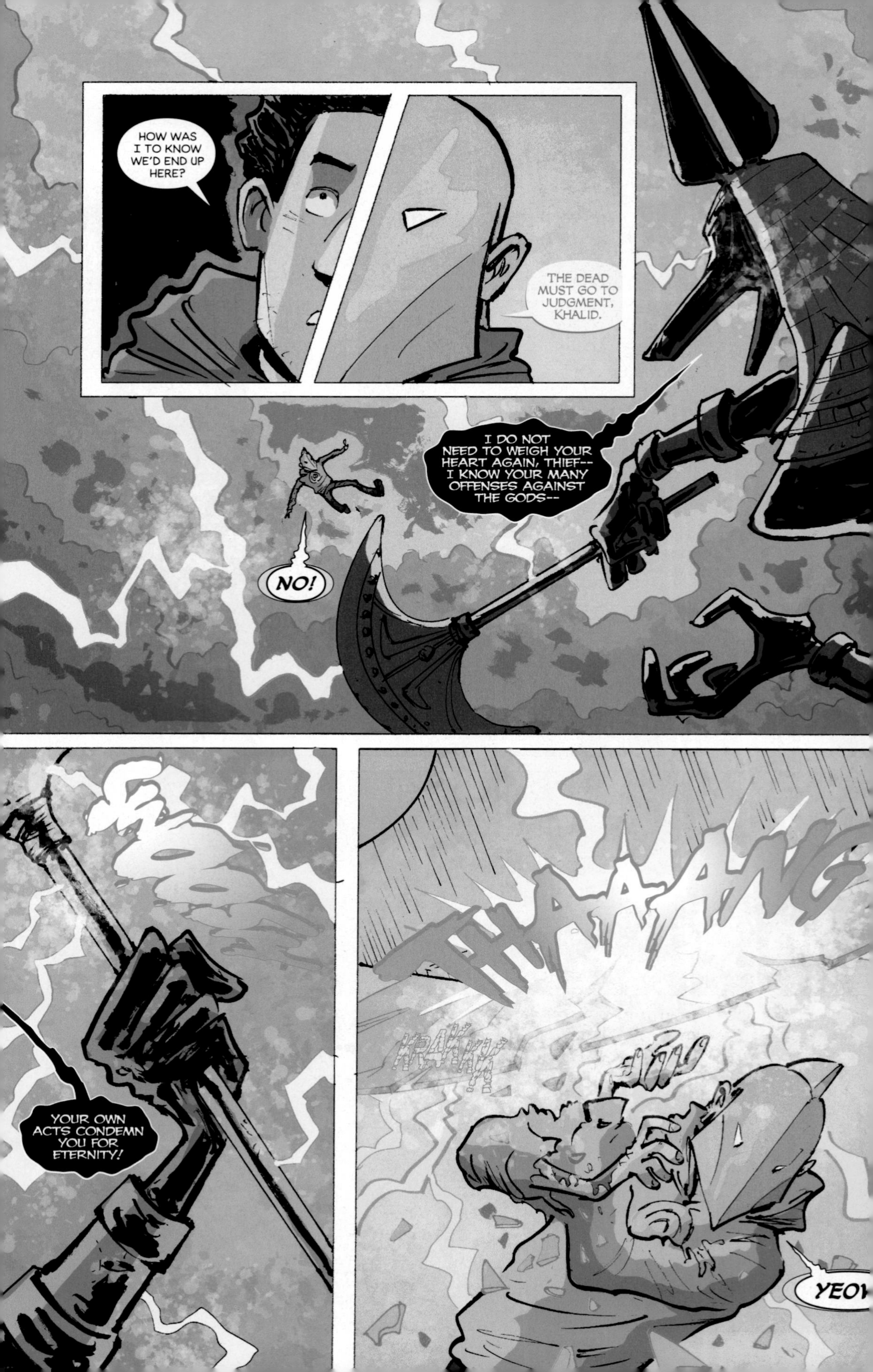
HOW WAS I TO KNOW WE'D END UP HERE?
THE DEAD MUST GO TO JUDGMENT, KHALID.
I DO NOT NEED TO WEIGH YOUR HEART AGAIN, THIEF-- I KNOW YOUR MANY OFFENSES AGAINST THE GODS--
NO!
YOUR OWN ACTS CONDEMN YOU FOR ETERNITY!
THAAANG
YEOW

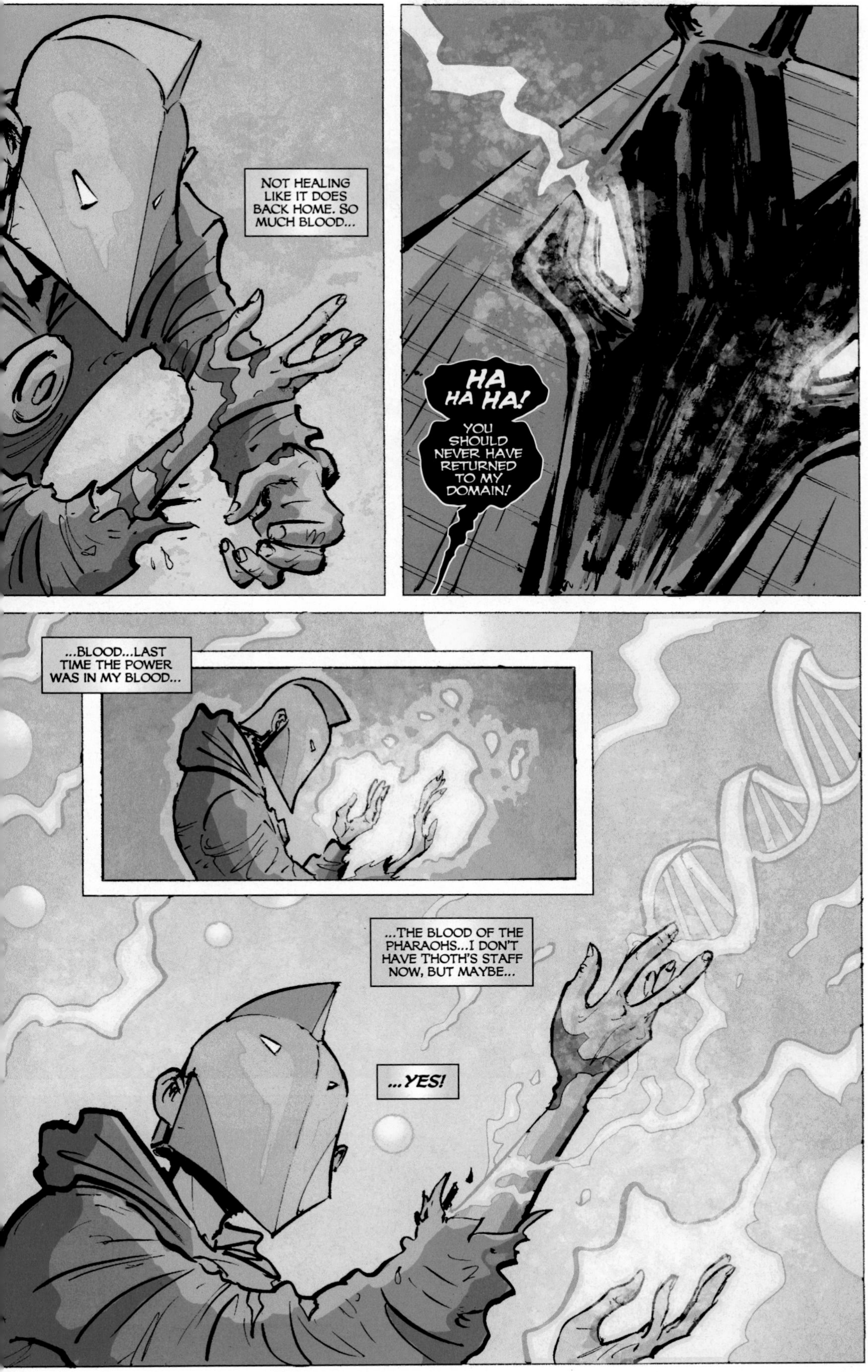
NOT HEALING LIKE IT DOES BACK HOME. SO MUCH BLOOD...
HA HA HA!
YOU SHOULD NEVER HAVE RETURNED TO MY DOMAIN!
...BLOOD...LAST TIME THE POWER WAS IN MY BLOOD...
...THE BLOOD OF THE PHARAOHS...I DON'T HAVE THOTH'S STAFF NOW, BUT MAYBE...
...YES!

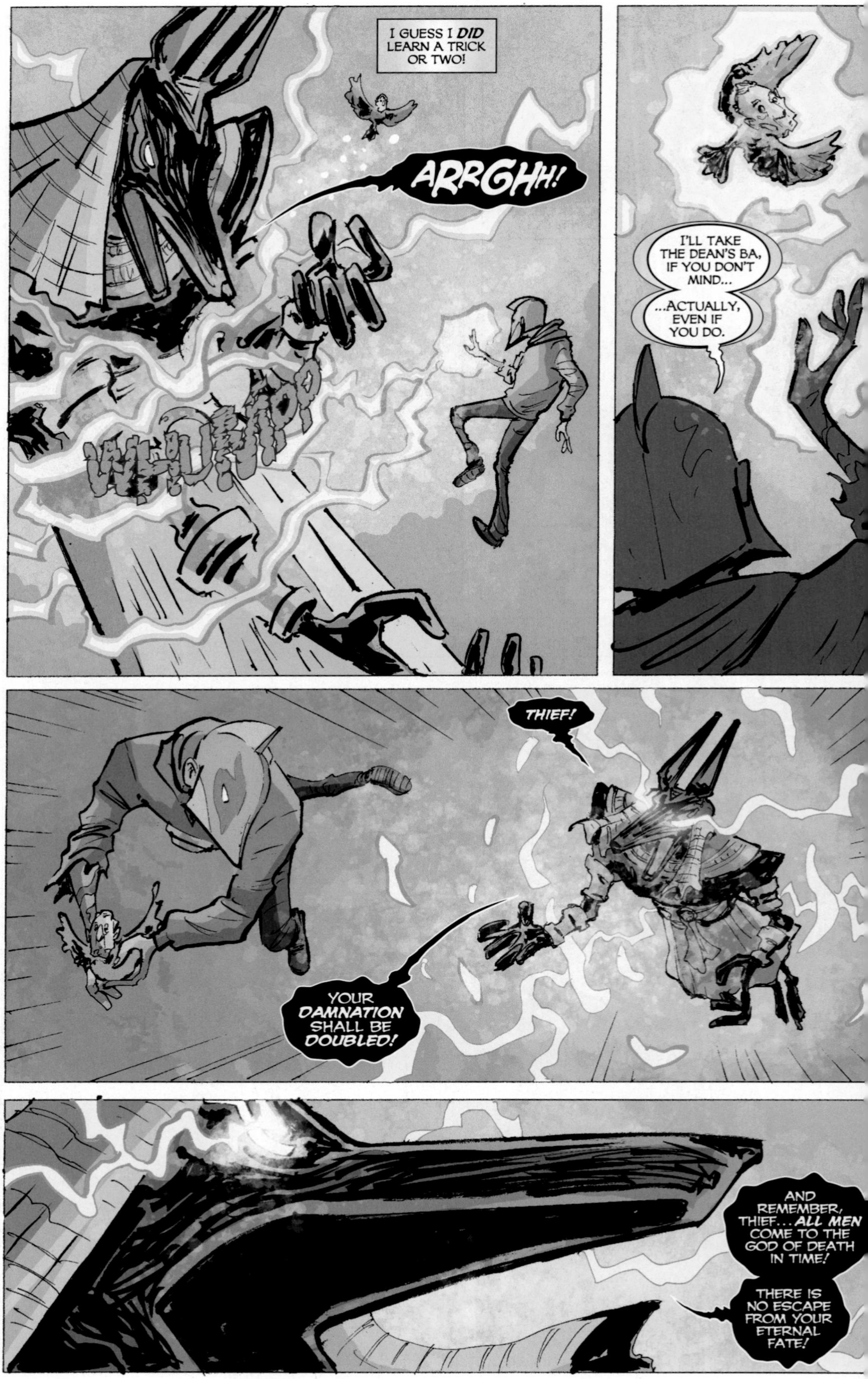
I GUESS I DID LEARN A TRICK OR TWO!
ARRGHH!
I'LL TAKE THE DEAN'S BA, IF YOU DON'T MIND...
...ACTUALLY, EVEN IF YOU DO.
THIEF!
YOUR DAMNATION SHALL BE DOUBLED!
AND REMEMBER, THIEF... ALL MEN COME TO THE GOD OF DEATH IN TIME!
THERE IS NO ESCAPE FROM YOUR ETERNAL FATE!

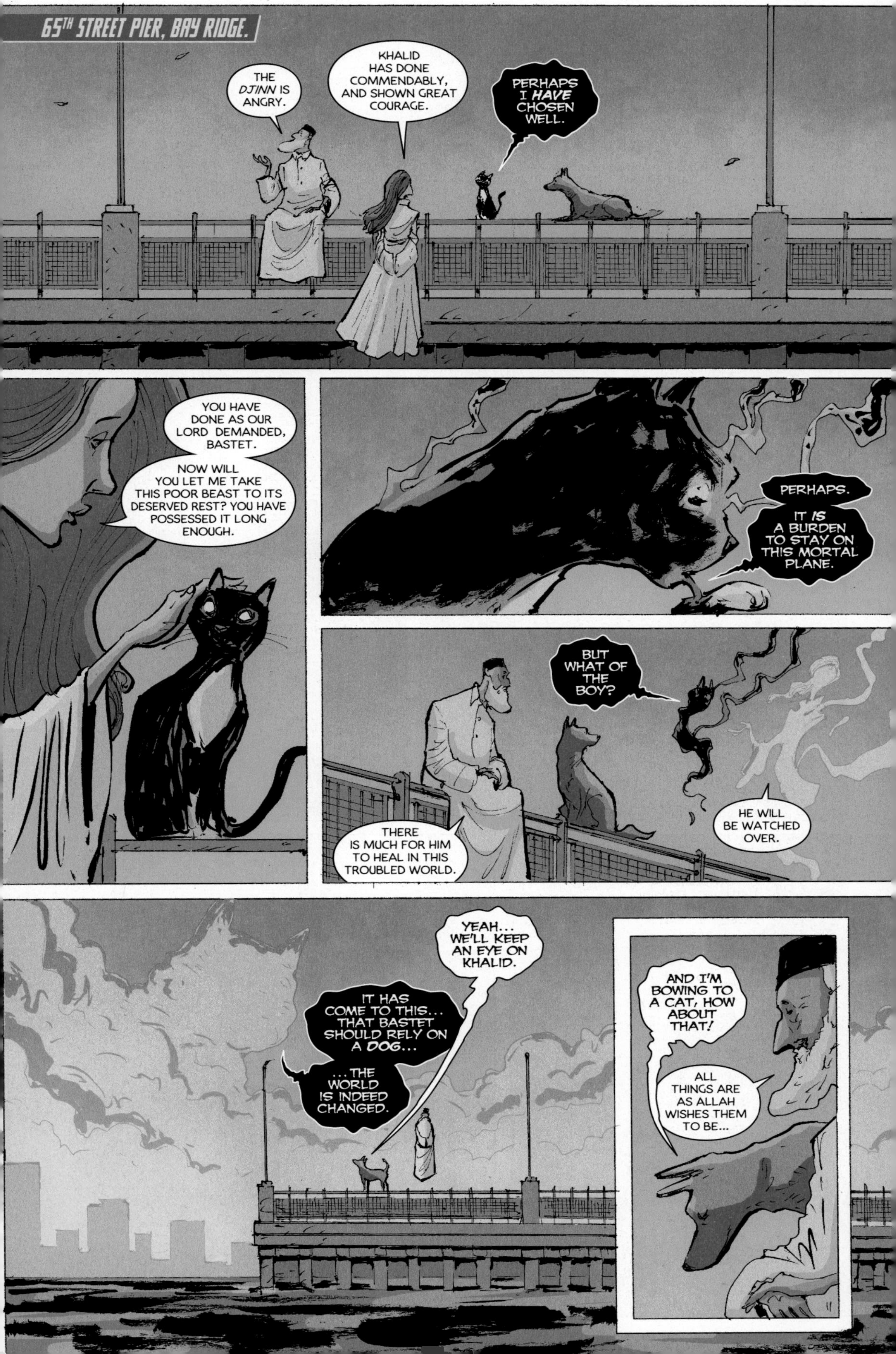
65TH STREET PIER, BAY RIDGE.
THE DJINN IS ANGRY.
KHALID HAS DONE COMMENDABLY, AND SHOWN GREAT COURAGE.
PERHAPS I HAVE CHOSEN WELL.
YOU HAVE DONE AS OUR LORD DEMANDED, BASTET.
NOW WILL YOU LET ME TAKE THIS POOR BEAST TO ITS DESERVED REST? YOU HAVE POSSESSED IT LONG ENOUGH.
PERHAPS.
IT IS A BURDEN TO STAY ON THIS MORTAL PLANE.
BUT WHAT OF THE BOY?
THERE IS MUCH FOR HIM TO HEAL IN THIS TROUBLED WORLD.
HE WILL BE WATCHED OVER.
IT HAS COME TO THIS... THAT BASTET SHOULD RELY ON A DOG...
...THE WORLD IS INDEED CHANGED.
YEAH... WE'LL KEEP AN EYE ON KHALID.
AND I'M BOWING TO A CAT, HOW ABOUT THAT!
ALL THINGS ARE AS ALLAH WISHES THEM TO BE...

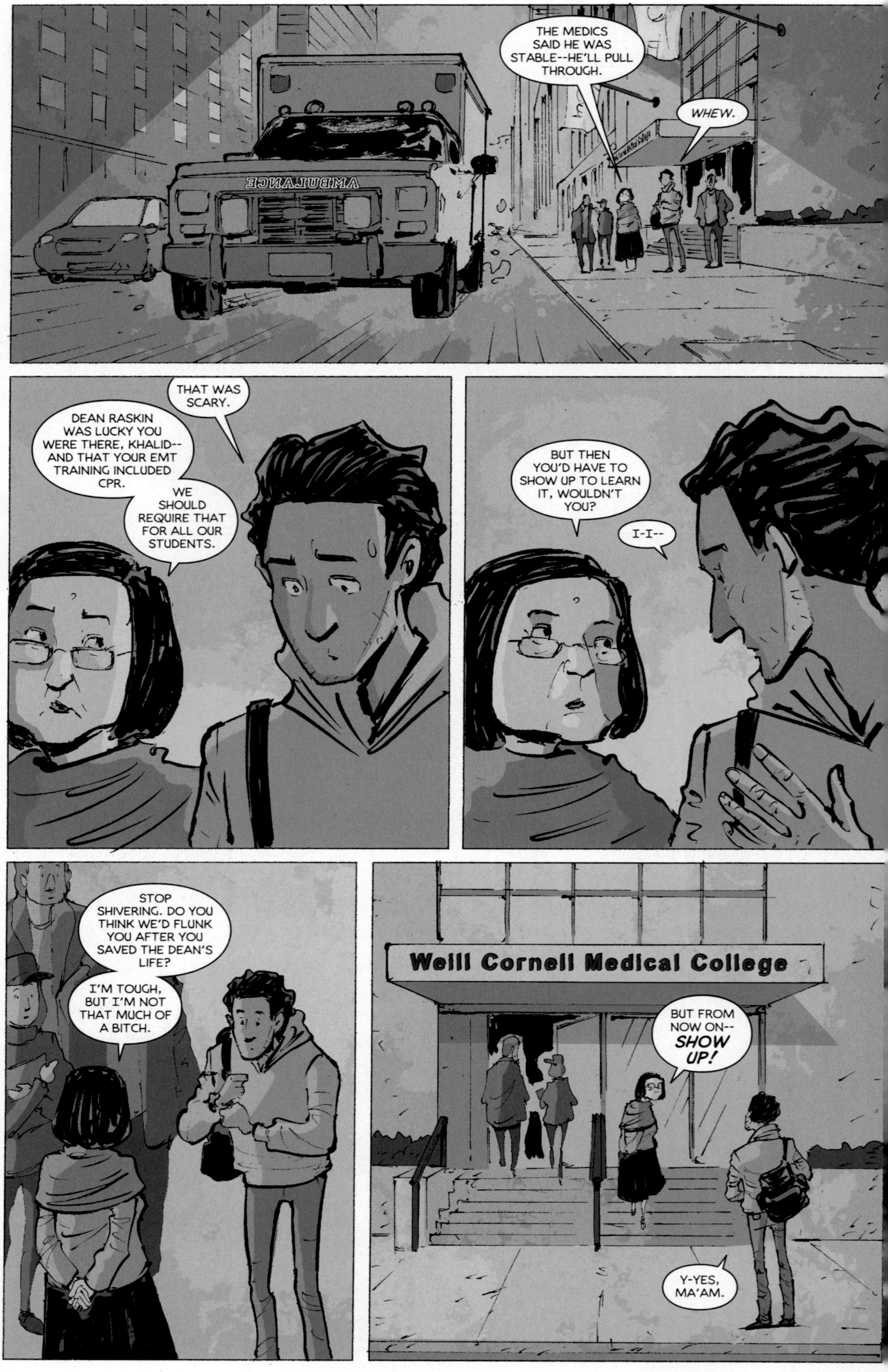
THE MEDICS SAID HE WAS STABLE--HE'LL PULL THROUGH.
WHEW.
AMBULANCE
THAT WAS SCARY.
DEAN RASKIN WAS LUCKY YOU WERE THERE, KHALID-- AND THAT YOUR EMT TRAINING INCLUDED CPR.
WE SHOULD REQUIRE THAT FOR ALL OUR STUDENTS.
BUT THEN YOU'D HAVE TO SHOW UP TO LEARN IT, WOULDN'T YOU?
I-I--
STOP SHIVERING. DO YOU THINK WE'D FLUNK YOU AFTER YOU SAVED THE DEAN'S LIFE?
I'M TOUGH, BUT I'M NOT THAT MUCH OF A BITCH.
Weill Cornell Medical College
BUT FROM NOW ON-- *SHOW UP!*
Y-YES, MA'AM.

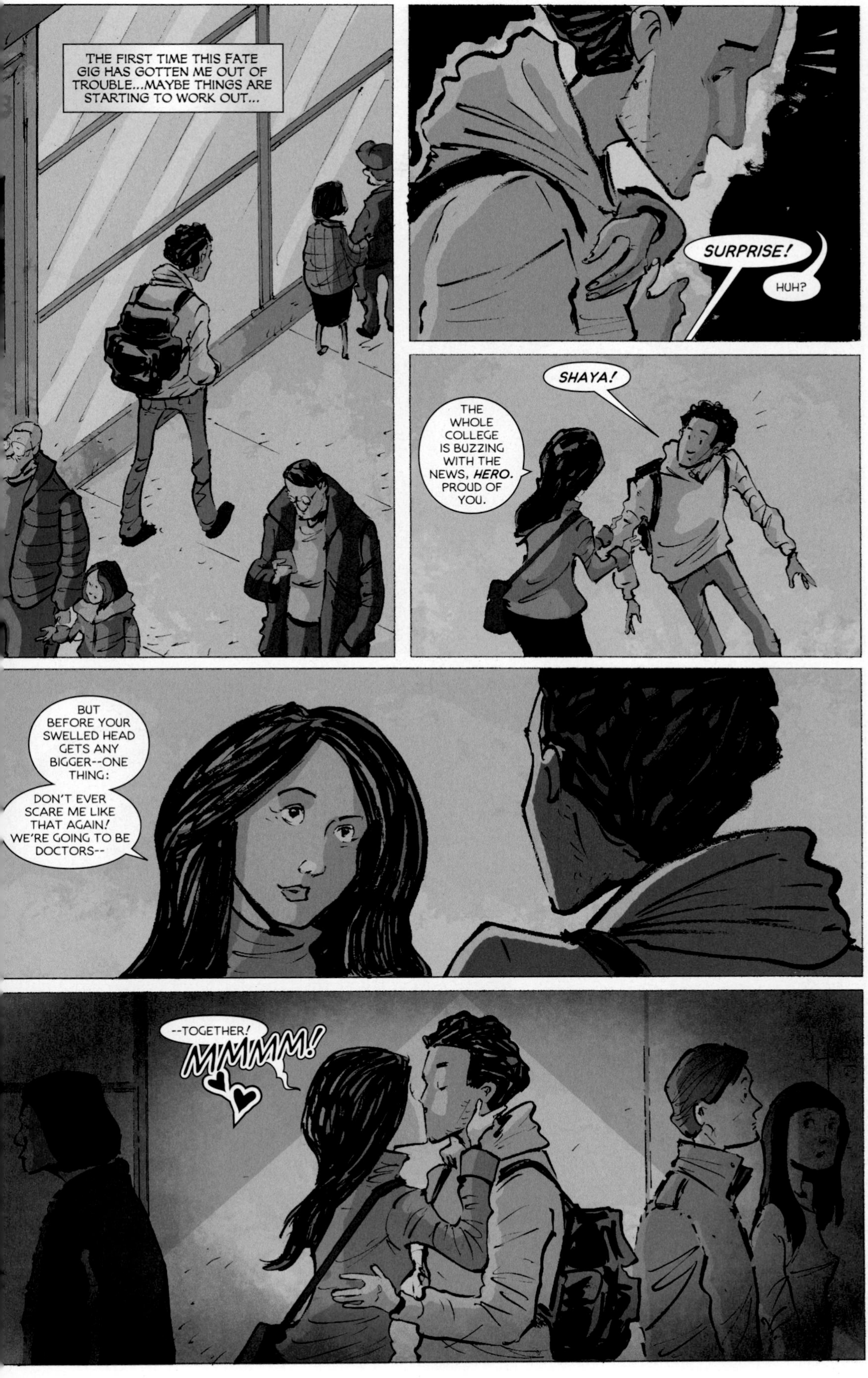
THE FIRST TIME THIS FATE GIG HAS GOTTEN ME OUT OF TROUBLE...MAYBE THINGS ARE STARTING TO WORK OUT...
SURPRISE!
HUH?
SHAYA!
THE WHOLE COLLEGE IS BUZZING WITH THE NEWS, HERO. PROUD OF YOU.
BUT BEFORE YOUR SWELLED HEAD GETS ANY BIGGER--ONE THING:
DON'T EVER SCARE ME LIKE THAT AGAIN! WE'RE GOING TO BE DOCTORS--
--TOGETHER!
MMMM!

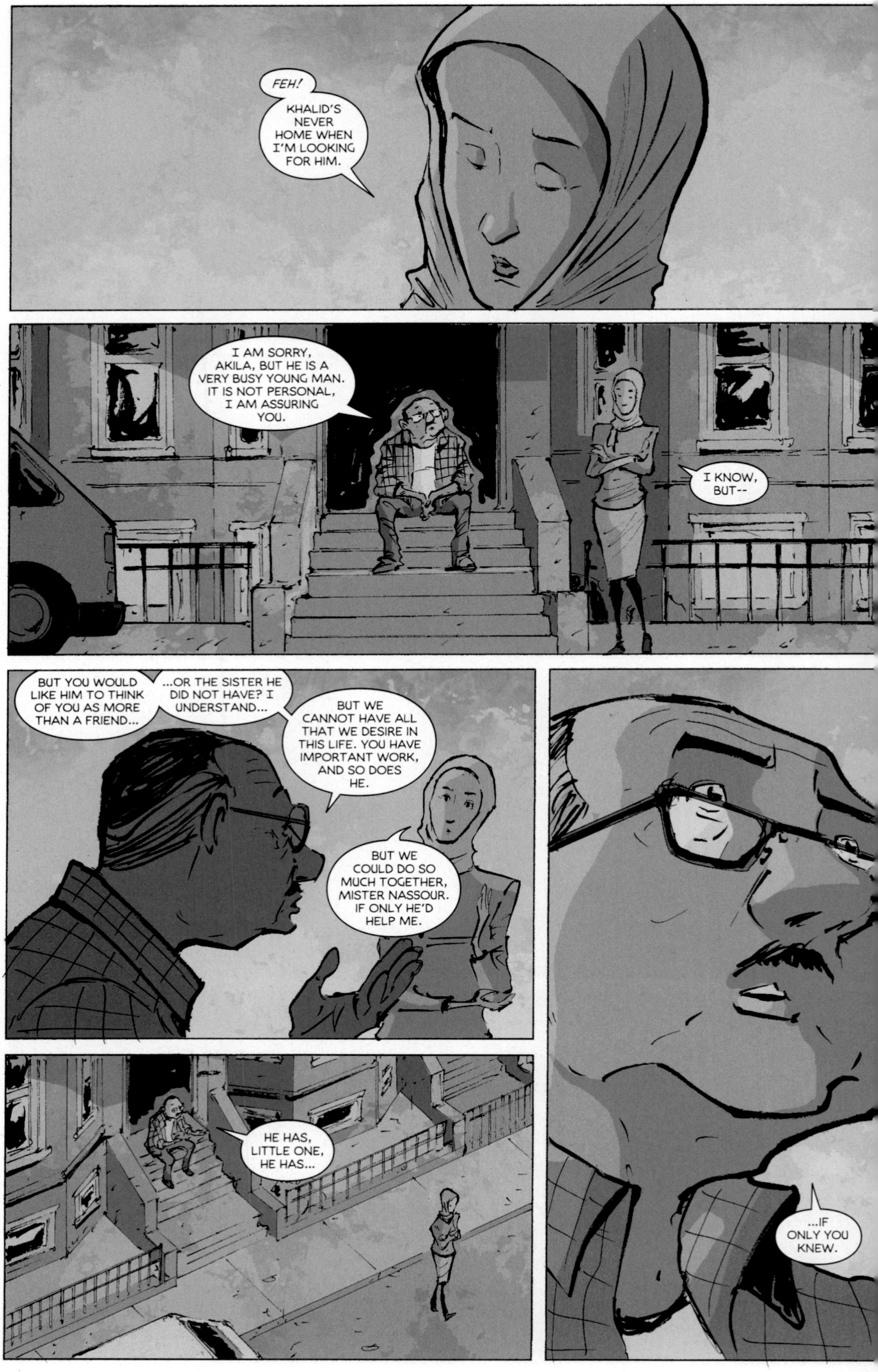
FEH!
KHALID'S NEVER HOME WHEN I'M LOOKING FOR HIM.
I AM SORRY, AKILA, BUT HE IS A VERY BUSY YOUNG MAN. IT IS NOT PERSONAL, I AM ASSURING YOU.
I KNOW, BUT--
BUT YOU WOULD LIKE HIM TO THINK OF YOU AS MORE THAN A FRIEND...
...OR THE SISTER HE DID NOT HAVE? I UNDERSTAND...
BUT WE CANNOT HAVE ALL THAT WE DESIRE IN THIS LIFE. YOU HAVE IMPORTANT WORK, AND SO DOES HE.
BUT WE COULD DO SO MUCH TOGETHER, MISTER NASSOUR. IF ONLY HE'D HELP ME.
HE HAS, LITTLE ONE, HE HAS...
...IF ONLY YOU KNEW.

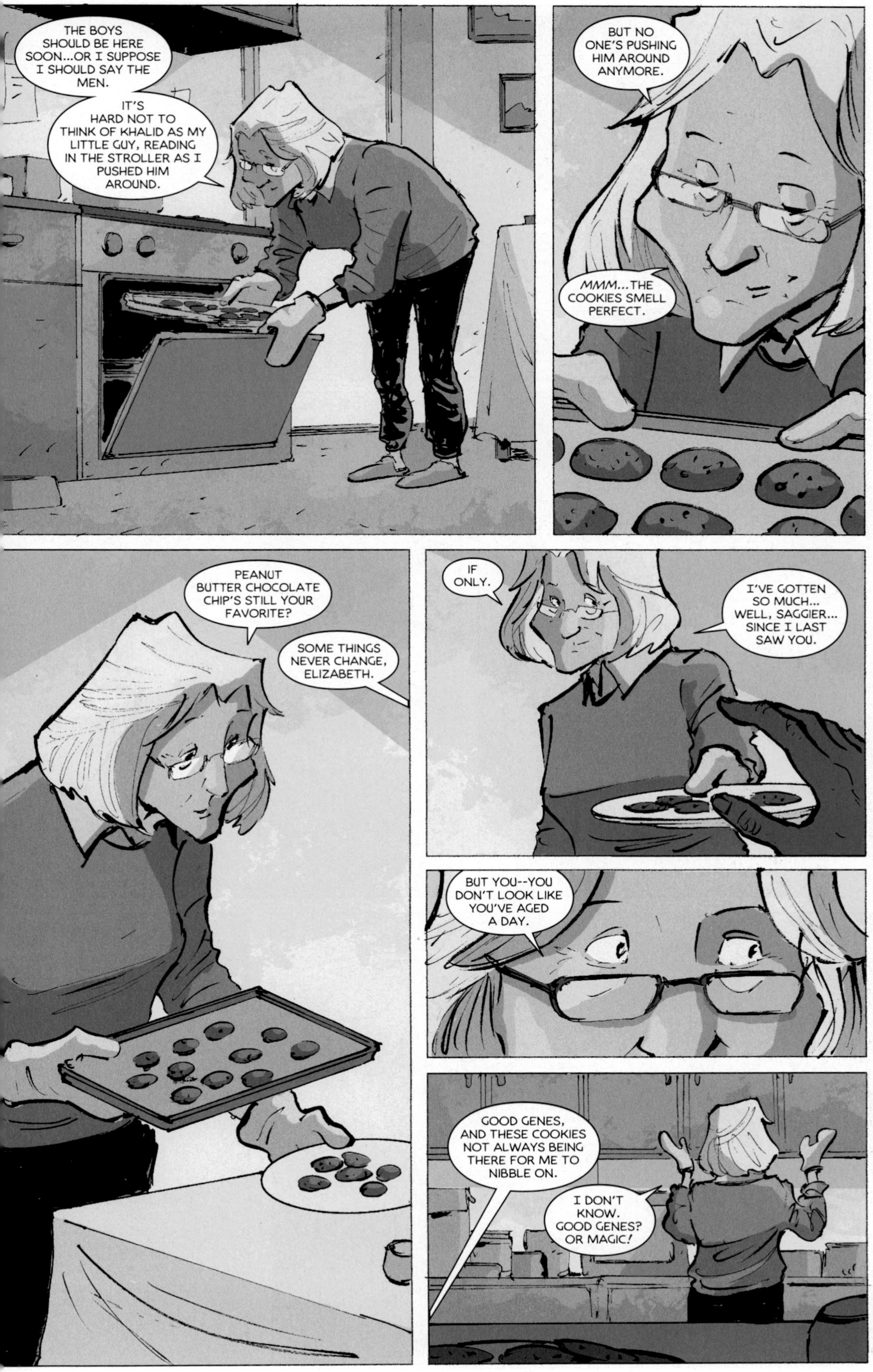
THE BOYS SHOULD BE HERE SOON...OR I SUPPOSE I SHOULD SAY THE MEN.
IT'S HARD NOT TO THINK OF KHALID AS MY LITTLE GUY, READING IN THE STROLLER AS I PUSHED HIM AROUND.
BUT NO ONE'S PUSHING HIM AROUND ANYMORE.
MMM...THE COOKIES SMELL PERFECT.
PEANUT BUTTER CHOCOLATE CHIP'S STILL YOUR FAVORITE?
SOME THINGS NEVER CHANGE, ELIZABETH.
IF ONLY.
I'VE GOTTEN SO MUCH... WELL, SAGGIER... SINCE I LAST SAW YOU.
BUT YOU--YOU DON'T LOOK LIKE YOU'VE AGED A DAY.
GOOD GENES, AND THESE COOKIES NOT ALWAYS BEING THERE FOR ME TO NIBBLE ON.
I DON'T KNOW. GOOD GENES? OR *MAGIC!*

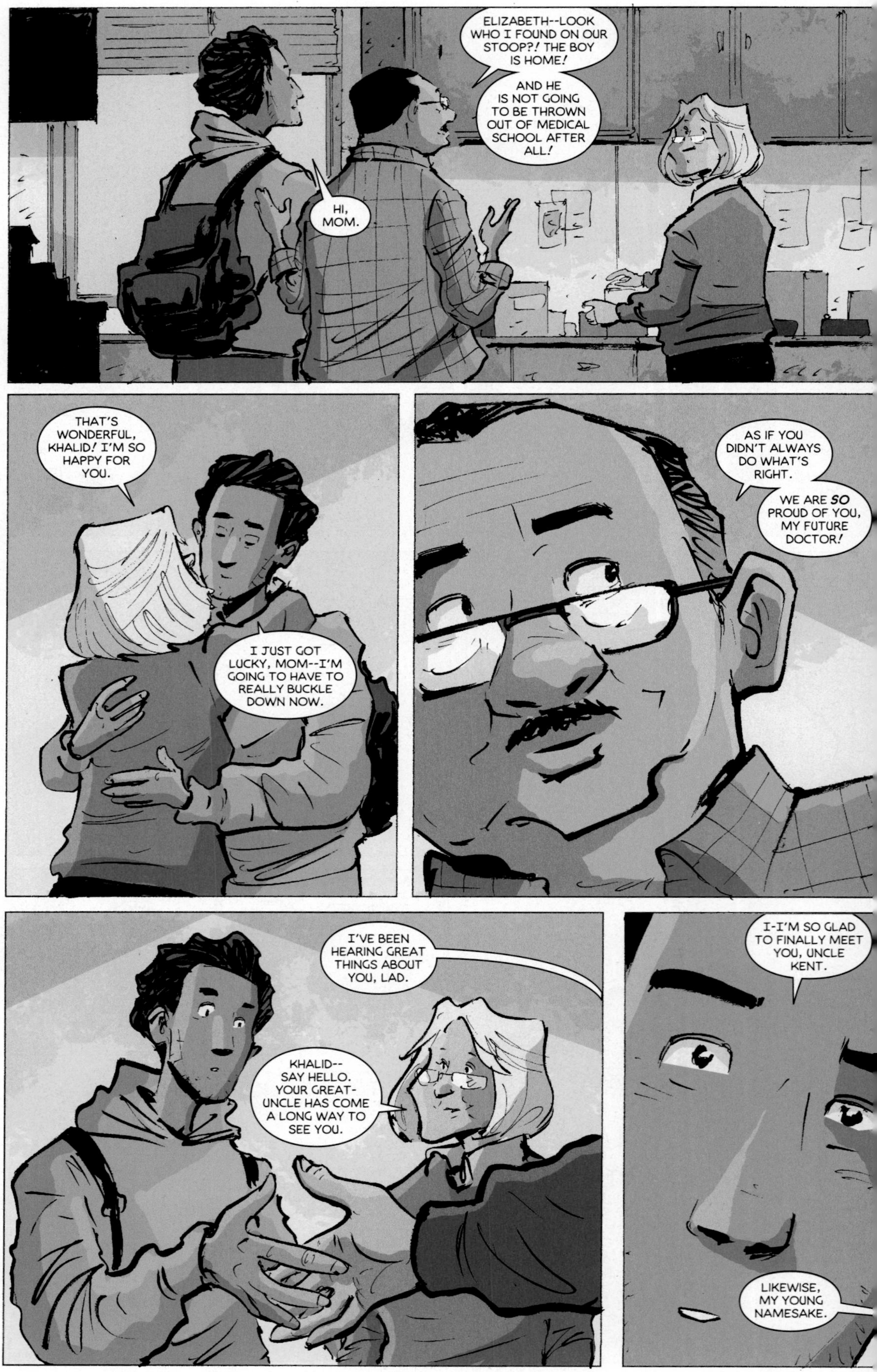
ELIZABETH--LOOK WHO I FOUND ON OUR STOOP?! THE BOY IS HOME!
AND HE IS NOT GOING TO BE THROWN OUT OF MEDICAL SCHOOL AFTER ALL!
HI, MOM.
THAT'S WONDERFUL, KHALID! I'M SO HAPPY FOR YOU.
I JUST GOT LUCKY, MOM--I'M GOING TO HAVE TO REALLY BUCKLE DOWN NOW.
AS IF YOU DIDN'T ALWAYS DO WHAT'S RIGHT.
WE ARE SO PROUD OF YOU, MY FUTURE DOCTOR!
I'VE BEEN HEARING GREAT THINGS ABOUT YOU, LAD.
KHALID-- SAY HELLO. YOUR GREAT-UNCLE HAS COME A LONG WAY TO SEE YOU.
I-I'M SO GLAD TO FINALLY MEET YOU, UNCLE KENT.
LIKEWISE, MY YOUNG NAMESAKE.

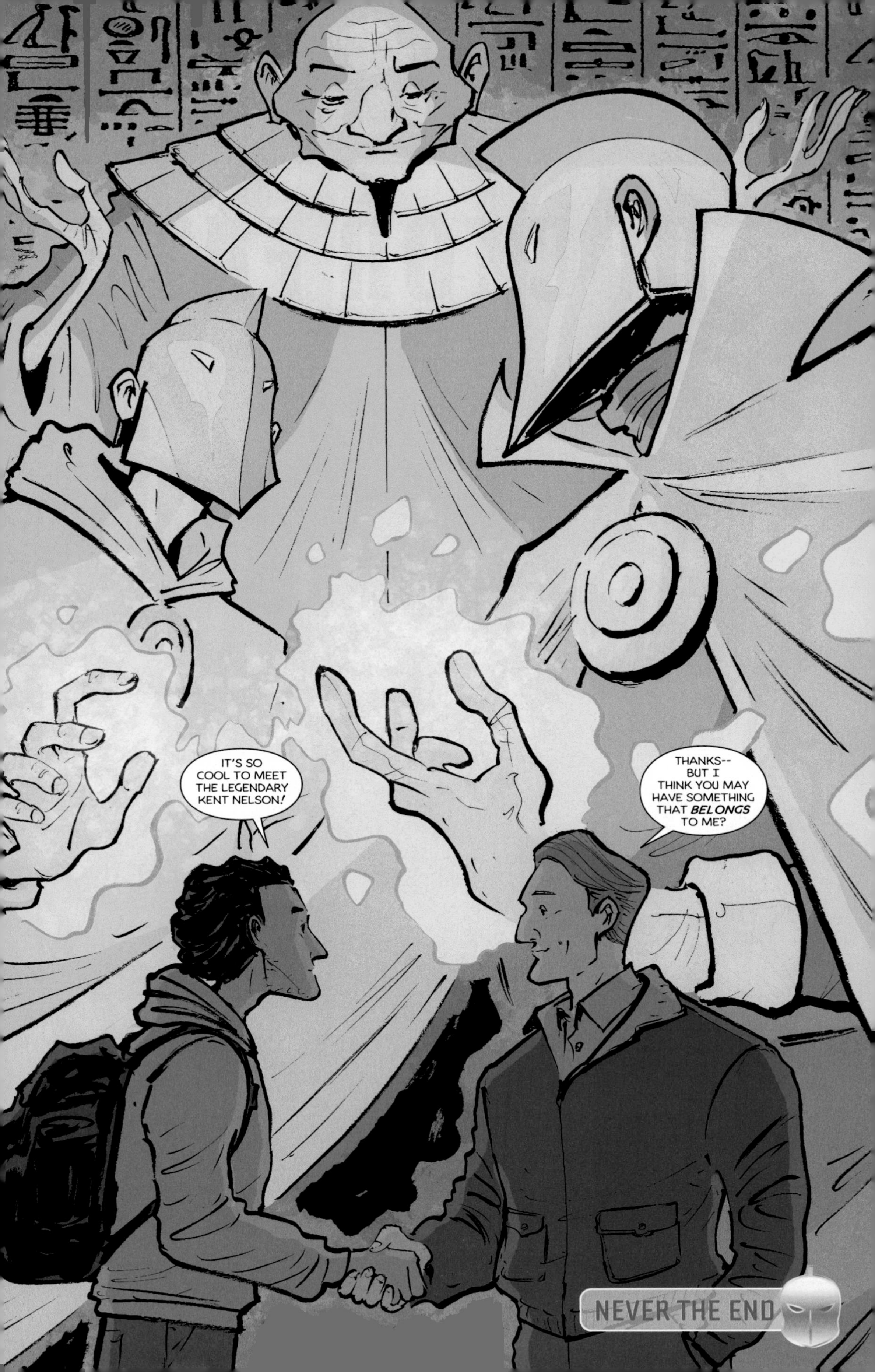
IT'S SO COOL TO MEET THE LEGENDARY KENT NELSON!
THANKS-- BUT I THINK YOU MAY HAVE SOMETHING THAT *BELONGS* TO ME?
NEVER THE END

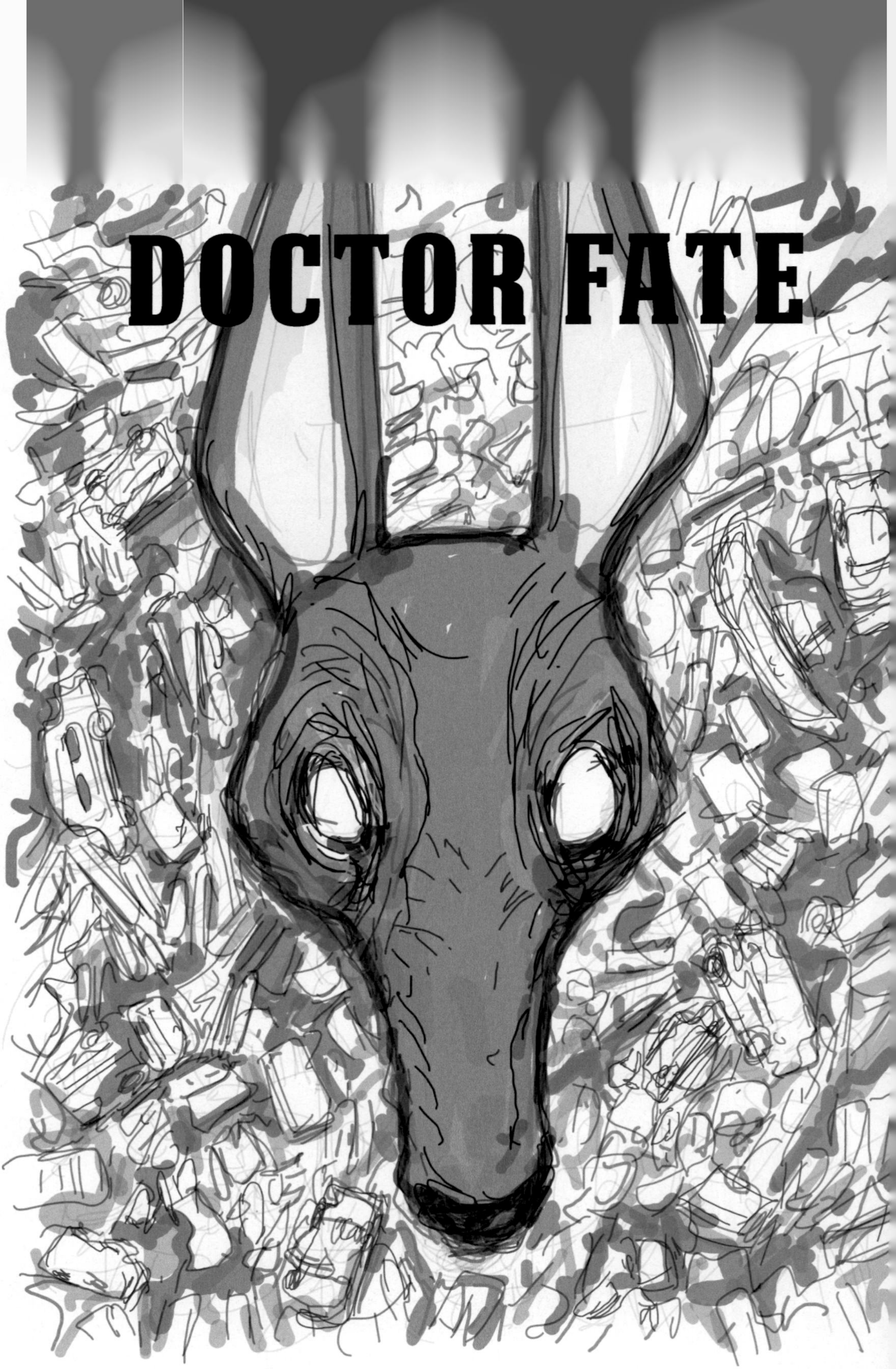
DOCTOR FATE

DOCTOR FATE

ASSEMBLY AND OPERATING INSTRUCTIONS

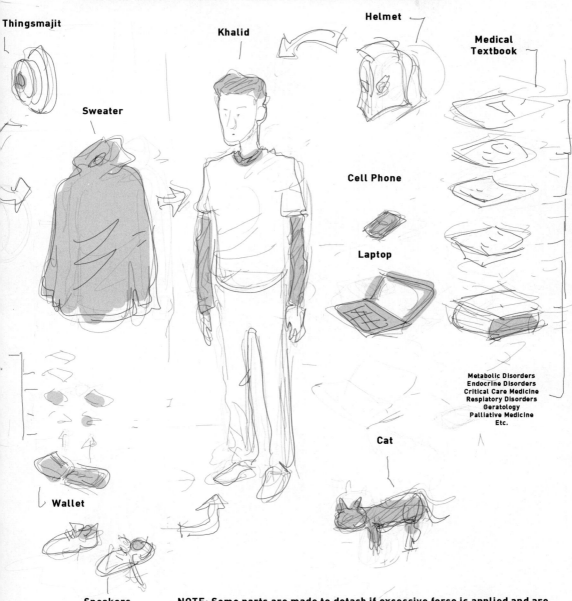

Thingsmajit

Sweater

Khalid

Helmet

Medical Textbook

Cell Phone

Laptop

Metabolic Disorders
Endocrine Disorders
Critical Care Medicine
Respiratory Disorders
Geratology
Palliative Medicine
Etc.

Cat

Wallet

Sneakers

NOTE: Some parts are made to detach if excessive force is applied and are desgned to be reattached if separation occurs. Other parts, not so much. Spirit Guide supervision may be necessary for younger children.

DOCTOR FATE

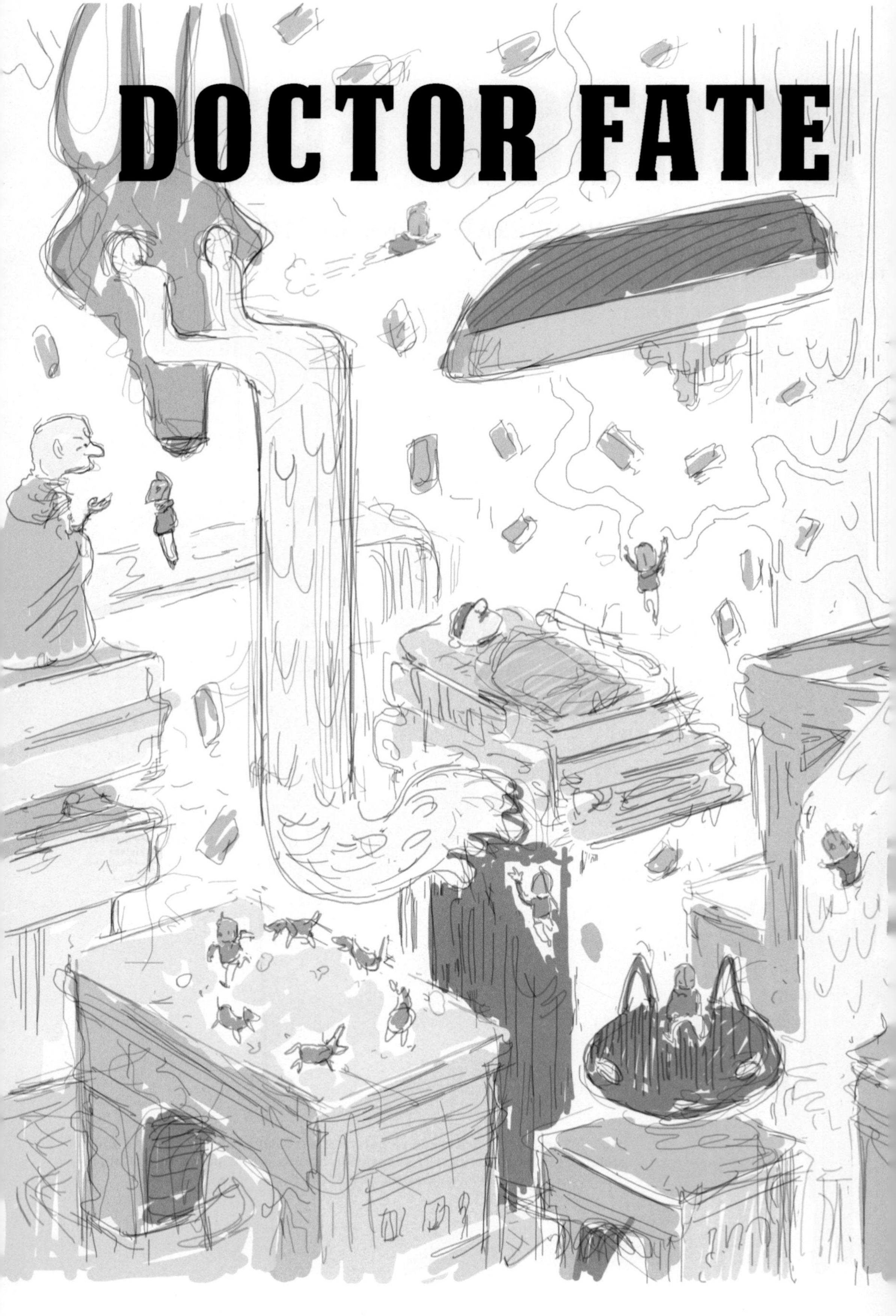

DOCTOR FATE

ASSEMBLY AND OPERATING INSTRUCTIONS

A.

B.

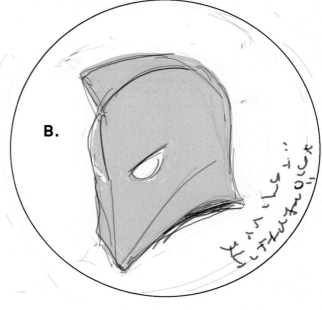

C.

D.

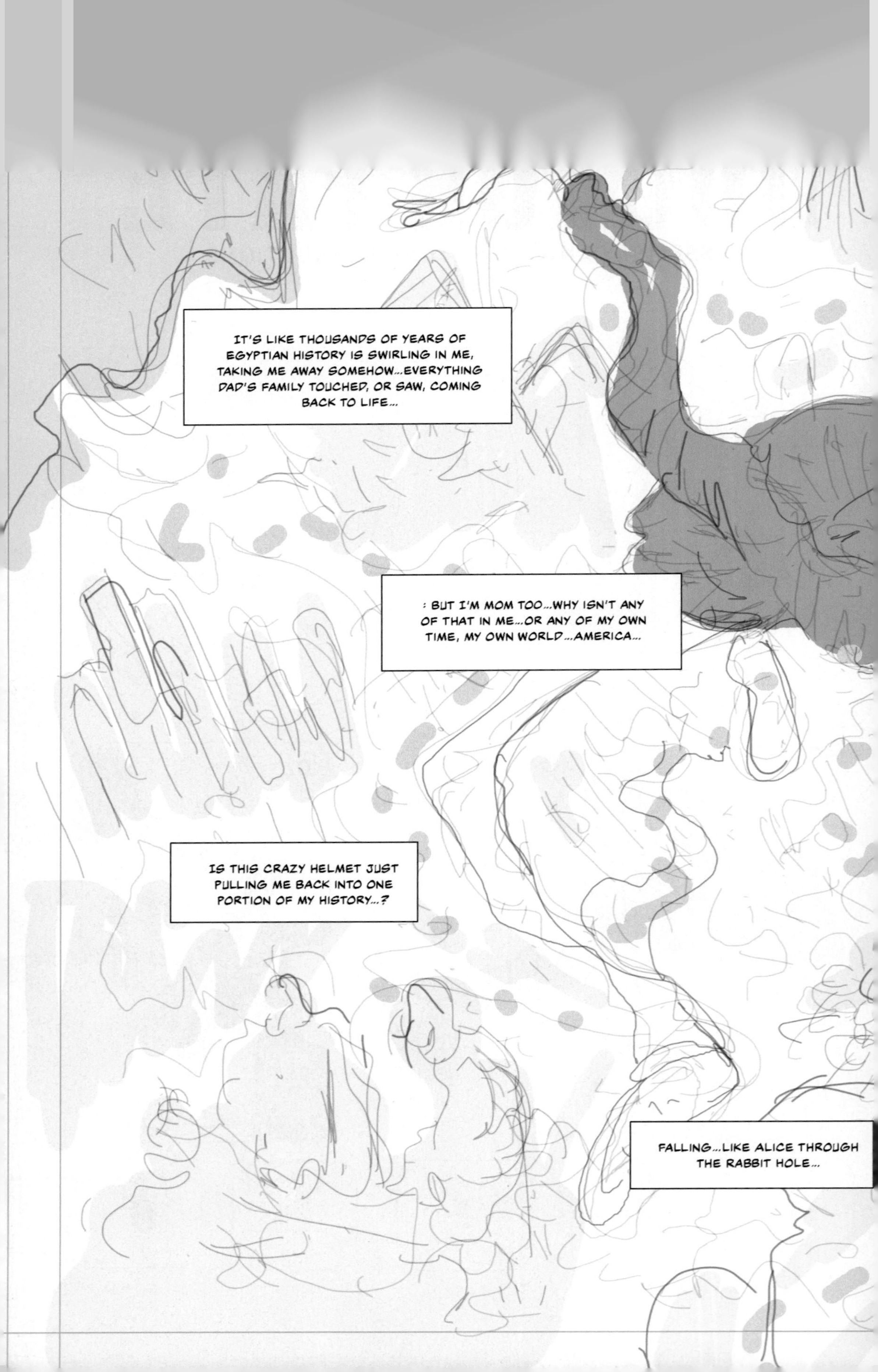
IT'S LIKE THOUSANDS OF YEARS OF EGYPTIAN HISTORY IS SWIRLING IN ME, TAKING ME AWAY SOMEHOW...EVERYTHING DAD'S FAMILY TOUCHED, OR SAW, COMING BACK TO LIFE...
: BUT I'M MOM TOO...WHY ISN'T ANY OF THAT IN ME...OR ANY OF MY OWN TIME, MY OWN WORLD...AMERICA...
IS THIS CRAZY HELMET JUST PULLING ME BACK INTO ONE PORTION OF MY HISTORY...?
FALLING...LIKE ALICE THROUGH THE RABBIT HOLE...

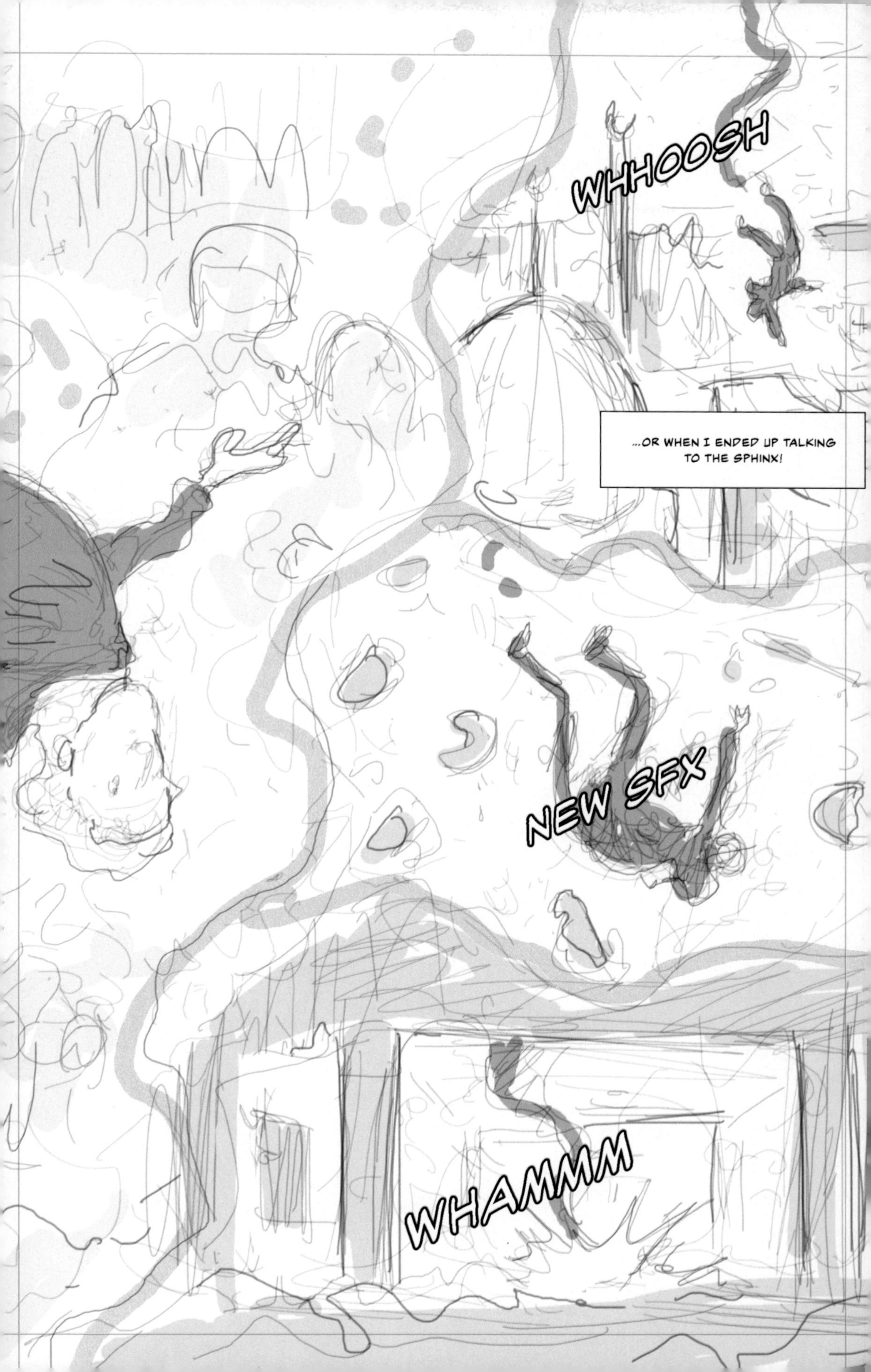
WHHOOSH
...OR WHEN I ENDED UP TALKING TO THE SPHINX!
NEW SFX
WHAMMM

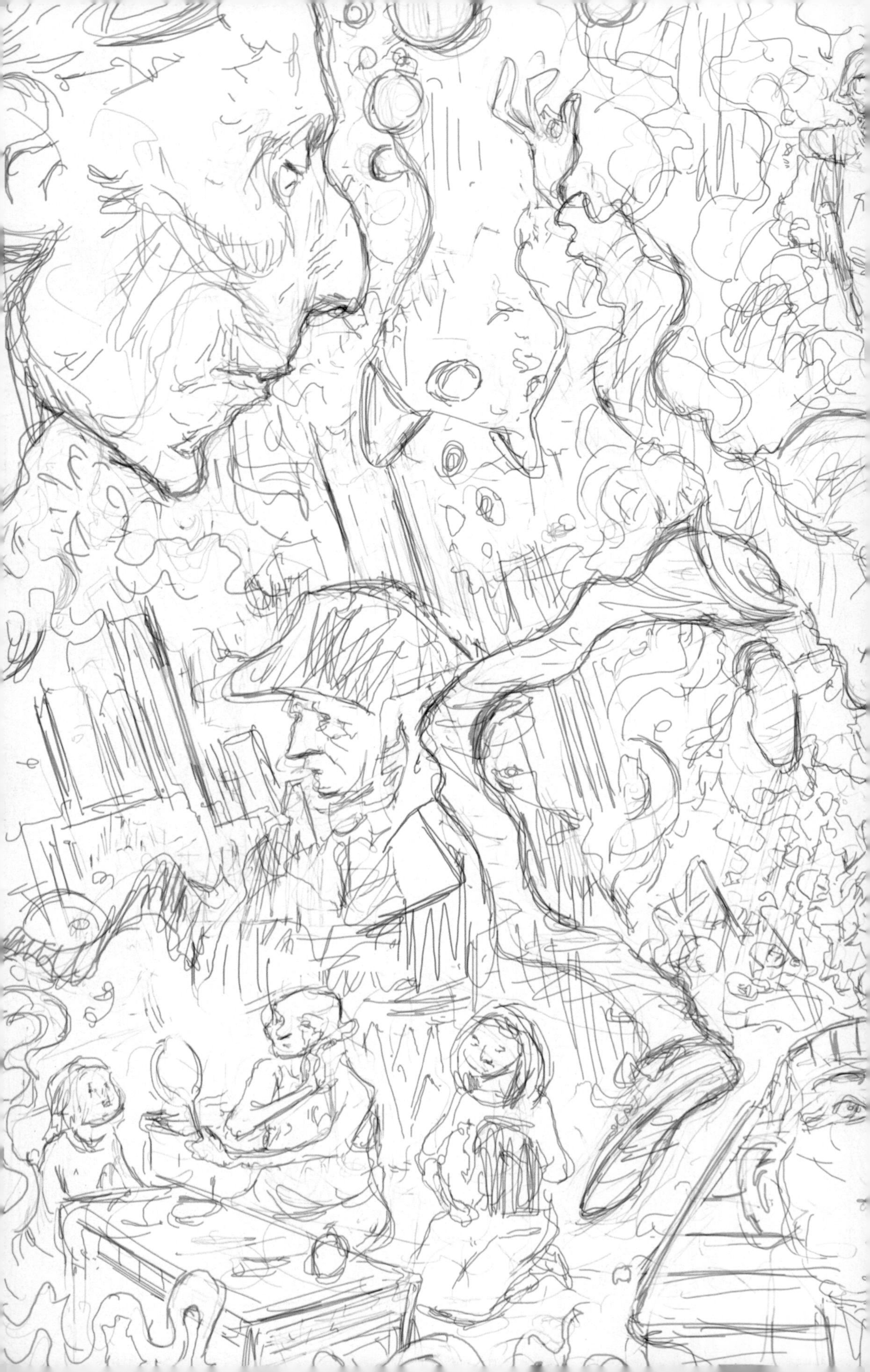

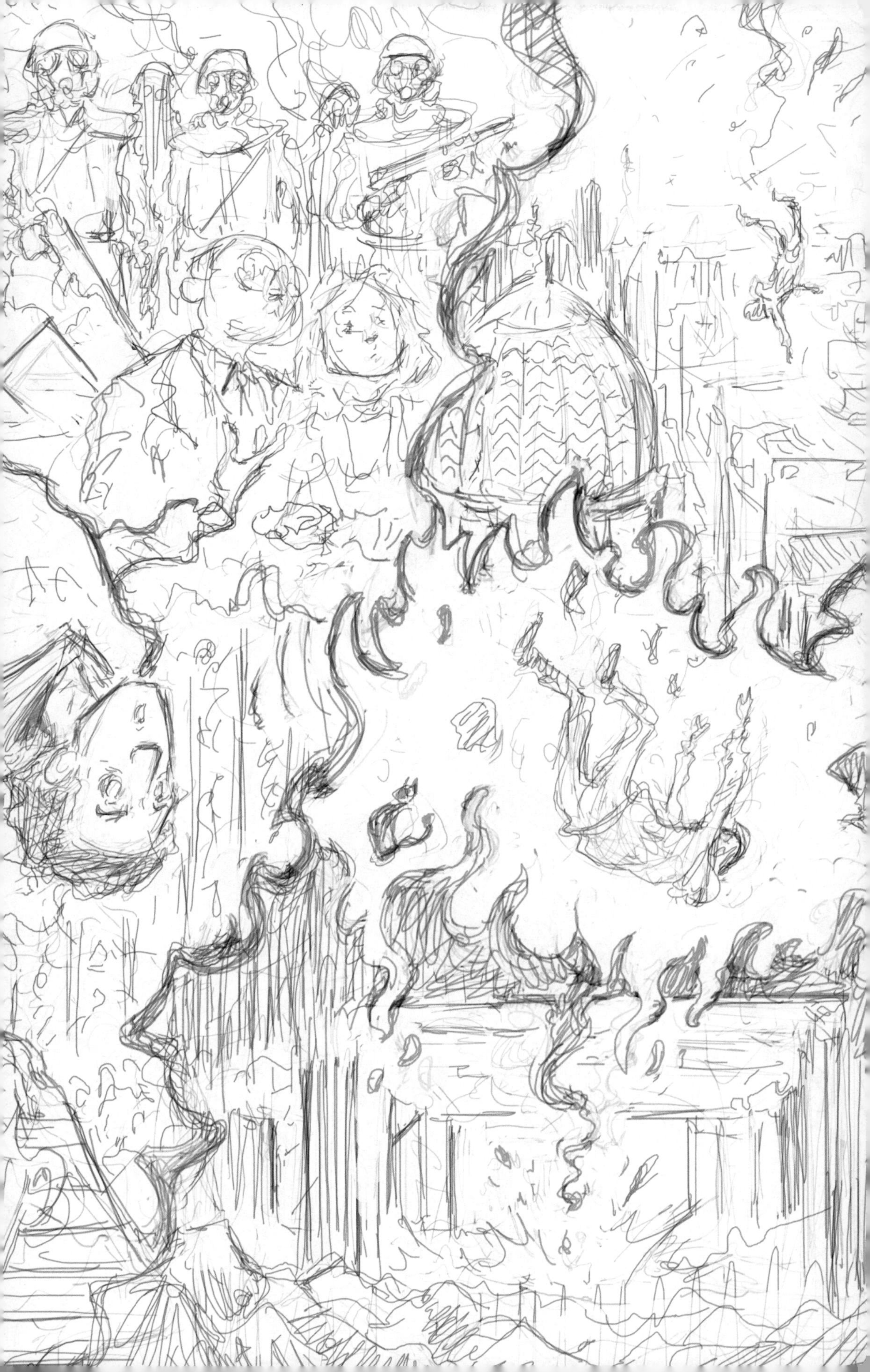

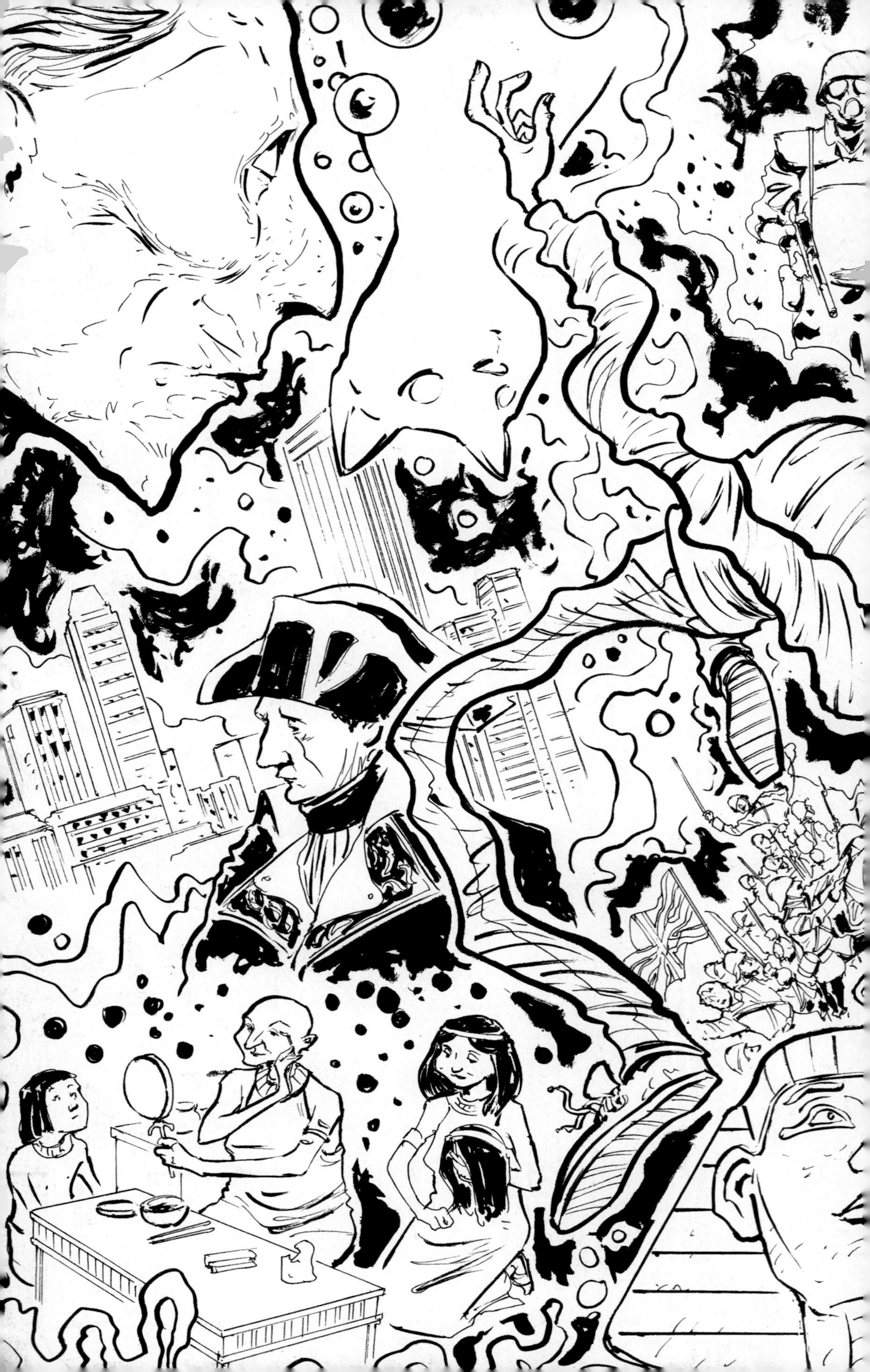

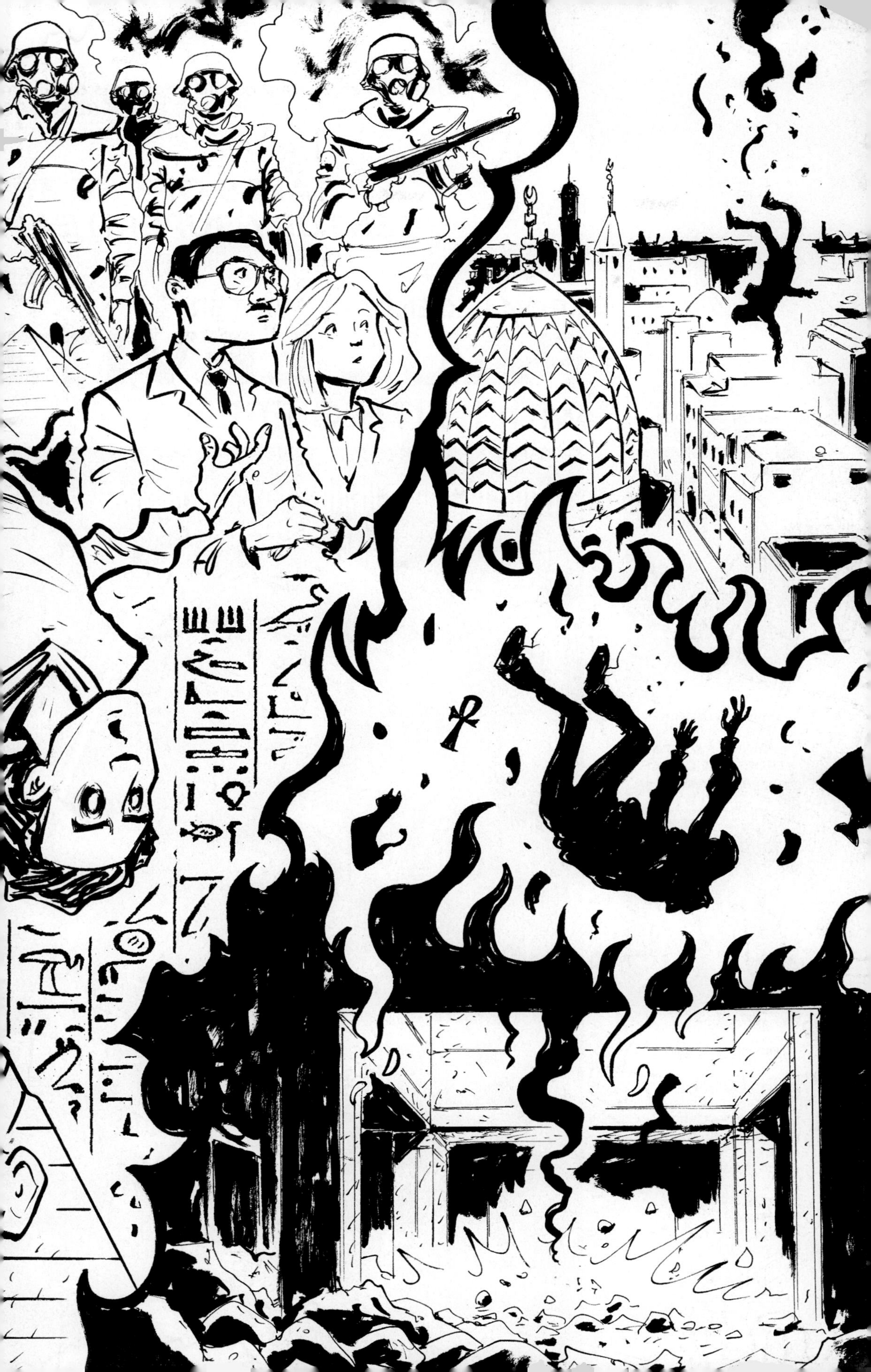

DC COMICS™

"One of the greatest comic book runs of all tim[e]"
—COMIC BOOK RESOURC[ES]

TALES OF THE 31ST CENTURY SUPER-TEAM

FROM LEGENDARY WRITER
PAUL LEVITZ
with KEITH GIFFEN

LEGION OF SUPER-HEROES: THE CURSE

with KEITH GIFFEN

LEGION OF SUPER-HEROES: THE CHOICE

with YILDIRAY CINAR

ALSO AVAILABLE

LEGION OF SUPER-HEROES: EYE FOR AN EYE
with KEITH GIFFEN

LEGION OF SUPER-HEROES: CONSEQUENCES
with YILDIRAY CINAR

LEGION OF SUPER-HEROES: WHEN EVIL CALLS
with PHIL JIMENEZ & YILDIRAY CINAR

"One of the best comic stories ever told."
—WASHINGTON EXAMINER

"Waid's charged dialogue and Ross' stunning visual realism expose the genius, pride, fears and foibles of DC's heroes and villains."
—WASHINGTON POST

ALEX ROSS

with MARK WAID

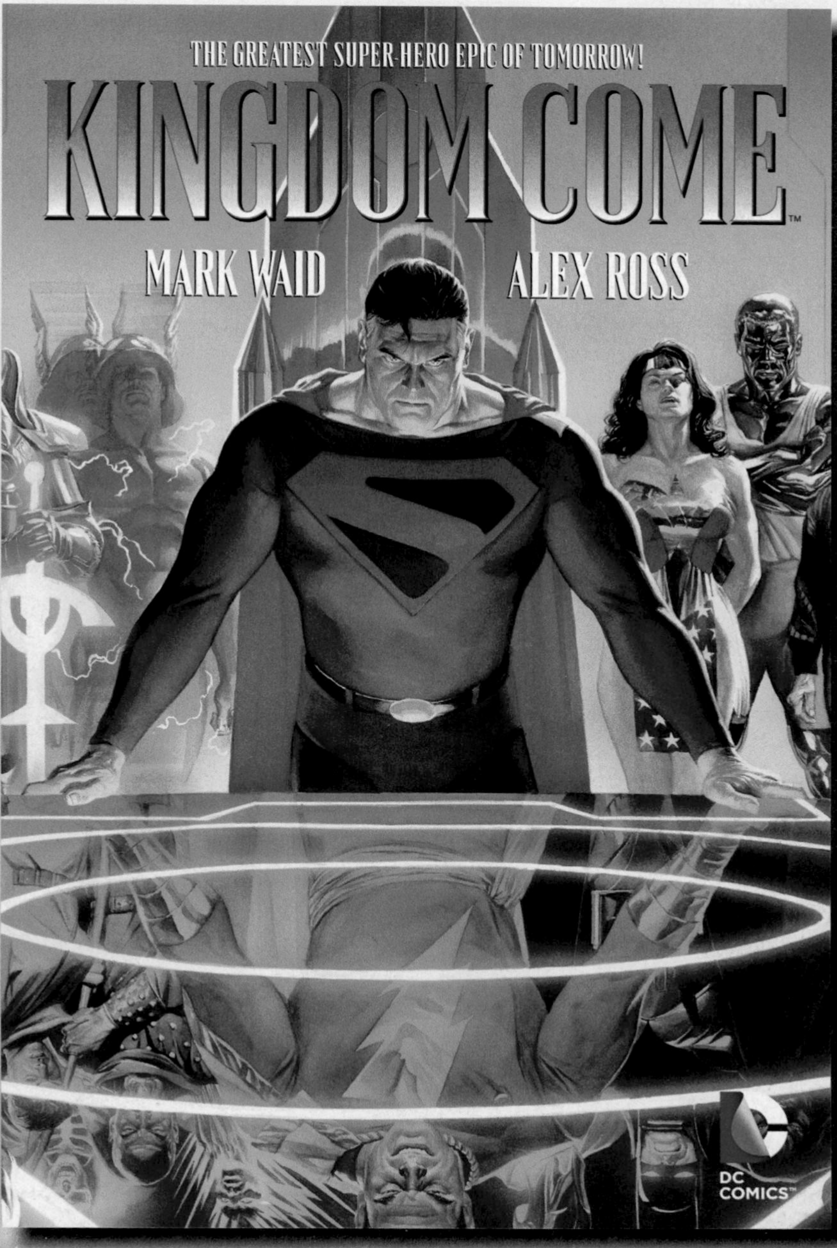
THE GREATEST SUPER-HERO EPIC OF TOMORROW!
KINGDOM COME
MARK WAID
ALEX ROSS
DC COMICS

JUSTICE

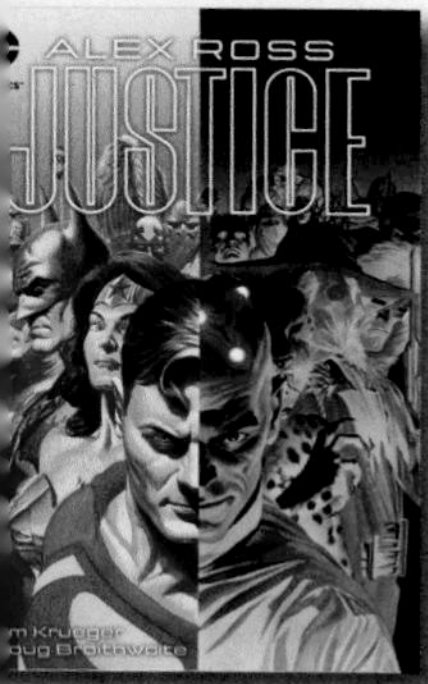
ALEX ROSS

with JIM KRUEGER
& DOUG BRAITHWAITE

THE WORLD'S GREATEST SUPER-HEROES

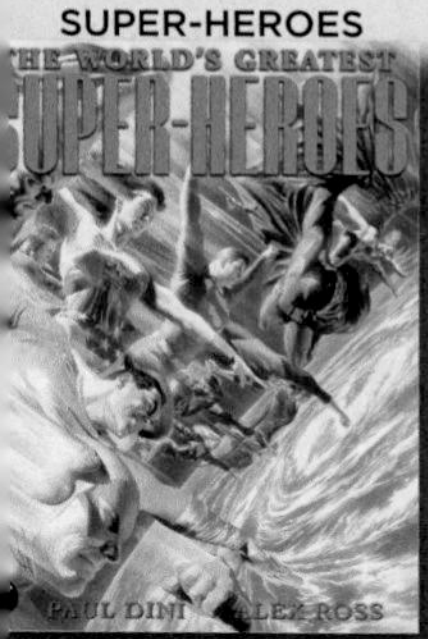
PAUL DINI
ALEX ROSS

with PAUL DINI

STICE SOCIETY OF AMERICA:
HY KINGDOM COME
PARTS 1-3

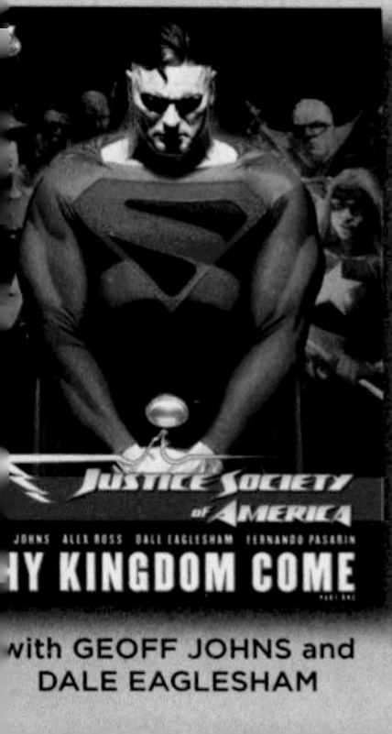
JUSTICE SOCIETY of AMERICA

with GEOFF JOHNS and
DALE EAGLESHAM

DC
COMICS™

"Worthy of the adjective, but in a good w
—THE NEW YORK TIM

"There are some threats that are too much
even Superman, Batman and Wonder Won
to handle. That's when you call the peo
who make magic their method."—CRAVE ONL

START AT THE BEGINNING

JUSTICE LEAGUE DARK
VOLUME 1: IN THE DARK

JUSTICE LEAGUE
DARK VOL. 2: THE
BOOKS OF MAGIC

with JEFF LEMIRE

JUSTICE LEAGUE
DARK VOL. 3:
THE DEATH OF MAGIC

with JEFF LEMIRE

CONSTANTINE
VOL. 1: THE SPARKLE
AND THE FLAME

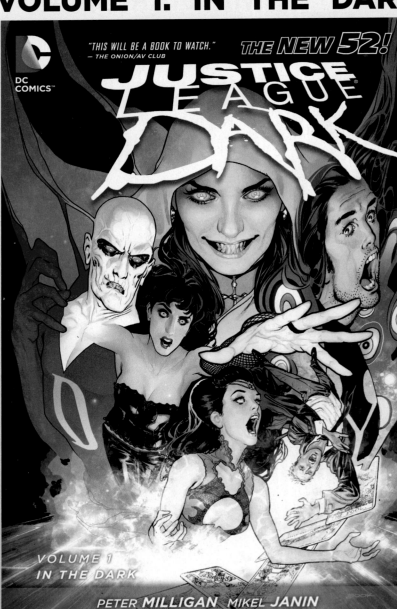

"THIS WILL BE A BOOK TO WATCH."
— THE ONION/AV CLUB

THE NEW 52!

VOLUME 1
IN THE DARK

PETER MILLIGAN   Mikel JANIN